TELEVISION
AND
CHILD DEVELOPMENT

LEA's Communication Series
Jennings Bryant/Dolf Zillmann, General Editors

For a complete list of titles in LEA's Communication Series, please contact Lawrence Erlbaum Associates, Publishers at www.erlbaum.com

TELEVISION
AND
CHILD DEVELOPMENT

Third Edition

Judith Van Evra
St. Jerome's University
in the
University of Waterloo

2004

LAWRENCE ERLBAUM ASSOCIATES, PUBLISHERS
Mahwah, New Jersey   London

Lawrence Erlbaum Associates, Inc., Publishers
10 Industrial Avenue
Mahwah, New Jersey 07430

Cover design by Kathryn Houghtaling Lacey

Library of Congress Cataloging-in-Publication Data

Van Evra, Judith Page.
  Television and child development / Judith Van Evra.—3rd ed.
    p. cm. — (LEA's communication series)

  Includes bibliographical references and index.
  ISBN 0-8058-4863-0 (cloth : alk. Paper)
  ISBN 0-8058-4864-9 (pbk. : alk. Paper)
    1. Television and children. 2. Child development. I. Title. II. Series.

HQ784.T4V333 2004
302.23'45'083—dc22   2004041157
                                                          CIP

Printed in the United States of America
10 9 8 7 6 5 4 3 2

To my wonderful family

Contents

II   COGNITIVE ASPECTS OF MEDIA EXPERIENCE

Preface

Research into the relation between children's television viewing and their cognitive, social, and emotional development has increased significantly since the second edition of this book and has confirmed some old insights and added many new ones. Television continues to be a major part of the lives of most children and adolescents, but current research also reflects the explosive growth in new technologies and their widespread use by young people. The digital revolution and the ensuing proliferation of DVDs, realistic video games, cell phones, pagers, and other wireless devices have introduced a level of flexibility, convenience, and portability only envisioned very recently. Technological advances have led to slick and evocative productions in which reality and fantasy are mingled and often indistinguishable. Many of the basic parameters in this exciting field of research remain unchanged; but newer research studies have raised some important questions about earlier findings and suggest new avenues and directions for future research.

My purpose in this book is to present as current and complete a summary and synthesis as possible of what is already known about the media's role in and impact on children's cognitive, social, and emotional development and to discern the complex and significant interplay between other forces in a child's life and their use of various media. In this book I rely on information from communication literature as well as that from child development and other psychological domains and seek to integrate these diverse sources into a coherent conceptualization of the major variables operating in children's media experience.

Much of the basic organization of the original book is retained in this edition, but there are significant changes both in content areas and in chapter organization. Research findings and changing trends in television content and viewing patterns are updated, and sections on new technologies and their impact are greatly expanded. Seven entirely new chapters include information on research methodology; cultural diversity, and stereotypes; health-related matters and lifestyle choices, including sexual behavior, drug and alcohol use, and nutrition and body image; media's impact on various social–emotional aspects of a child's development; and separate chapters on technology use for information and entertainment. Finally, an entire chapter is now devoted to intervention possibilities and parent strategies and education. Summaries and discussion questions are included at the end of each chapter.

Part I of this third edition begins with a review of the major theoretical perspectives from psychology and communication that have been used to predict and explain many of the research findings, including social learning and social cognitive theory from the psychological literature and cultivation and uses and gratifications theories from the communication literature. In Part I, an integrative approach is offered by which the bodies of literature from communication and psychology can be bridged to better understand and explain media's impact on children and adolescents and the variations and differences among them in its influence. In another chapter, basic research designs and methodologies are reviewed.

Part II is devoted to a look at the cognitive aspects of children's media experience. It includes a chapter on their processing of information to understand just what and how they learn from the media, which material affects them, and how child and content variables interact to influence this process. Knowledge of what children actually attend to is basic to our understanding of how much they understand and what they are likely to remember. Consideration of television's effects on children's cognitive development generally, as well as on their reading and academic performance specifically, is included.

Part III deals with media's impact on various areas of children's and adolescents' social and emotional development and behavior, with chapters on violence; advertising; cultural diversity and stereotypes; lifestyle and health-related choices such as use of alcohol, tobacco, and drugs; sexual behavior; and nutritional issues and body image. One chapter is devoted to the impact of media on various other aspects of children's and adolescents' social and emotional development, and family issues in relation to media use are addressed in a separate chapter.

Part IV is devoted to the role of specific technologies in the lives of children and adolescents and their impact on the development of beliefs, knowledge, attitudes, and behavior. Separate chapters are devoted to use of technology for information, such as the Internet and computers in classrooms, and to its use for entertainment, including computer and video games, music videos, the Internet, and chat rooms.

Part V includes a chapter review of intervention strategies including media literacy and parent education as well as other interventions. In the final chapter an overview of the findings and trends of research to date is offered, and the many questions that remain for future research to address are discussed.

I hope that by understanding more about how, and to what extent, television and other media actually affect children and adolescents and what role other variables may play in mediating their impact, we can maximize technology's potential for enriching children's cognitive, social, and emotional development while at the same time minimizing any negative influence.

ACKNOWLEDGMENTS

My sincere thanks and appreciation go to all of the enthusiastic and capable people at Lawrence Erlbaum Associates with whom I have had the pleasure of working on the development and production of this third edition. These include Karin Wittig Bates whose confident, enthusiastic, and friendly emails, clear and patient responses to questions, and very helpful suggestions guided the development of this edition and made working on the book a pleasure. Thanks also to all of the other wonderfully capable and great-to-work-with editorial, production, and promotional staff including Linda Bathgate, Sara Scudder, and Susan Barker, to Jennings Bryant and Dolf Zillmann, General Editors of the Communication Series, and Alan Rubin, Advisory Editor of the Mass Communication subseries, and to all those adopters and respondents who provided invaluable feedback on their experience with the previous edition. Finally, special and heartfelt thanks to all of my family for their interest and support during my work on the book, and especially to my husband whose comments and suggestions were indispensable and whose patience and good humor helped to make the hard work involved in developing this edition such a satisfying and rewarding endeavor.

Introduction

In a study conducted for the Kaiser Family Foundation by Rideout, Foehr, Roberts, and Brodie (1999), *Kids and Media @ the New Millennium*, a national sample of over 3,000 children gave information about their media use patterns. Twenty percent of the children completed detailed diaries about their media use, including their use of TV, computers, movies, video games, music, and print media. The study also included questionnaires and in-home interviews with parents. The findings about current use of the media by children and adolescents are compelling. Some of the highlights include the following:

- The typical American child spends an average of almost a full work week using media outside of school, and most use more than one at once; children 8 years and older spend an average of 6¾ hours a day using media, most of which is televiewing. Only 5% spend less than an hour a day with media.
- More than one in six watch television for 5 hours a day.
- Even young children between 2 and 7 years old use media for 3½ hours a day, and fewer than 10% use it for less than an hour.
- Nearly one third of children in the study live in homes with four or more TVs; 12% have five or more.
- Over 40% of children live in homes where the TV stays on "most of the time," and two thirds of children say it is on during meals.
- Sixty-one percent of children 8 and over have no rules about what or how much they watch at home, and they watch with their parents only about 5% of the time (Rideout et al., 1999).
- Even 1-year-olds watch TV an average of 6 hours a week (Talbot, 2003).

Given a conservative estimate of 2½ hours of watching television each day over a lifetime and assuming 8 hours of sleep a night, the average American would spend 7 years out of the approximately 47 waking years humans have by age 70 (Kubey & Csikszentmihalyi, 1990).

According to Rideout et al. (1999), children between the ages of 8 and 13 years, known as "tweens," spend the most time with media, about 6¾ hours a day. They spend as much time as older children watching movies, playing on the computer, and going online, but they spend much less time listening to audio media such as the radio or CDs. More than a fourth of these tweens watch TV for more than 5 hours a day.

The Kaiser Foundation report (Rideout et al., 1999) suggests that those children who spend a lot of time with one type of media will also spend more time with other types as well. Children who used a computer for entertainment more than an hour a day also watched more TV and read more than children who did not use computers at all. "High" computer users were also twice as likely to watch TV for more than 5 hours a day and read more than 1 hour a day than children who did not use computers at all.

TV is truly ubiquitous in American homes. Not only do 99% of American families have TV sets; the average family has two or three (Annenberg Public Policy Center, 1999). Rideout et al. (1999) also showed that the average American child grows up in a home with three TVs, tape players, and radios; two VCRs and DVD players; a video game player; and a computer. More than half have a radio, TV, tape player, or CD player, and about one third have a video game player and a VCR in their own room, making their rooms "media central." Even many preschoolers have TVs in their rooms, and in 1999, car manufacturers began to offer backseat video screens with 400,000 mobile units installed in 2002 with multiple screens in some cars (Talbot, 2003). Children and adolescents are never far from multiple media in their lives.

Even very young children are immersed in an electronic media world. Data from a new Kaiser Foundation study (Rideout, Vandewater, & Wartella, 2003) revealed that nearly half of children 6 years old and younger have used a computer and nearly a third have played video games. Children in that age group spend about as much time with screen media as they do playing outside and about three times as much as time reading or being read to. Rideout et al. found that on a typical day 83% of children in that age group used any screen media and nearly three fourths watched TV, videos, or DVDs. Moreover, they are active in their media use with more than two thirds of them turning on the set, changing channels, and asking for favorite shows or videos (Rideout et al., 2003).

Children are also alone with the media for large proportions of the day, and two thirds of children 8 years or older have a TV in their bedrooms, and one in five children have a computer in their bedrooms. Almost half have Internet access. Despite all of this access, however, they spend less than a half hour a day using computers for fun compared to nearly 3 hours with TV (Rideout et al., 1999).

In their national MediaQuotient study of family media habits, Gentile and Walsh (2002) found that children who do have sets in their bedrooms perform more poorly at school and engage in fewer nonelectronic media activities such as reading or playing games. They also watch 5½ more hours of TV a week than those without sets in their room and there is less parental monitoring of their viewing.

The Kaiser Foundation data (Rideout et al., 1999) suggest that despite a wide array of new technologies to choose from and new media to use, most children today spend their time in much the same way they did a generation ago—listening to music, reading, and watching TV—and young children continue to read for fun. In a typical week they watch TV for 19 hours, listen to music for 10 hours, and read for pleasure for more than 5 hours. They spend from 2 to 2½ hours using computers for fun or playing video games. About 80% of children will read or be read to on any given day not counting time spent reading for school or homework, but once they become teenagers, the amount of time they spend reading drops. Roberts and Christenson (2001) have suggested that children spend even more time listening to music, 3 to 4 hours a day, as compared with TV viewing, 2 to 3 hours a day, especially for adolescents, and spend relatively little time viewing music videos compared with the time they spend listening to music.

Moreover, when children use the new media, they tend to supplement rather than replace their use of other media forms, and there are few differences between children in rural or urban areas in how they use media (Rideout et al., 1999). Affluence and family income do make a difference, however. Children who live in poor neighborhoods spend more time with the media than those from wealthier communities, including watching more TV. They are also more likely to have a TV in their bedroom and less likely to have rules about their viewing and to live in homes where the TV stays on most of the time. However, this group is also less likely to have a computer in the home. White children and high-income children are more likely to use computers (Rideout et al., 1999).

Recent data from Statistics Canada ("Unequal Access," 2003) on nearly 30,000 students from 1,117 Canadian schools reported that 88% of 15-year-olds, almost 9 out of 10, had access to a computer in their homes compared with 69% who used the Internet in 2000. More than three fourths of them used the computers at home for access to information from the Web, e-mail, instant messaging, word processing, and game playing. However, students from lower income families were less likely to have a computer available at home, although 65% of adults earning less than $20,000 annually had Internet access at work, school, or public places such as libraries and Internet cafes.

Although it is difficult to know just how much all of this media content is actually partially or fully attended to, what is learned, what is remembered, what impressions are gleaned, and what images are formed, such questions are especially important in relation to child viewers because they still are in very active stages of development. Their attitudes, beliefs, and ideas about the world, as well as physical, cognitive, and social skills, are taking form; and they absorb information from everywhere.

The considerable number of hours spent viewing television or using other media means that the media constitute a disproportionately large potential informational and attitudinal source. This is an important finding because adolescents, for example, use the media to get information about sex, violence, drugs, and relationships (Gruber & Grube, 2000). The most frequently studied areas of influence include violence and aggressive behavior, consumerism, school performance, fear and anxiety, stereotypes, prosocial behavior, sexuality, obesity, and tobacco and alcohol use, and heavy viewers are more at risk than light viewers (Strasburger, 1993).

Concern often has centered on the short-term and long-term effects of TV viewing on the development of children of all ages. Much of the early research focused on preschoolers who are in the most rapid stage of social, cognitive, and emotional development. Programs like *Sesame Street* alerted consumers to the creative learning as well as entertainment possibilities that exist through the television medium. The wholesome values and educational tools that *Sesame Street* seemed to provide eased the concerns of many parents about television viewing in young children. They allowed and encouraged their children to watch it with almost the same sense of good parenting with which they gave their children vitamins or read them stories.

Others worried about the possibility of becoming too dependent on television as a way to entertain their children or about the effects on young children of passively engaging in this activity in lieu of active and imaginative play with other children. Other questions relating to children's television viewing experience also commanded increasing attention. How do children respond to violence that they see enacted daily either in the news or in prime-time programming? Which children choose to watch violent television? What perceptions of adult men and women are children developing from viewing situation comedies, soaps, and commercial advertising? Do they understand, and how do they interpret, the many sexual innuendos and jokes that play an increasingly significant part of many shows? How do television portrayals affect their perception of ethnic minorities or of individuals from other socioeconomic levels? How does television viewing facilitate or interfere with relationships with parents and siblings or with peers? How much television is "safe"? When is it "harmful"? Parental concerns, coupled with those of psychologists and educators, have generated a huge amount of research.

Now parents and educators raise the same questions about the other media that play such a huge role in their children's lives. Now they wonder about the impact of the violence and stereotypes in video games and music videos, the time their children spend online and what the nature of their Internet contacts and activity is, what influence socioeconomic level might have on their exposure to and access to media, and how much control they should, or even can, exert. They wonder how to maximize the positives of media use and minimize the negatives.

To evaluate the media's actual impact on child and adolescent development, then, it is essential to study not only the types of content to which children are being exposed or the amount of media use in which they are engaged but also how differences in their developmental level and background variables influence children's media experiences and affect media impact.

Much has been blamed on television viewing and other media use—obesity, low metabolism, poor family relationships, lower academic achievement, aggressive behavior, insensitivity to others, and weakened attention and concentration, to name a few. It is not difficult to see that while children are viewing television or playing video games, they are not exercising, playing outdoors with friends, reading, helping with chores, or practicing piano. Others have noted the positive effects media use can have on children's development. Even children who have less access to TV or other media are affected directly or indirectly in, perhaps, exclusion from various peer interactions related to media use or in the changing behaviors and values of peers and others in society that are brought about, facilitated, or accelerated by the media.

The thousands of studies that have focused on the effects of media use on children's development cover a very broad range of research topics. They include the relation between aggressive behavior and television violence, changes in levels of prosocial behavior such as sharing and cooperation, and other aspects of a child's socialization. Others have considered the influence of media stereotypic portrayals on children's gender-role development and occupational choice as well as on their attitudes toward various age groups and minority populations. Some have studied the ways in which television viewing and computer use enhances or interferes with reading and learning and on how children process television information. Newer studies have emphasized the role of the media in the decision making of children and adolescents regarding lifestyle choices and health issues such as drug, alcohol, and tobacco use, nutrition and body image, and sexual behavior. Finally, some have focused on the sheer magnitude of media presence in our lives and how it affects individuals of all ages.

Researchers in both communication and developmental psychology have emphasized the complexity of the television experience and the interactions among child, program, technical, familial, experiential, motivational, and contextual variables. Much developmental research to date has focused on child variables such as age, sex, socioeconomic background, and intellectual level as though television content was all much the same. Other psychological research has focused primarily on the television content such as whether it is violent, stereotypic, or prosocial as if the audience was a largely homogeneous group. Still other research, particularly from the communication field, has emphasized technical characteristics and formal features of television itself as well as programming issues, motivations for viewing television, and the context of viewing. What is essential is a careful look at the interactions among all of these factors and characteristics and an integration of communication and developmental approaches. Building a bridge between these two broad perspectives leads to a more thorough and meaningful understanding of children's media use and its impact. Failure to build such a bridge between relevant bodies of research or focusing on one at the expense of the other provides a seriously incomplete picture of children's media experience; it is not unlike clapping with one hand.

For the most part, many specific problems have been addressed using very diverse methods, populations, program content, and conceptual models.

Strasburger (1993) identified five crucial issues in efforts to understand the impact of the media on children and adolescents. They are the following:

1. How much influence do the media have?
2. Are all children equally susceptible?
3. How valid is the research?
4. What can be done to improve the quality of television?
5. What is the role of the primary-care physician?

Some variables are simple to identify and measure. Age and sex can be specified clearly and easily. Intellectual level and socioeconomic background, although somewhat less objective, can be coded according to relatively common standards and practices. However, when faced with the need to measure such variables as violence, gender-role stereotyping, attention, comprehension, attitudes toward television, impact of advertising, or modeled behavior within the family, one encounters fundamental differences in assumptions, definitions, and varying emphases among researchers. It is an even more taxing matter to assess the interaction of such variables as age, gender, intellectual functioning and level of cognitive development, socioeconomic background, and school or employment status in evaluating media use and media impact, not to mention all of the formal features of television and the variations in program content and format. Yet the interactions between the various media and the many facets of child development require such efforts.

Finally, the mere inclusion of many variables in specific studies does not guarantee clear, interpretable results; appropriate research designs and statistical analyses are required to evaluate not only the potency and significance of each of the variables but, more important, their complex interactions. In fact, some of the newer research studies that have used ever more sophisticated and complex methods of investigation and data analysis have led to the clarification of trends that are emerging in the research to date on children's media use and the future directions that are taking shape.

PART I

Theoretical Perspectives and Research Methodology

CHAPTER ONE

Theoretical Perspectives

CHAPTER ONE

Theoretical Perspectives

The wealth of research data on all aspects of children's development and their media experience has led to the development of various theoretical interpretations and explanations within both the communication literature and the psychological and child development literature. Three major theoretical perspectives are discussed in the following paragraphs, and an integrative approach is proposed.

SOCIAL LEARNING AND SOCIAL COGNITIVE THEORY

Historical Background

Social learning theory was one of the first to be used to explain television's impact on children. Much of the early work in this area, spearheaded by Bandura's (e.g., Bandura, 1967) work in the 1960s, pointed to observational learning and imitation of modeled behavior as the critical components of television's impact. In the classic studies by Bandura, children who viewed violence directed against a Bobo doll were observed in later play sessions. Those who had seen the aggressor punished did not engage in aggressive behavior following the viewing; the others did. In other words, the children imitated the model unless they were deterred through the effects of vicarious learning. Both groups "learned" the aggressive behaviors, but only one group actually imitated them in the later play sessions. The other group inhibited them until the postviewing conditions were changed, and then they too engaged in more aggressive behavior, thus demonstrating their latent learning of the aggressive response.

Bandura (1967) himself related one of the most graphic and entertaining accounts of modeling in the following quote:

> I remember reading a story reported by Professor Mowrer about a lonesome farmer who decided to get a parrot for company. After acquiring the bird, the farmer spent many long evenings teaching the parrot the phrase, "Say Uncle." Despite the devoted tutorial attention, the parrot proved totally unresponsive and finally, the frus-

trated farmer got a stick and struck the parrot on the head after each refusal to produce the desired phrase.

But the visceral method proved no more effective than the cerebral one, so the farmer grabbed his feathered friend and tossed him in the chicken house. A short time later the farmer heard a loud commotion in the chicken house and upon investigation found that the parrot was pummeling the startled chickens on the head with a stick and shouting, "Say Uncle! Say Uncle!" (p. 42)

Basic Processes

Bandura (1977) made it clear, however, that modeling is not just simple imitation; behavior that follows exposure results from the derivation of rules for appropriate behavior by observation, the context of the behavior observed, and the likely consequences or rewards following the behavior.

Bandura's (1986, 1994) social cognitive theory expanded the earlier social learning model and has been widely used to explain the process by which viewers might learn aggression from media violence. According to this perspective, novel behaviors are acquired either directly through experience or indirectly through the observation of models. Observational learning is governed by four subprocesses: attention, retention, behavior production, and motivation. The attentional process determines what is observed and what information is extracted from the modeled events. This process is influenced by such factors as the observer's cognitive skills and capability, values, and preferences, as well as by the event's salience and the functional value of it to the viewer. It is also influenced by viewers' preconceptions and networks of interactivity that determine their access to various models.

The second subprocess is retention in which viewers restructure the information to allow for retention. According to Bandura (1994), retention is "an active process of transforming and restructuring information about events for memory representation in the form of rules and conceptions" (p. 68). Retention is facilitated by restructuring information about models into memory codes that can be rehearsed, enacted, and recalled. The third subprocess, behavior production, involves translating symbolic notions or ideas into appropriate, specific behavior or courses of action. This process is influenced by a person's actual ability to enact what has been observed and may necessitate skill development.

The fourth subprocess is motivation, and a distinction is made in social cognitive theory between acquisition or learning and performance. Individuals do not perform everything they learn. Whether a learned behavior is actually performed depends on one's motivation to perform, and this motivation can be direct, vicarious, or self-produced. According to Bandura (1994), individuals are more likely to perform modeled actions that are valued rather than those acts that are not rewarded or are punished. Moreover, they can guide their own behavior by observing rewards and punishments experienced by others performing the modeled behavior, much as they would if they experienced the consequences directly. This is known as vicarious reinforcement. Personal standards also determine which observationally learned behavior will actually be pursued.

In social cognitive theory, then, a child's cognitive representation of expected positive results for aggressive behavior motivates the behavior. The positive outcomes can include tangible rewards, psychological rewards such as control over someone, self-esteem, or social reactions such as peer status (Guerra, Nucci, & Huesmann, 1994). Cognitive representations of expected negative outcomes, on the other hand, can inhibit aggressive behavior. These can include punishment, disapproval, injury, or disrupted social relationships. "With development, aggressive behavior is increasingly governed by normative standards of acceptable conduct. These standards serve as guides for information processing in different situations, and ultimately influence social behavior" (Guerra et al., 1994, p. 18).

Variables Affecting Modeling

Similarities between a viewer and the model, the credibility of the model, the context of the viewing, and similarities and differences between the televised models and real-life models in a child's environment are also important determinants of which behaviors are actually imitated. A child's motivational state, the perceived reality of what is being observed, and the number of other experiences that provide competing models and information are additional significant influences on the imitation of television models that social cognitive theory predicts.

According to Bandura (1994), the influence of TV has more to do with the content that is viewed than the sheer amount of viewing. Models can be inhibitors or disinhibitors, teachers or tutors, social prompts, or emotion arousers, and they can shape conceptions of reality values. The different functions can operate separately, but they often operate together. For example, a model of aggression can be both a teacher and a disinhibitor, or the behavior of others can prompt behavior in observers that was learned previously but not acted on.

According to script theory, children do not simply imitate behavior that they view. Rather, they acquire behavioral scripts through observational learning that can then be activated by cues in the environment or activation of memory (Huesmann, 1988). Thus, televiewing affects behavior by activating certain scripts in the viewer such that the behaviors seen on television are associated in the viewers' minds with other thoughts, events, or conditions.

The determinants of imitation, then, are complex and involve significant cognitive activity, learning, and semantic associations.

Evaluation

Despite the consistency of many findings, there are limitations and problems with using only social learning and social cognitive theory to explain the data. First, not all children imitate what they see regardless of context, observed consequences, and prior learning. Moreover, as the relation reported often is based on correlational data, causation cannot be demonstrated definitively. Although viewing violence on television may lead to imitation of that content and increased aggression, for example, it also is possible that aggressive children may choose to watch more violent programs. Independent factors that lead both to viewing high levels of violence and to increased aggressive behavior need to be investigated further.

Social learning and social cognitive theory have been used effectively to interpret the short-term effects that have been demonstrated in the many laboratory experiments that have been conducted (e.g., Comstock & Scharrer, 1999; Comstock & Strasburger, 1993b). The long-term effects of viewing and the relative influence of many other factors that contribute to the appearance of specific behaviors are less clear. Clearly, the elements of observational learning, modeling, vicarious reinforcement, and imitation are essential components of a child's viewing experience, but they are mediated by a host of other variables.

CULTIVATION THEORY

The cultivation hypothesis as espoused by Gerbner, Gross, Morgan, and Signorielli (1980, 1982, 1986) asserts that heavy television viewing leads to or cultivates perceptions of the world that are consistent with television's portrayals. The more time spent viewing television, the more likely the viewer is to accept televison's version of things, especially in areas in which the viewer has little direct experience such as in the expectation of violence or in getting information about other groups with whom the person does not interact. Cultivation theory predicts or expects frequent viewers to give more "TV" answers or answers consistent with television's portrayal of the world as shown in content analyses than of the real world as shown by actual statistics (Wright, 1986).

Basic Assumptions

According to a cultivation perspective, the amount of viewing or exposure is a very important variable in television's impact on thought and behavior. Heavy viewers differ systematically from light viewers in beliefs, values, and assumptions that may relate in consistent ways to the groups' life situations and views (Gerbner et al., 1982). Cultivation theory assumes that heavy viewers are also less selective in their viewing, engage in habitual viewing, and experience a good deal of sameness of content. Moreover, television's impact is greatest when it functions as the only information source and when it is relevant to the person. Lighter viewers are more likely to have many other diverse sources of information such as social interaction, reading, and vocational experience that take up much of their time and displace televiewing time. They have a greater number of behavioral models, and they are also perhaps less likely to take television content seriously. Heavy viewers have few other sources of ideas and thus are more likely to report reality perceptions that are consistent with television portrayals (Gerbner et al., 1980).

However, television does not act in a vacuum; nor does it act on everyone in the same way. Not only do heavy viewers at one developmental level have a different experience than heavy viewers at another level; those of a different gender, or socioeconomic level, or family background also experience television differently. Any potential cultivation effect must be evaluated against the significance and impact of these other factors on a child's development and experience.

Television dramatically changes children's access to information about the world, and because of their more limited experience and knowledge base and in the absence of competing information, television may have a particularly potent effect on them. Huston et al. (1992) reported that children who are heavy viewers of television show a high level of concern about getting sick and have higher perceptions of medical relief and over-the-counter remedies. It is essential, then, to look at the developmental differences over the long run between children who have been "brought up on television"—those for whom television has portrayed and defined "reality" to a larger extent—and those whose television experience has been more limited, either to a certain period of their lives in terms of total amount of viewing or as an informational source.

Perceived Reality

An important variable in any cultivation effect is perceived reality. If the television content is seen as realistic, it is more likely to be taken seriously. Moreover, viewers who perceive and believe in television as a source of useful information that can help them vicariously to solve problems and to cope likely also perceive television to be fairly realistic (Potter, 1986).

The concept of perceived reality, however, appears to be more complex than has usually been thought. Potter (1986, 1988), for example, has discussed the importance of identity or "the degree of similarity the viewer perceives between television characters and situations and the people and situations experienced in real life" (Potter, 1986, p. 163). Individuals high on this dimension feel close to television characters, have a strong sense of reality about them, and feel about them the way they feel about real friends. They believe that television characters are similar to individuals they meet in real life, and they are likely to be more susceptible to television's influence.

The explosive growth of "reality TV" raises some interesting questions in this context. Do heavy viewers of such programs feel that participants actually represent real-life experiences? Or do they assume that these are characters and behaviors at the far end of the normal curve for those characters or activities being portrayed? The popularity of these shows and the apparent strong involvement of viewers with the characters and their actions suggests that the level of perceived reality is high, but more research is needed.

Finally, Kubey and Csikszentmihalyi (1990) pointed out that television and film are likely to have more of a homogenizing effect than print because people's perception of content on television is more likely similar to each others' than is true of print. Viewers know exactly what a character looks like, for example, and don't have to construct an image in their mind.

Mainstreaming and Resonance

According to Gerbner et al. (1980) there are varying patterns of associations between amounts of viewing and conceptions of reality for different social groups that can be explained in relation to two systematic processes: mainstreaming and resonance.

Mainstreaming refers to an overall effect of television in which viewing may override differences in behavior or perspective that arise from other cultural, social, and demographic influences in "a homogenization of divergent views and a convergence of disparate views" (Gerbner et al., 1986, p. 31) or the cultivation of common outlooks in heavy viewers. That is, heavy viewers, even in high-educational and high-income groups, share a commonality that light viewers do not (Gerbner et al., 1980).

According to cultivation theory, television has the power to cultivate mainstreamed perceptions or outlooks (such as fear or mistrust) and to assimilate groups into a mainstream who ordinarily diverge from it. There is more interpersonal distrust among heavy viewers, an idea that people cannot be trusted or that they will take advantage of others, and "a heightened and unequal sense of danger and risk in a mean and selfish world" (Signorielli, 1987, p. 267). Heavy viewers in one study (Shrum, 1996) gave significantly higher estimates of the frequency of real-world crime, particular occupations, and marital discord than did light viewers.

Others have found very different reactions and perceptions among viewers. For example, Rubin, Perse, and Taylor (1988) found that respondents felt safe and connected to others regardless of exposure levels, and in fact, higher exposure was associated with perceived safety. Moreover, in contrast to what cultivation theory would predict, heavy and ritualistic viewing was not associated with negative effects, which depended, rather, on specific content (Rubin et al., 1988).

Resonance, on the other hand, refers to situations in which television information about specific issues has particular salience, and what is seen is congruent with a person's actual experiences, with reality, or with the individual's perceived reality (Gerbner et al., 1980). That combination then may give added weight to the television message and lead to an increased effect. The "congruence of the television world and real-life circumstances may 'resonate' and lead to markedly amplified cultivation patterns" (Gerbner et al., 1980, p. 15). Thus, resonance occurs when a topic in the television world has special salience or personal relevance for a group (e.g., overvictimization of the elderly), and it is in that situation that correlations with heavy viewing are clearest.

Research (Bar-on, 2000; Potter, 1986, 1988; Rubin, 1986; Van Evra, 1998) indicates that young children find television content more realistic and/or have greater difficulty distinguishing realistic material from unrealistic material, so its impact on them should be stronger. This impact is enhanced even more by the fact that they have fewer alternative or competing sources of information with which to compare television's messages. In situations in which parents or peers have minimal input or influence, television is more likely to have an effect. Thus, personal interaction and affiliation reduce cultivation, presumably by providing alternate sources of information (Gerbner et al., 1986).

In an updated and expanded theory of the cultivation process, Gerbner, Gross, Morgan, and Signorielli (1994) maintained that cultivation is a complement to other approaches to media effects, not a substitute:

> Yet, we have found that long-term exposure to television, in which frequent violence is virtually inescapable, tends to cultivate the image of a relatively mean and dangerous world. Responses of heavier compared to matching groups of lighter viewers suggest the conception of reality in which greater protection is needed, most people "cannot be trusted," and most people are "just looking out for themselves." (Gerbner et al., 1994, p. 30)

Gerbner et al. (1994) described "the shift from 'effects' to 'cultivation' research" (p. 20) and suggested that TV helps to shape predispositions that affect later media influence. Television is an integral part of a dynamic process and does not simply create or reflect images and beliefs. TV viewing shapes and is part of outlooks, and there is an interaction between viewer characteristics and viewing certain content and among contexts and messages (Gerbner et al., 1994). Cultivation is not unidirectional, but its "pull" depends on where viewers are in relation to the mainstream of the TV world. "In a relatively stable social structure, cultivation implies a commonality of outlooks and resistance to change" (Gerbner et al., 1994, p. 25).

> As successive generations grow up with television's version of the world, the former and more traditional distinctions established before the coming of televison—and still maintained to some extent among light viewers—become blurred. Cultivation implies the steady entrenchment of mainstreatm orientations for most viewers. That process of apparent convergence of outlooks we call *mainstreaming.* (Gerbner et al., 1994, p. 25)

Gerbner et al. (1994) explained how differences between symbolic and objective reality can demonstrate how TV "facts" are incorporated into the beliefs of heavy viewers about the world. For example, TV drama sharply underrepresents older people, and TV characters are much more likely to encounter violence compared to individuals in the real world—more than half on TV and fewer than 1% of people in the United States in any 1 year (Gerbner et al., 1994). However, Gerbner et al. (1994) said cultivation also looks at how these so-called facts affect viewers even when they say they know it's fiction.

According to Gerbner et al. (1994), "lessons" learned repeatedly from TV can affect one's worldview.

In a "drip effect," one picks up knowledge and information even if one is viewing television primarily for entertainment. This suggests, according to Salomon (1981a), that perhaps repeated exposure to undemanding material makes it part of one's schemata and thus influences one to be exposed further to similar material. This is consistent with the cultivation effect proposed by Gerbner et al. (1980, 1994).

New Technologies and the Cultivation Effect

New technology may change how television viewing could cultivate beliefs about social reality as Gerbner suggested because of the diversity of programming and increased viewer control and selectivity (Perse, Ferguson, & McLeod, 1994). Perse et al. found more interpersonal distrust with higher exposure to broadcast-type channels but less mistrust and less fear of crime with greater exposure to more specialized cable channels. Cable had the greatest impact on television's mainstreaming effect, but Perse et al. also found an inverse relation between fear of crime and ownership of VCRs. Perse et al. suggested that cable may pull away from dominant themes of networks or may offer other themes that are reassuring or that increase perceptions of self-efficacy. Cable also may weaken a mainstreaming impact over time. That is, new technologies change the homogenization of heavy viewing, but heavy viewers are less likely to own a VCR and may use cable for "more of the same." Perse et al. urged more study of the impact of new technology on traditional ideas about media effects.

Evaluation

Not everyone agrees with the validity of the cultivation theory conceptualization, however, and cultivation analysis has been criticized on methodological grounds. Rubin et al. (1988) concluded that factors such as response bias may explain cultivation effects that had previously been seen as a function of levels of exposure to television. Moreover, cultivation studies have omitted attention to antecedent and intervening variables, and factors like program choice or perceived reality may override television content in structuring one's perceptions (Rubin et al., 1988). In addition, as it is basically a correlational analysis, causal direction is not easily established. Although heavy viewers may develop a certain perception of the world, their perception of the world also may determine their viewing habits and program choices. Finally, heavy and light viewers differ in other ways as well, and some subgroups seem to show an effect, whereas others do not (Dominick, 1987).

Other variables such as age, socioeconomic level, gender, and perceived realism predicted faith in others better than television exposure, and there is a need to study further the impact of viewer choice and individual differences on perception, especially with the greater diversity of communication alternatives (Rubin et al., 1988).

Shrum (1995) applied social cognitive theory to cultivation research and found that heuristic processing strategies are more likely to be used when involvement in a judgment task is low or when one feels pressure to make a judgment quickly. This, according to Shrum (1995), has implications for cultivation effects because both of those conditions exist in the survey research that is used in much of the published cultivation research. Shrum (1995) suggested that passive viewers are more likely to show a cultivation effect (when measured by first-order judgments such as prevalence estimates of people or behaviors or objects) because of heuristic processing, so viewer involvement is important. Virtually all people overestimate such things as violent crime and prevalence of certain occupations in the workforce such as police. This may not have anything to do with television viewing, however; the important difference is the one between the estimates of heavy and light viewers (Shrum, 1995).

Amount of viewing alone, however, does not appear to be the most important cause of a cultivation effect, and any cultivation effect that is observed is a function of more complex variables than simple level of viewing (Potter, 1986). Levels of identification with television characters and levels of perceived reality also need to be taken into account (Potter, 1986), as do developmental factors. Four-year-old heavy viewers do not receive and respond to the same information as 14-year-old viewers or 40-year-old viewers. Their needs and their motivation for viewing differ widely, their ability to comprehend and retain television information is very different, and their experience and the scripts by which they interpret television material are widely disparate.

Interactions among such variables as cognitive maturity, attention, experience with television, viewing context, family attitudes, and other social/emotional variables need to be addressed in any effort to understand whether and how a phenomenon such as a cultivation effect occurs in children's television viewing experience.

USES AND GRATIFICATIONS THEORY

A uses and gratifications approach focuses on users' motivations and needs, their media preferences, the use they make of the media, and their patterns of use. It assumes that individuals interact actively with the media and purposefully select media or messages from among alternatives to meet their needs (Rubin, 1994). The motives for viewing may vary with television content and among viewers (Rubin, 1984), but children and adolescents as well as adults use media content to satisfy personal needs or wants (Rubin, 1985).

Rubin (1994) argued that much of the criticism of uses and gratifications has resulted from initial assumptions and early research in the 1970s and does not take subsequent research into account. He said that contemporary studies answer the criticism and show systematic progression and further conceptual development including attention to theoretical links among uses of media and effects and more knowledge about audience members as "variably active communicators" (p. 432).

Given the complexity of the uses and effects process, careful consideration of antecedent, mediating, and consequent conditions is necessary (Rubin, 1994).

Motivations for Viewing

Comstock and Scharrer (1999) concluded that the data show three broad categories of motivation for viewing ranked in importance:

1. Escape: View to relax and enjoy, change mood, escape from pressures and reduce stress but especially to spend time in an undemanding way, more an "escape from" than an "escape into."
2. Self-evaluation: View to keep up and to see how well they measure up, comparing themselves to those on the screen of similar gender, age, or race.
3. Information seeking: View to keep up with the medium, to see how television treats various topics.

The gratifications derived from viewing have remained stable over decades, but the main function is to help viewers avoid or escape from aversive stimuli and to spend time in a pleasant and nondemanding way:

> Television programming satisfies popular tastes, is attractive, diverting, and interesting, but not demanding. The viewer, and particularly when the viewing is ritualistic, expends little in terms of involvement emotionally, cognitively, or psychologically, and much only in terms of time. (Comstock & Scharrer, 1999, p. 83)

Developmental level is an important variable in a uses and gratifications approach, and developmental changes in the use of television as a medium have emerged in many studies. The use of television for excitement, for example, decreases between age 9 and 17 (Rubin, 1985). Young children watch more perhaps because they lack other information and experience and because they more often see it as realistic and therefore more relevant. An age cohort is also an indicator of what role individual and social factors play at different developmental levels (Rubin, 1985).

Important differences also exist between heavy viewers and nonviewers in motivation toward or away from television. Foss and Alexander (1996) found that heavy viewers generally attribute their reason for viewing to external circumstances (e.g., being ill, having time, nothing better to do). Both groups felt that television viewing could have negative consequences such as addiction, but heavy viewers felt immune because they viewed television just for escape and relaxation. Nonviewers chose not to watch so that they would not succumb to addictive effects or become passive or noncritical thinkers. Heavy viewers saw television as unimportant and simply a means to relax; nonviewers also saw television as unimportant but chose to spend their time doing other things. Agreement on the basic themes of motivation, consequences, and importance and on the addiction meta-phor still led to very different behavior in the two groups.

Instrumental and Ritualistic Viewing

In a further analysis of audience motives, Rubin (1984, 1986; Rubin & Perse, 1987) distinguished between an active audience that selects specific programs and views purposefully or instrumentally and one in which viewers watch nonselectively and ritualistically. The distinction between instrumental and ritualized types of viewing is also related to amount of viewing and content preferences.

Instrumental viewing, for example, refers to a goal-directed use of the media such as for information. It is selective, purposeful, and infrequent, and it does not show high regard for television as a medium (Rubin, 1984). Viewing is more selective and intentional or purposeful, and there is greater involvement. Ritualized viewing, on the other hand, is a more habitualized, frequent, and nonselective use of television such as for diversion or to relax or pass time, and television is valued as a medium (Rubin, 1984). Thus, the activity of the audience may vary by degree and kind. All audiences are not active for the same reason or in the same way. Audience activity is a variable concept, and individuals might view television instrumentally or ritualistically depending on time, background, and situation (Rubin, 1984).

In ritualistic viewing, according to Comstock and Scharrer (1999), the medium has priority over specific programs, and the motivation is to watch TV and then choose a particular program as the best available. In instrumental viewing, on the other hand, the intrinsic value of the content is more important than the medium, and specific programs attract the viewer. Instrumental viewing is related to lower amounts of viewing and greater preference for interest-based content such as sports, informational programming, and more serious entertainment, but ritualistic and instrumental viewing can alternate within viewers. Most viewers and viewing are ritualistic, and viewing is given passing attention (Comstock & Scharrer, 1999).

Interestingly, Metzger and Flanagin (2002) looked at the extent to which new technologies are used actively and instrumentally or passively and ritualistically. They found that traditional media are used more passively and less instrumentally and more for relaxation and entertainment. TV is used ritualistically, but some traditional media are used very instrumentally (e.g., the phone) or not ritualistically (e.g., a newspaper). The new media, on the other hand, involve more instrumental goals than ritualized ones. Users of the new technologies have more active goals, and there is much more versatility for them in the new technologies. There is inconsistency in orientation, however, in that some new technologies are used ritualistically too, such as the conversational aspects of the Web and Internet. Older users tend to make more instrumental use of the new techniques, and the greater instrumental use of new techniques may mean higher potential for media effects (Metzger & Flanagin, 2002).

Selective Exposure

Zillmann and Bryant (1985b) suggested that viewers are sensitive to the effects of various program characteristics and that they use that knowledge to choose messages that are most capable of achieving desirable results. That is, they emphasize and focus on exposure to content involving comforting messages and tend to minimize exposure to programs with disquieting information; they use or select messages for their therapeutic value (Zillmann & Bryant, 1985a). Individuals who are in a bad mood or want to extend a good one are more likely to choose humor and comedy, for example (Zillmann, 1985). Such selective exposure occurs under or as a function of all kinds of conditions and moods, including fear, stress, and boredom (Zillmann & Bryant, 1985a). Even children as young as 4 or 5 years old were found to use TV to improve their moods (Zillmann & Bryant, 1994), and much media use is beneficial. "It is adaptive, recreational, restorative, and in this sense, therapeutic" (Zillmann & Bryant, 1994, pp. 457–458). The therapeutic value of television entertainment lies in its power to improve one's mood, to calm down, to reduce boredom, or in other ways to derive psychological benefits from viewing it (Zillmann & Bryant, 1986). Selective exposure can use television to produce excitement, to sooth and calm, to involve or distract, to change one's mood, to cheer one's self up, and to provide comfort (Zillmann & Bryant, 1994). It all depends on the needs and motivation of the viewer.

Kubey (1986) stressed the importance of examining the actual experience of individuals in a wide range of activities—of which television viewing is one—to try to discern correlates and causal directions, and studying moods should help to establish when and why individuals view television. Kubey and Csikszentmihalyi (1990) employed three dimensions: location (where participants were when they were beeped), activity (what they were doing when they were beeped), and companionship (whether they were alone or with someone and, if so, with whom when they were beeped). Kubey and Csikszentmihalyi found a relation between amount of viewing and discomfort during solitary and unstructured time, especially for those with marital disruption or breakup and for less affluent and less educated viewers. Such viewers are more likely to continue viewing to avoid time alone with feelings and thoughts and turn to TV when they feel bad and others are not around (Kubey, 1986).

Henning and Vorderer (2001) postulated that individuals with a lower need for cognition or thinking would watch more TV because they feel less pleasure when there is nothing to do but think. The TV, however, is always there and is a distraction and provides escape. Henning and Vorderer concluded that there was a significant negative effect of a need for cognition on the amount viewed, which suggested more viewing as escapism, and that finding was true for both genders in this student sample. There was no support for the idea of social escapism, according to Henning and Vorderer, as income, life satisfaction, and strain did not significantly affect amount of TV viewing.

Media Practice Model.   Brown, Steele, and Walsh-Childers (2002) used their Media Practice Model to go beyond a uses and gratifications perspective to assert that what is learned from media depends not only on viewers' motivation and needs in the viewing situation but also on their sense of self, or identity, and their "lived experience." The lived experience accounts for all of the other factors, such as developmental stage, gender, race, or socioeconomic level and other factors that differentiate one person's experiences from another's. Brown et al. (2002) noted that adolescents' developing identity is a big factor in the media choices they make, interact with, and apply in their lives. Whereas most studies assume more similarity in media choices and interpretation of content, this model assumes that choices and interactions with media are based on who the person is or wants to be at the time (Brown et al., 2002).

Evaluation

Despite its explanatory power on many fronts, however, uses and gratifications theory also has come under serious criticism by some researchers. Kubey and Csikszentmihalyi (1990), for example, noted that the assumptions underlying a uses and gratification approach assume voluntary use of the media to satisfy needs and do not take into account the fact that users do not always have a choice about what is viewed. Family members may view a program because that is what other family members are watching. In addition, Kubey and Csikszentmihalyi said insufficient consideration is given to the fact that viewers have many needs at the same time, and they might be satisfied by a wide range of programs. They also claimed that uses and gratifications theory ignores the fact that many people are affected in similar ways, and there are general media effects that in their view hold the greatest potential for studies of mass communication.

Ruggiero (2000) argued, however, that a uses and gratifications approach is even more significant in an era of computer-mediated communication and that it has always provided an important perspective to each emerging new mass medium, most recently the Internet. Ruggiero urged expansion of the uses and gratification model to include such concepts as interactivity and to explore the interpersonal aspects of current communication.

AN OVERVIEW AND INTEGRATION

Each of the theoretical perspectives discussed in the previous sections has a very different focus or emphasis. A cultivation approach stresses the media content and the impact it has because of its power to cultivate attitudes among heavy viewers. Other theoretical perspectives place more emphasis on viewer characteristics and motivations and on the processes and interactions involved in the viewing experience. Social learning and social cognitive theory, for example, focus on both the content and the viewer and on the modeling, vicarious reinforcement, and other processes that determine viewers' imitation of observed behavior.

Discussions about information-processing abilities, perceived reality, and social learning processes focus on the viewer's cognitive processes as intervening variables between the medium and behavioral effects. Studies (e.g., Austin, Roberts, & Nass, 1990; Desmond, Singer, & Singer, 1990; Messaris, 1986; Nathanson, 1999, 2001) of family influence and mediation point to the environment in which children watch television and place television within a socialization context. Finally, a uses and gratifications approach emphasizes the interaction between the television message and viewer characteristics, needs, and motives. It deals with the motivations of viewers, the uses they make of television, and the needs they satisfy through their use of the media. It looks at what people do with the media rather than what the media do to them (Wright, 1986). Further, a uses and gratifications model addresses the functional alternatives to one's use of the media, the social and psychological environments of viewers, and their communication behavior and its consequences (Rubin, 1986).

Looking at the television viewing experience from only one of these perspectives leads to an incomplete understanding and perhaps misinterpretation of much research data. What is needed is a means by which these various theoretical perspectives and emphases can be integrated into a consistent and coherent conceptualization of what actually happens during and as a result of a child's television viewing and how those events are caused, mediated, facilitated, or impeded.

If one takes into account the diverse theoretical views and empirical data described throughout this book, two rather distinct viewing patterns emerge that help to integrate many of the research findings. These patterns consist of viewing variables that tend to cluster together and reflect very different viewing experiences.

In the first one, television is viewed seriously in an effort to derive information and knowledge from what is being viewed. A considerable amount of mental effort is invested, and logical and critical skills are brought to bear in goal-directed viewing. Such viewers have more intense and focused attention and stronger motivation to extract relevant information from the television content. Under those conditions, television would be expected to have maximum impact in that content area: It is being taken seriously. Whether that influence is positive or negative depends on the content that is being viewed. Moreover, if they engage in heavy viewing and hence displace opportunities for comparing television information with that from other sources, one would expect those viewers to be particularly vulnerable to television's influence and to the cultivation of attitudes and outlooks by the television portrayals.

This interpretation is entirely consistent with script theory in that individuals with little information in an area would have only a limited script (little alternate information) and would depend more heavily on the television experience for information to develop a script for a given area or topic. If the television portrayal is the only, or the major, model for a child (or for viewers who are disadvantaged, in underrepresented minority groups, poorly educated, or lower functioning) or if it is the only or major source of information for a script, that viewer will be more likely to take it seriously, to emulate the television model, or to internalize the television script.

On the other hand, if viewers already have a rich variety of informational sources and are viewing television simply for diversion or entertainment and not for information, they are more likely to experience the television content in a more emotional and less critical way, to exert less mental effort, and to take it less seriously. They would seem to be less susceptible to television's influence or to cultivation of attitudes by its content. Even if they engage in heavy viewing, its impact might be less than if they were using television as a serious and primary source of information, although subtle messages still are conveyed.

The considerable significance of developmental level must be taken into account, however. In the absence of other informational sources and without extensive experience, as is the case with young children, viewing large amounts of television for entertainment might also serve an important informational function. Young children may use entertainment to gain information they need. If they have few other avenues to learn about a content area, heavy viewing, even for entertainment, would likely provide them with information, and would increase television's impact on them.

One way to interpret the data, then, is to underscore the complex interaction that appears to exist between cultivation and uses and gratifications approaches, an interaction that is made more complex by developmental differences among viewers. When television is used differently—to satisfy specific needs—other aspects of the viewing experience also differ significantly. In addition, perceived reality mediates whether the portrayals viewed actually have an impact, particularly if there are few competing views from other informational sources. Even in the case of light viewers, then, when television is being used for information and when the content is perceived to be very realistic, one would expect it to have more effect than if it is being used for diversion and/or if it is perceived to be less realistic. These complex interactions are illustrated in Fig. 1.1.

Thus, the use made of television and the seriousness of one's involvement in it may be more important than sheer level of exposure. Cultivation theory suggests that heavy viewers are most influenced by television's messages. Yet perhaps the amount of viewing is secondary to the motivation for viewing, at least for older children who have other experiences and sources of information to counter television's messages.

The cultivation effect that is often associated with heavy viewing, then, may be greater in some viewer groups, not only because they watch more television but also because they are members of groups (e.g., ethnic minorities, disadvantaged individuals, young children, elderly, poorly educated) who use television very differently; they more often rely on television as a source of information, and they have fewer or less diverse alternative sources. Even if those heavy viewers use television

18

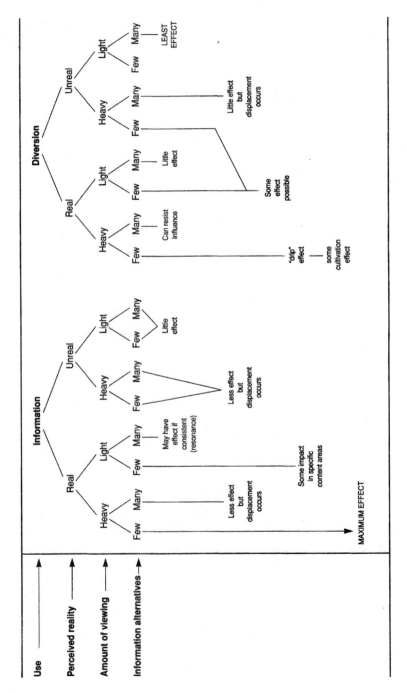

FIG. 1.1. Interactions among use and amount of viewing with perceived reality and information alternatives. Developmental level, socioeconomic level, race, gender, and other factors determine use made of television, perceived reality, amount viewed, and informational alternatives.

primarily for entertainment, if they perceive it to be realistic and if they have little competing information, they are still likely more vulnerable to its influence.

Because individuals view specific programs for various reasons and at different times, they may use television for one purpose on one occasion or for a given program or time period and use it for another reason at another time.

With increasing maturity, then, and the greater likelihood of having alternative sources of information, television may have less impact. One would expect television to be taken less seriously with age, to be perceived as less realistic, and to be used more often for diversion, entertainment, and escape, although socioeconomic status (SES), gender, content, and format variables also affect its influence. For children who have reasonable educational and interpersonal opportunities, television should play a less central role in their lives and socialization as they mature and as their range of experiences expands.

For those older children and adults who do not have other sources of information, however, or who have not developed skills to obtain it, television would be expected to continue to be a primary source of information and to exert a stronger influence. For children from disadvantaged homes, then, or for children with reading problems or whose parents are not involved in their viewing and are not thereby providing alternative information (i.e., for children who watch a considerable amount of television to get the information that they need), the potential for influence and cultivation of attitudes is much greater. Such a distinction among groups of children also helps to clarify seemingly conflicting views among researchers about how seriously children take television or how much they are affected by it.

When one studies viewers who are using television as a serious source of information, all of the characteristics, intervening variables, and processes that are involved in the information processing of television material are relevant and important and further complicate the issue. The effects of formal features on attention, for example, the varying levels of comprehension, the factors that influence retention, the importance of verbal encoding and rehearsal, the effects of age and previous experience on a child's interpretation of television content, and many other variables interact to determine the level and accuracy of the information that the child derives from the viewing experience. Therefore, even when a child is using television seriously to obtain information, many developmental and experiential factors influence the actual quality of the information obtained. Two children viewing the same program for the same purpose (e.g., for information) might well get very different input from the experience depending on their age, sex, socioeconomic level, cognitive maturity, general experience, and family background. The study of television's impact on children, then, is clearly an extraordinarily complex and challenging task.

Cultivation theory has been criticized as relying too heavily on correlational findings in its claim that heavy viewers are more likely to develop attitudes consistent with television portrayals when in fact, it is perhaps those attitudes that lead to heavy television viewing. An emphasis on the purpose of the viewing, however, provides an intervening variable to help explain the relation between amount of viewing and attitudes. Whether heavy viewing leads to the development of a cultivated perception of the world or whether one's perception leads to heavy viewing, the reason for viewing, the use made of television, and the seriousness with which it is taken, as well as other sources of competing information are important factors in predicting the extent of its influence.

Viewing preferences are also important. If one is seeking information, the content selected may be rather different than if one is watching for entertainment or diversion, although individual viewers vary in their judgments about which content is informational and which is entertaining. Hence, patterns of viewer preference also affect the influence that television has, not necessarily directly through the content perhaps but also through the purpose for which the viewer watches that content.

Television content itself can be seen as varying along informational and entertainment dimensions, but its interpretation and the use made of it also can vary depending on the motivation of the viewer. On the surface, one might assume, for example, that shows such as news programs and documentaries would appeal primarily to individuals seeking information; shows such as situation comedies would appeal primarily to those looking for diversion. However, young and inexperienced children, socially inhibited children, or shy adults, that is, those with limited alternative information and strategies, might rely on situation comedies for information as well as a model for social interaction or as a source of strategies in their own interpersonal relationships.

Such television portrayals, then, in the face of less competing information, and especially if viewed alone without input from others about the relative effectiveness of those interactions, should exert a far greater impact than is ordinarily associated with them. Conversely, some viewers are likely to watch documentaries solely for diversion or entertainment rather than to obtain information. There may also be a kind of blending of the two as "infotainment" (Morgenstern, 1989) in which information is presented entertainingly. Morgenstern (1989) pointed out that most Americans connect with reality through television rather than through newspapers and that the television medium is "where relentless sensationalism is now blurring the line between information and entertainment" (p. 28).

The fact that empirical data do not consistently support cultivation theory (Berkowitz & Rogers, 1986) may be because the purpose of viewing or the use made of television and developmental differences among viewers were not taken into account at the same time. Identical content viewed for different reasons and by viewers with very different levels of information and experience should have quite different effects. Moreover, the importance of other variables that have been found in a considerable amount of research, such as age, gender, viewing context, SES, and minority status may well lie, at least in part, in their impact or influence on the use that is made of specific television content at any given point in time.

Conceptualizing the research data in this way allows for integration of many seemingly contradictory findings into a more consistent explanatory picture of television's impact.

SUMMARY

Various theoretical perspectives and models for explaining and interpreting the complex interaction of variables and events that influence children's television experience have been put forward over the years. The earliest of these in the psychological literature was a social learning perspective, which emphasized observational learning and modeling of behaviors viewed on television. This was expanded to social cognitive theory to include the role of such cognitive processes as attention, retention, and motivation in one's media experience.

Some research in the communication field has emphasized television's potential for the cultivation of attitudes and behavior change in viewers. Other research has stressed the needs and motivations of viewers, the context of viewing, the use that is made of television viewing, and the gratifications that viewers obtain from their television experience. Perceived reality of the content and the availability of and access to alternative and competing sources of information as well as the purpose for viewing are critically important variables in the assessment of television's impact. Knowledge of the interactions among media components and content; viewer variables, perceptions, and motivations; and characteristics of the viewing context are essential factors in any efforts to understand children's television experience.

DISCUSSION QUESTIONS

1. Discuss the relative strengths and shortcomings of each major theoretical perspective.
2. How could the diverse theoretical perspectives be combined or integrated to interpret research data that suggests a causal relation between exposure to violence in the media and aggressive behavior?
3. Discuss the relative importance of age and gender differences in each of the theoretical perspectives.

CHAPTER TWO

Research Methodologies

RESEARCH DESIGNS
   Experimental Studies
   Correlational Studies
   Quasi-Experimental Studies

RESEARCH SETTINGS
   Laboratory Studies
   Naturalistic Settings and Field Studies

RESEARCH TIMELINES
   Longitudinal Studies
   Cross-Sectional Studies
   Short-Term Longitudinal or Sequential Designs

PARTICIPANT POPULATIONS AND SAMPLE SELECTION

DATA COLLECTION
   Self-Report Measures
   Observational Data
   Interviews
   Media-Use Diaries
   Experience-Sampling Method

DATA ANALYSIS
   Content Analyses
   Meta-Analysis
   Statistical Techniques and Data Manipulation

SUMMARY

DISCUSSION QUESTIONS

Research Methodologies

Many questions remain about the nature and extent of media influence on children and adolescents. The number of content, viewer, and contextual variables and their interactions in this field is enormous. The study of content variables is in many ways the easiest, although it is still a huge task. Content can include everything from animation to live news broadcasts, from advertisements for makeup to graphic violence, and from sitcoms to historical documentaries. The content of TV programs, video games, magazine articles, and other media can be coded, graphed, analyzed, and compared, and accurate statistics can be derived about the number of portrayals of men versus women, Blacks versus Whites, number of incidents of violence, commercials per hour, or other variables.

The study of the viewers or users of media is more difficult as behaviors, attitudes, beliefs, moods, motivations, and values are harder to code and quantify. The interaction of viewed content and viewer characteristics introduces significantly more complexity into the research. The problems are compounded even further when variations in the context for media use are added in, such as whether viewing or playing video games is done alone or with siblings, parents, or peers; whether the media are used at home or at school or in an arcade; what incidents have occurred before, during, or after media use; and what media such as a TV or radio are on as background. Possible cohort effects further complicate the design and affect the nature of the conclusions that can be drawn.

Research into the interactions among all of these factors is essential to get a clearer picture of the actual impact of media use on children and adolescents. Do children who are younger react differently to advertising or violence when they view alone than when they view with older siblings? How do teens from different backgrounds differ in how they are affected by advertising or by family portrayals on TV? Are they influenced differently by video game violence if they are alone or with a group of friends? The viewing experience of a 4-year-old boy watching a violent show alone likely is quite different from that of a 10-year-old girl viewing the same program with her mother. If one then adds to that picture variations in their socioeconomic level, family background, and school experience as well as differing motivations for viewing and other variables in all of the possible combinations and permutations, the magnitude of the problem facing researchers is very apparent.

The selection of appropriate research methods to try to study these questions and to try to clarify significant variables and confounding factors is one of the most basic blocks of the research foundation. The wrong method or design can lead to invalid, meaningless, or nongeneralizable conclusions. Yet designing studies to ferret out meaningful associations and drawing valid conclusions from such complex phenomena presents a most formidable challenge to researchers. Specific research questions as well as practical and ethical constraints should guide the selection of appropriate methods of both data collection and data analysis. Proper methods maximize the amount of valuable information that can be obtained and the number of valid conclusions that can be drawn. Palmer (1998) talked about variable X, a variable outside the design chosen that may be causing the observed differences, but it is controlled by the diversity of methodologies used. When very different ones lead to similar conclusions, the likelihood of a common outside variable becomes very remote.

Qualitative research has come to mean methods that differ in important ways, and it includes naturalistic research, phenomenological research, and case study or life history research, all of which use observation, interviews, and interpretation and analysis (Lindlof & Meyer, 1998). According to Lindlof and Meyer, the interpretive turn in studying television and social behavior started in the late 1970s because of limitations in existing approaches. There were limitations of experimental designs, for example, such as artificial conditions that were necessary but prevented generalization to more natural viewing situations.

This chapter includes a summary of the main types of research designs commonly used and a discussion of the strengths and weaknesses of each. Reference to these designs in the research cited throughout the book illustrates how the choice and use of the various designs affects the interpretation of data and the conclusions that can be drawn from the studies that are reviewed.

RESEARCH DESIGNS

Experimental Studies

Experimental studies are carried out to try to establish cause and effect relations among variables, and they have distinct advantages. Hypotheses are generated and various factors that might affect relations among relevant variables are controlled for. Participants are matched on relevant variables that might affect results such as age, IQ, educational background, or gender. They are then randomly assigned to experimental or control groups to control bias and confounding factors. One can also control for factors such as the effects of being observed by giving the control group attention but not the experimental treatment.

This design works well for some topics of study but is totally inappropriate for others. It is very difficult, for example, to use this method to study developmental processes. For ethical and methodological reasons, children cannot be randomly assigned to certain groups such as socioeconomically advantaged or disadvantaged groups. They of course cannot be assigned randomly to age groups to see what effect age has on the variables under study.

Children cannot ethically be assigned to groups that might cause harm or keep them from getting the best treatment or intervention that is available. In addition, such research designs may not accurately reflect the complexities of the real world and therefore lack generalizability to that world. Therefore, sometimes "quasi-experiments" are carried out to circumvent these difficulties, and they are discussed later in this section.

According to Ward and Greenfield (1998), the strengths of the experimental design are its high internal validity, the random assignment of participants, and the deliberate manipulation of independent variables so there is greater control and precision. Ward and Greenfield (1998) cited the following as methodological gaps:

1. Not using popular network programs.
2. Not using programs chosen by viewers as stimuli.
3. Not looking at the impact of genre or format or formal features and focusing just on content.
4. Not using a wide range of ages for developmental research. There is more research on young children and on undergraduates with little focus on adolescents, which makes discerning developmental trends difficult.
5. Not looking at the different impacts of underrepresentation of a group as compared with misrepresentation of the group.
6. Not looking at the importance of individual viewer perceptions of stimuli. There is much variation in interpretations of even obvious behavior, and different interpretations can mediate other effects so individual perceptions can be used as mediating variables to study the impact on related behavior and attitudes. For example, would stereotyped content have greater impact if the viewer thought the character's behaviors were justified?
7. Not comparing the effects of content that appears in multiple media such as characters that appear in a TV program or movie and then also in comics, video games, or other media. (The "Harry Potter" phenomenon comes to mind, with characters appearing first in the books and soon after in movies and computer games and software, not to mention Lego sets, lunch boxes, knapsacks, and all of the other marketed spin-offs.)

Ward and Greenfield (1998) said that the priming paradigm can be extended to bridge these methodological gaps. Different dependent variables could be used. One could have participants watch stereotyped content, for example, and then question their justifications for later behavior regarding differences in how they interpreted their own behavior depending on the kind of material involved in priming them. One could prime stereotypes of viewers before viewing, for example, to see how their perception of content is affected. In any case, new questions should be addressed and research should not be limited by what has already been done (Ward & Greenfield, 1998).

Correlational Studies

Correlational studies focus on the relation between specific variables and how they covary. For example, heavy smoking is correlated or associated with a high risk of lung cancer. This is a positive correlation because both factors vary in the same direction. Higher rates of smoking are associated with higher rates of lung cancer. Negative correlations exist when two factors vary in opposite directions. As one rises, the other decreases. For example, as one adopts a healthier lifestyle, including good diet and exercise, the risk of heart disease decreases. One goes up, the other goes down; they are negatively associated or correlated.

Correlational studies can only demonstrate associations and relations between variables, however. They cannot establish causality or causal direction such as whether variable A caused variable B or vice versa or whether both were affected by a third variable. They are necessary when ethical constraints and other factors prevent researchers from assigning children to certain groups. Children and adolescents could not be assigned randomly to smoking and nonsmoking groups, for example; existent groups must be used.

Although correlational studies cannot establish causation, they are enormously helpful in developing our knowledge about relations among variables and in generating hypotheses to be tested in future research. Sophisticated statistical analyses can also be done on data to discern trends that lend support to causal hypotheses.

Quasi-Experimental Studies

These are studies that use already existing groups to study specific phenomena. For example, groups of children from affluent and from poor homes might be exposed to a specific teaching technique to see what effect it has on their learning and achievement. The children can be matched for age, gender, and intellectual level to control for some important variables, but they cannot be randomly assigned to poor and affluent groups. This method can expand our knowledge about the possible interaction of variables. A significant problem arises in the interpretation of the data, however, because these groups often differ systematically in other ways than the dimension being studied, which can affect the relations being studied. Such studies, then, allow testing of specific hypotheses, but possible confounding variables or cohort effects can make the data difficult to interpret.

RESEARCH SETTINGS

Laboratory Studies

Studies done in a laboratory setting allow the most rigorous control of variables. As only a limited or finite number of variables can be controlled, however, the possibility of confounding by other variables exists. Moreover, the laboratory setting is least like a natural setting, making some generalizations to broader, real-world settings questionable.

Naturalistic Settings and Field Studies

These studies are conducted in the most life-like setting, a setting where a behavior such as TV viewing or other media use normally and naturally occurs. Control of all of the variables that may affect the findings is impossible, however. Children viewing violence in a laboratory setting set up and controlled by researchers is a very different experience from viewing in their own living rooms with their families and with all of the usual interruptions, concurrent activity, household cues, and family attitudes.

According to MacBeth (1998), natural and field experiments do allow causal inferences to be made. Natural experiments use intact, preexisting groups that vary naturally rather than because of assignment to groups in the research. Field experiments also use preexisting groups but assign them to different conditions rather than naturally varying ones. One way to rule out the effect of maturation, for example, is to include a couple of groups in a pretest to see if cross-sectional differences are similar to pretest and posttest longitudinal differences (MacBeth, 1998).

RESEARCH TIMELINES

Longitudinal Studies

Longitudinal studies are carried out over a long period of time. They are necessary to actually follow changes in individuals over time. The same participants are studied over an extended period to follow actual changes in those individuals as they grow and mature. The acquisition of knowledge about changes in behavior and thought processes over time helps to define broader developmental changes and processes. Moreover, changes in groups of individuals who vary in important ways such as gender and who have different experiences can be compared. Longitudinal studies can help to show how media portrayals are integrated into children's and adolescents' developing beliefs and intentions to act on them (Gruber & Grube, 2000).

Such studies, although providing invaluable information, also have serious limitations. They take a long time, and new variables cannot be introduced as they come to light. Moreover, participants may leave and drop out of studies, changing and skewing the sample. Factors that differentially affect who drops out may not be apparent, and thus, bias can be introduced into the study. Longitudinal studies do not get around the cohort problem entirely either because individuals are still selected at certain ages and may share certain experiences.

Cross-Sectional Studies

Cross-sectional studies are easier to devise and require snapshots in time, so they are quicker to carry out. These studies use groups at different ages rather than the same individuals at different ages; therefore, developmental processes can be inferred but cannot actually be studied in individuals. Problems can include cohort effects (in which a whole group shares some similar experience that affects the outcome) and limited ability to control important confounding variables.

Short-Term Longitudinal or Sequential Designs

These studies take different groups at different ages as in cross-sectional studies, but they follow them over a period of time that is shorter than longitudinal but longer than a simple snapshot as occurs in cross-sectional studies. One example is a time-lag study, a kind of cross-sectional study in which different groups (cohorts) are compared to get around the cohort problem. For example, one might study preschoolers born in one year with preschoolers born in subsequent years over a specified period of time to try to discern developmental processes over time.

PARTICIPANT POPULATIONS AND SAMPLE SELECTION

Children and adolescents can be studied in small groups or an *n* of 1 such as in case studies or in large groups that are representative of even greater populations and randomly selected from those populations. The type of sample and the sample size dictate in part how generalizable the findings will be. If participants have been randomly selected from a large defined population, findings can be generalized to that population with a certain degree of probability. If participants have not been randomly selected, hypotheses can be generated that might help to explain the findings or that could inform future research, but broad generalizations cannot be made. Even if participants were randomly selected from a specific population, findings cannot be generalized to other populations because possible confounding variables would be introduced.

In choosing participants from a larger population, there must be appropriate geographical, gender, ethnic and cultural, socioeconomic, educational, and other representation, including proportions of each that occur in the larger population, before the findings can be extrapolated or generalized to the larger group.

Comstock (1998) reminded us, however, that we get protection from inability to generalize research findings from a number of sources, including (a) samples that are not biased for the question being addressed; (b) replication, as the ability to replicate findings protects against interpretation of artifacts and allows the study of applicability to other populations; (c) elimination of alternative explanations; and (d) theory. By testing propositions that have been derived from theory, we can build our knowledge, and new findings that fit into a pattern give the pattern greater credibility.

DATA COLLECTION

There are many ways to gather data on children and adolescents. The means by which data are collected depends in large part on the type of research design, on the specific hypotheses being tested or the questions being asked, and on specific participant variables. The age of the participants affects the type of data collection as well. Young children, for example, cannot be expected to keep diaries or complete surveys, and infants cannot describe their experiences. Parents need to provide that information except for observational data that can be obtained by researchers. The following represent some of the most commonly used data collection techniques.

Self-Report Measures

These include surveys and questionnaires completed by children and teens themselves or by parents for younger children. They can provide a considerable amount of valuable data, but they do have limitations. Participants may show a response bias in that they may tend to give primarily negative or positive responses in a kind of pattern of responding. Social desirability, or answering in a way that one thinks is the "right" way to respond or one that will present the most favorable image, can skew the results. Selective memory or retrospective memory distortions, such as the amount of time they actually spent watching television or playing video games or the content they viewed, may lead to inconsistent and inaccurate data.

Observational Data

Participants are observed in the laboratory or natural setting, and the relevant behaviors are recorded fully and carefully. The observations then can be scored or coded to provide information about patterns of behavior. The key to good observational data is to have specific and well-defined behaviors to be observed and to have as helpful and effective a way as possible to record and then code them. Changes in behaviors such as in frequency, intensity, or duration need to be recorded carefully to be of any use in data analysis and interpretation. Possible problems in differences between observers can be avoided by testing out the observational signs and codes beforehand and making sure correlations between the responses of various observers are sufficiently high to allow useful interpretation of the results.

Interviews

Similar caveats as for observational data apply here. Careful definitions, consistency in questions and coding of responses, and objectivity are essential.

Media-Use Diaries

Media-use diaries can provide useful documentation of one's viewing, reading, or game-playing behavior, but they rely on an individual's consistency and compliance. Accurate recording of responses may vary from person to person or even within the same individual at different times.

Experience-Sampling Method

The Experience-Sampling Method (ESM; Csikszentmihalyi & Larson, 1987; Kubey, Larson, & Csikszentmihalyi, 1996) can be used to obtain data in naturalistic settings on the frequency and patterns of various daily activities and interactions, on psychological states, and on thought patterns. ESM data is based on self-reports of individuals at random points through their waking hours and measures variability within people over time (Kubey & Csikszentmihalyi, 1990). This method elicits not only information about time spent but more information about viewers' subjective experience of various activities (Kubey & Larson, 1990). Evidence for its validity exists in the correlations with physiological measures, psychological tests, and behavioral indexes (Csikszentmihalyi & Larson, 1987).

DATA ANALYSIS

Data analysis is a crucial part of the research process. It affects how much information can actually be gleaned from the data and the kind of conclusions that can be drawn.

The simplest types of data analyses are the measures of central tendency such as comparisons of means and standand deviations or medians on various factors being measured to see differences between groups and whether the differences are significant. Levels of statistical significance allow one to state at a specified level of probability that the results are not due to chance variation.

Content Analyses

Content analyses break down the content of a show or game or article to provide information about relevant variables such as the number of violent events in a TV show, the number of males and females in advertising, and the relative frequency of specific events. These variables provide data on what is viewed but not on what effects there are on viewers (Strasburger, 1993). They do provide important information on the nature of the content to which children and adolescents are exposed and on changes that occur over time.

Meta-Analysis

Meta-analyses combine the results of many studies on a topic and attempt to discern trends in the research by combining these findings. They are very useful for getting more global pictures of the research and can lead to broader conclusions from many studies than from single ones. As whole bodies of evidence can be studied to analyze trends, results, and the "weight of the evidence," meta-analyses are "the great synthesizers" (Palmer, 1998, p. 63).

Statistical Techniques and Data Manipulation

There are many kinds of sophisticated statistical analyses that can be done to further refine the types of conclusions that can be drawn. They help researchers discern trends or causal sequences when actual experiments are not feasible.

SUMMARY

The choice of research design and methodology has a direct influence on the validity and generalizability of one's research findings and interpretation of data. Experimental designs allow for the greatest control of possible confounding variables. Because of the random assignment of participants to groups, the control of relevant variables, and the manipulation of other variables or conditions, causal statements can be made with greater confidence. However, experiments are usually conducted in laboratory or contrived settings and cannot incorporate all of the complex variables that determine behavior in the natural environment.

The natural setting for research provides the most realistic background, but control of relevant variables is more difficult, and the data usually lead to findings of correlation or association rather than causality. Causal interpretations are limited because of the inability to manipulate variables and to randomly assign participants to various groups. Ethical questions and constraints often require the use of naturally occurring groups rather than random assignment of children to groups that could be harmful or that would preclude sound treatment.

Methods of sample selection and data collection and variations in timelines of studies such as whether they are cross-sectional or longitudinal also affect the interpretation of data. Various research designs and sophisticated statistical analyses have been developed to try to circumvent some of these problems.

DISCUSSION QUESTIONS

1. Discuss some of the major methodological problems involved in studying developmental changes in children's media use and preferences.
2. Discuss the relative merits of cross-sectional and longitudinal studies for research on children's vulnerability to media violence.
3. What are some of the ethical constraints on choice of research design and methodology? How could these be handled?

PART II

Cognitive Aspects of Media Experience

CHAPTER THREE

Information Processing

ATTENTION
  Comprehensibility of Content
  Auditory and Visual Attention
  Stimulus Characteristics and Developmental Level
  Gender Differences

COMPREHENSION
  Information Processing of Content
  Amount of Invested Mental Effort (AIME)
  Developmental Differences
  Conceptual Changes
  Stimulus Modalities
  Formal Features
  Realism of Content
  Methodological Issues

RETENTION
  Mediating Variables
    Formal Features
    Developmental Differences
  Recognition Versus Recall
  Motivation for Viewing

LINGUISTIC AND HOLISTIC ASPECTS
  Stimuli and Processing Interactions
  Differences in Retention

SUMMARY

DISCUSSION QUESTIONS

Information Processing

ATTENTION

The question of whether children are passive or active viewers of television fare has important implications for their cognitive processes including attention, comprehension, and retention. Disagreement continues in the current research literature as well as historically between those who view the television viewer as an essentially passive individual who absorbs information and television content indiscriminately and those who see the viewer as an active, constructionist individual whose own characteristics and past experience determine what is attended to and retained. Current research supports the view that children's expectations, needs, motivation, set, activity, cognitive skill, and experience all serve as determinants of attention.

Comprehensibility of Content

Many studies have noted the significant reciprocity between levels of attention and the comprehension, or anticipated comprehension, of television content. Children's assessment of the comprehensibility of television content affects the levels of attention they direct to the material (Lorch, Anderson, & Levin, 1979; Pingree, 1986). Even 2-year-olds direct attention to television because they are strongly motivated to understand it (Hawkins & Daly, 1988). Content beyond their level of comprehension, however, may lead to reduced attention by children, as does engaging in other activities while viewing (Comstock & Paik, 1991; Wright, St. Peters, & Huston, 1990).

Monitoring comprehensibility is one of several cognitive activities in viewing. If a television segment is clearly not understandable by a child, there is little reason for that child to continue attending visually even though much effort has been invested initially (Pingree, 1986). When Hawkins, Kim, and Pingree (1991) studied the visual attention of children aged 3, 5, and 6 years, the children showed early increased attention to random segments shown them as though they were trying to deal with difficult content. When language in a segment was incomprehensible, however, attention at all ages decreased and stayed low, and there was little developmental change in the results.

Older children increase their visual attention and put more effort into incomprehensible or challenging sections than do 5-year-olds (Pingree, 1986), and older children who watch educational and child-informative programs that are appropriate for their level of comprehension and who coview with a parent may learn to attend more closely (Wright et al., 1990).

Thus, attention is guided actively by the child's assessment of the comprehensibility of the content and attempts to comprehend it, situational and contextual variables including the presence of other viewers, and other activities in which the child may be engaged.

Auditory and Visual Attention

Levels of auditory and visual attention vary greatly depending on program content, the age of the viewer, and the viewing context. Children also monitor television auditorially while they are engaged in other activities. When they note something of interest and something they can understand, they give it their visual attention as well (Lorch et al., 1979). If the content becomes redundant or incomprehensible, they return to their other activities. A reduction in the comprehensibility of the audio portion has a strong effect of reducing visual attention (Anderson & Collins, 1988). Even preschoolers can use cues from auditory input while engaging in other activities to tell when visual attention is necessary, and they can spontaneously adjust their visual attention (Pezdek & Hartman, 1983; Pingree, 1986).

Visual attention to television likely accounts for only about two thirds of the time spent with the television set, as children may spend considerable time with television doing things other than looking at it (Anderson & Collins, 1988; Anderson, Field, Collins, Lorch, & Nathan, 1985). Thus, "heavy viewers" (i.e., those spending a lot of time with television) are not necessarily heavy viewers in the amount of time spent attending to television (Anderson et al., 1985). In one study (Anderson et al., 1985), for example, a child who spent almost 40 hours a week with television (heaviest viewer) only looked at it for about 3½ hours (light viewer). Thus, visual attention is a reliable indicator of television viewing, but it may not be a valid one.

Important interactions operate as well, and even the percentage of visual attention is not a clear determinant of influence or involvement. Children who glance briefly at a television program and then look away to think about what they have seen may actually be using a relatively greater amount of mental effort, or children may use different levels of effort with equivalent levels of visual attention (Pingree, 1986). Moreover, viewers who appear to be attending may actually be daydreaming about something totally different (Lull, 1988a).

It is clear, then, that studies that define attention as visual orientation to a television screen may overlook important auditory perceptual activities that also affect attention and comprehension, and they also may miss other cognitive activity in which a child is engaged. Behaviors other than visual attention need to be considered in addressing a child's meaningful attention and involvement with television content. Such findings highlight some of the methodological problems that can lead to inaccurate conclusions.

Stimulus Characteristics and Developmental Level

Attentional level is not just a matter of whether the stimuli are visual or auditory. Much depends on the nature of the stimulus and its complexity. Many studies have focused on television's formal characteristics and features that attract a child's attention to the television. The importance of the formal features of television (e.g., pace, cuts, sound effects, the presence or absence of dialogue) as distinguished from its content has been well established (Huston, Greer, Wright, Welch, & Ross, 1984; Huston & Wright, 1983). Important age differences in attention to such features exist, however. Young children are much more attentive to highly perceptually salient features including animation, peculiar voices, lively music, rhyming, auditory changes (Anderson & Levin, 1976), and sound effects (Calvert & Gersh, 1987).

As children become older and more knowledgeable about and experienced with television, the cognitive demands of a program become more important. Salient features still attract their attention as well, at least initially, but they tend to use more highly developed conceptual skills to guide their attention and response to content. Older children also do not require the same focused attention that is needed by younger children to obtain information. They can attend in a less focused way or while doing other things and still obtain a considerable amount of information from the TV content.

Miron, Bryant, and Zillmann (2001) considered arousal level in its relation to attention and vigilance as the relative benefit of arousal through moderately fast-paced programs, and the negative effects of very fast programming because of limited processing capacity. They concluded that the optimal pace may depend on the type of programming, with arousal benefits of rapid-pace programs associated with entertainment. For educational programming, the main concern should be information load. Miron et al. also noted that technological advances toward higher image and sound fidelity have reduced the sensory gap between reality and TV content and shifted concern more toward the distinction between realistic and unrealistic programming.

Gender Differences

In one of two studies of gender differences in attention by Alvarez, Huston, Wright, and Kerkman (1988), 5- and 7-year-olds were shown four animated programs with combinations of high and low violence and high and low action. Visual attention was greater in boys than girls, but that did not mean greater comprehension. Boys showed more attention to high violence than low, and their attention did not change across conditions. Girls, on the other hand, attended more to low-action programs than high.

In Alvarez et al.'s (1988) other study of children ages 3 to 11, boys showed significantly more attention than girls across experiments, and most content and form characteristics did not explain the gender differences. Alvarez et al. found weak support for the greater appeal of violence and animation for boys, and they concluded that girls focus more on verbal or auditory content and boys more on visual content.

COMPREHENSION

Age differences in levels of comprehension, both for central learning and for incidental learning, have been reported frequently. Although understanding is clearly related to age and experience with the medium, other variables such as amount of effort invested, reason for viewing, input from others, and socioeconomic level also affect how much and which content a child can grasp and master.

According to Clifford, Gunter, and McAleer (1995), from age 8 to midteens, children's information-processing skills as well as social and intellectual schemas are developing. Clifford et al. focused on the cognitive impact of programs with informational content to see what information viewers absorbed, how they thought about issues that the programs raised, and whether short-term changes occurred as a result of exposure to those issues. This approach assumes that television effects are mediated by a child's understanding of the content, whether they believe it, and whether it is consistent with what they know.

The basic premise of Clifford et al. (1995) was that what children get out of television depends heavily on what they bring to it, and age and experience are important. Moreover, according to Clifford et al., children's cognitive processes and the constructs they use to understand and interpret television programs are different from the ones adults use. They found few gender differences, and prior viewing and amount of viewing had little relation to comprehension, although background knowledge did (Clifford et al., 1995). As much of television programming shows people in social interaction, children's comprehension of television may be influenced by their ability to understand such character depictions (Babrow, O'Keefe, Swanson, Meyers, & Murphy, 1988). Their comprehension of much of television's content, then, also depends on their more general interpersonal experience.

Information Processing of Content

The information-processing problem facing the child viewer, as described by Anderson and Smith (1984), is a very demanding one. The television content is highly varied and open to several levels of analysis, and the content that the child perceives may not be what the producer intended. They also must learn to understand the formal features of television that maintain attention, mark important content, and transmit meaning. Finally, important differences exist in the viewing environment or the context in which television is viewed, including such factors as the choice of other activities, distractions, others watching, general family or cultural attitudes, and other demands (Anderson & Smith, 1984).

Because much of the material necessary for full comprehension of television programs is not presented explicitly and requires drawing of inferences such as causation, motivation, time passage, and others, a distinction must be made between the specific cognitive activities involved in processing television information and the amount of effort applied to those activities (Hawkins & Pingree, 1986). Fowles (1992) noted that children will absorb more than adults per hour of TV because they are always trying to learn about the world, but compared to the number of hours they sit there, they learn a small amount, and at a slower rate as they get older and more discriminating.

Amount of Invested Mental Effort (AIME)

According to Salomon (1981b, 1983, 1984), the amount of mental effort invested in television viewing (AIME) is affected by a viewer's perception of what is demanded, and symbol systems on television require less mental effort to extract meaning (i.e., they emphasize experiential aspects, imagery); they may allow "shallower" processing than reading, regardless of content. In fact, this characteristic may be part of television's appeal (Cohen & Salomon, 1979). In other words, the imagery and symbols on television generally allow viewers to derive meaning with less effort than they would require to derive meaning from reading. Reading requires more focused concentration, a greater facility with language and recall of vocabulary, and a mastery of all of the skills that comprise reading. In reading, the mental schema or perspective that a reader brings to the material affects the likelihood of remembering elements of a story, and processing with more AIME leads to better learning, recall, comprehension, and inferences (Cohen & Salomon, 1979).

According to Salomon (1984), AIME depends on a viewer's perception of material, what effort it deserves, the likely payoff of more effort, and belief in one's own efficiency; that is, the issue of AIME indicates that children interact with the medium. They must make judgments about the level of effort required for a task. Children do, however, use many cues to decide what level of processing is required to comprehend the information presented (Wright et al., 1984). Moreover, their assessment of how much effort is needed to understand material, either printed or televised, affects the depth of information processing that they actually use and thereby fulfills their expectations (Salomon & Leigh, 1984). For example, they are likely to read comic books with less invested effort, making that particular reading activity more like television viewing. In fact, one might view comics, with their heavy visual and pictorial component, as more like television than they are like ordinary books.

If children are not instructed to react differently than usual, less effort is invested and little inferential knowledge is extracted. Children can change their processing, however, exert more effort, and show increased understanding when they are told that they will be tested for recall of content (Anderson & Collins, 1988). They can also be encouraged to invest more effort and to look at television programs with a more critical eye. Effortless processing of television information, then, is based on children's preconceptions and expectations, not on the inherent nature of television.

Developmental Differences

There are, of course, important developmental differences in children's understanding of television. Imagine the task facing a very young child who is attempting to comprehend what he or she is watching, and compare it with the events that the same child perceives and experiences in real-life interactions:

> They [television personalities] have no substance, they're only human-seeming shadows moving on glass, but they can go anywhere and do anything—one minute a male and female shadow will be in a bar and zap! a second later they're in a bed together. They disappear at regular intervals and in their place come earnest ones talking about suppressing our odors or keeping us regular. Then the first ones are back, acting as if they never left. They dance, they sing, they drive very fast. They seem sure they can make us laugh, cry and watch them, but if we don't, they vanish. ("Celebrating Television," 1989, p. 6)

In one study (Barr & Hayne, 1999) infants ranging in age from 12 to 18 months were shown behaviors or actions either in a live demonstration or on a videotape. They were all able to reproduce the actions that had been modeled live, but their ability to imitate the same actions demonstrated on a tape varied with age and task differences (Barr & Hayne, 1999). In another study demonstrating similar age differences, Troseth and DeLoache (1998) compared 2-year-olds with 2½-year-olds on their ability to retrieve a toy that they had watched being hidden, either directly or on a video. The 2½-year-old children could find the toy based on watching a video of the toy being hidden, but the 2-year-olds could not. The 2-year-olds did much better, however, if they watched the toy being hidden directly through a window or if they thought they were watching it directly (watching a monitor through a window). Troseth and DeLoache concluded that young children have difficulty using information from symbolic representation of a real situation. This is relevant because we often assume that video displays and their connections to reality are obvious to viewers regardless of age, whereas this is sometimes true but sometimes not (Troseth & DeLoache, 1998).

Children's ability to understand emotional components of what they see is also clearly related to their developmental level. Three-year-olds think television characters are real and they do not understand narrative or dramatic structure; they may not understand sarcasm and irony until late childhood or perhaps early adolescence (Young, 1990). On the other hand, Pexman, a Canadian researcher, found that children as young as 5 could understand sarcasm such as might come from Bart Simpson, but they just do not find it funny until much later ("Sarcasm," 2003). That is, they understand the mean–nice dimension and know that one can insult someone, but it takes longer for them to see how that can be used to be funny or to make someone look less clever. Pexman's data suggests that children can start to appreciate sarcastic humor at about 10 or 11 years of age, although older siblings and exposure to various television programming might affect a child's ability to learn to interpret sarcasm. As sarcasm is a mainstay of much TV, younger children may miss some of the humor in those shows, as they respond more to visually obvious humor such as slapstick, messiness, or falling down. Some have alleged that there are too few targeted programs for children between 6 and 9 that would include humor that was more sophisticated than that aimed at preschoolers but not as cynical as that aimed at adults ("Sarcasm," 2003).

In one recent study (Reuters, 2003), children as young as 12 months were observed to make decisions based on the emotional reactions of adults around them. The researchers showed videotapes of actors reacting to normal household objects such as a bumpy ball, garden hose attachment, and red letter holder. When babies were given the same objects to play with, the 10-month-olds were not influenced by the videos but the 12-month-olds were. They played happily with objects to which the actors had reacted positively or neutrally but avoided those to which actors had reacted with fear or disgust (Reuters, 2003).

Significant differences in accuracy of temporal judgments also exist as a function of age (Hirsch & Kulberg, 1987). Hirsch and Kulberg found that children tended to underestimate longer, 45-second segments and overestimate those of shorter, 15-second duration. Those who watched less television performed better in estimating the length of television segments. That is, participants, especially preschoolers, performed less accurately in direct proportion to the amount of television that they reportedly watched. This was less the case for older children whose skills at estimating time lengths were more clearly established. Hirsch and Kulberg concluded that children's age and the amount of television they watch during preschool are significant factors in the development of their ability to make temporal judgments.

Flashbacks and replays as indicators of temporal shifts in television content are incomprehensible to young children. Of the 4- to 9-year-olds in one study (Rice, Huston, & Wright, 1986), for example, the older children were more likely to detect a replay, whereas younger children saw them merely as repetitions, suggesting that they are likely to be rather confused about much on television—or at least might misinterpret and distort a good part of what they see. Ten-year-olds could understand flashbacks better than 6-year-olds (Calvert, 1988). Young children, then, may misinterpret content in flashbacks and view replays as new or ongoing events instead of one event being described repeatedly. This becomes especially important in exploring the impact of news coverage that includes endless replays of specific footage such as the terrorist attacks of 9/11 or other disasters. Given the huge number of replays of disasters such as the 9/11 attacks, the lack of understanding of replays and the belief that what they see represents ongoing events would make the material even more frightening and upsetting.

Conceptual Changes

Children's comprehension of TV content clearly improves with age also because they develop the ability to focus on information that is relevant to the plot and ignore information that is not (Kelly & Spear, 1991). Kelly and Spear found that children's comprehension and retention of content could be facilitated by placing a viewing aid within the television program itself in the form of short synopses of centrally relevant scenes to mimic chunking skills that older viewers use. Synopses placed after commercials helped second graders remember central content better than placement before commercials or none at all. In fact, in that condition, their recognition was similar to that of fifth graders, and the various conditions did not affect the comprehension of fifth graders. Kelly and Spear suggested that inclusion of such synopses after commercials could improve young children's comprehension without coviewing with adults.

Comprehension increases only gradually with age, and young children may get quite different information from television than older children who can process larger amounts of information more efficiently. Some research has suggested, however, that early studies may have underestimated children's levels of understanding and that children may comprehend a good deal more than has been thought. Anderson and Collins (1988) noted the ability of preschoolers to discern central content and to engage in many inferential activities, at least for short programs; but they have greater difficulty with and more frequently misinterpret full-length dramatic programs. Anderson and Collins suggested that children's improved comprehension of lengthier and more adult programs as they get older is due more to their increased experience with the media and to their growing general knowledge of the world than to shifts in their ability to discern central content or to make inferences.

Children's developing experience with TV affects their future viewing and comprehension (Crawley et al., 2002). When regular experienced viewers of the TV series *Blues Clues*, ages 3 to 5, were compared with inexperienced viewers, Crawley et al. found that the experienced group looked less but interacted more with new episodes and showed better comprehension of the familiar content. When the two groups were compared while viewing a different series, however, the experienced ones again looked less and interacted more, but the groups did not differ in comprehension. These results suggest that children's experience with *Blues Clues* seemed to affect their viewing style but only gave them a comprehension edge for that series and not with new and unfamiliar material (Crawley et al., 2002).

Stimulus Modalities

The modality involved in the television input is an important component of comprehension as it was with attention. Differences in comprehension appear to be due in part to differences in the types of stimuli to which children of varying ages attend, and there is controversy about the relative importance of auditory versus visual stimuli to young children in their television viewing and comprehension. Hoffner, Cantor, and Thorson (1988) reported that 5- and 6-year-olds had more difficulty understanding and integrating visual input than auditory, whereas older children (8–9 and 10–12) appeared to understand equally well in either format. When the younger participants in the Hoffner et al. (1988) study were given both visual and auditory input, however, they could sequence sentences as well as the older participants. Hoffner et al. (1988) suggested that the older children may have formed a visual representation while listening to auditory input, whereas the younger children may have needed visual support as well. Moreover, children may remember specific visual material better, but they need verbal information to derive meaning and understand complex visual information (Hoffner et al., 1988). It appears that supplementary auditory information, either in the form of spontaneous labeling by the child or labeling by an adult, facilitates the reception of input through that modality when stimuli are primarily visual.

In a study of 4- and 7-year-olds' comprehension of audiovisual and audio-only presentations (Gibbons, Anderson, Smith, Field, & Fischer, 1986), however, the visually presented actions were associated with better performance in the younger children but not in the older ones. The younger children also understood dialogue better when it was presented in the audiovisual condition than in the audio-alone condition. Perhaps some of the inconsistencies in the literature, then, regarding the relative importance of visual and auditory input in children's comprehension result from a confounding of these processing components and this possibility is explored later in this chapter.

Children attend most when both visual and auditory presentations are used, and narration improved visual attention and comprehension of visual content in one study (Rolandelli, Wright, Huston, & Eakins, 1991). However, children could understand the verbal content without looking; that is, their comprehension of auditory material did not depend on looking. Girls attended more to the auditory modality than boys, and boys were more dependent on looking. Narration, then, enhances visual attention and comprehension, it mediates attention and comprehension, and it seems to make programs more understandable and interesting for young children because it is appropriate to their language ability (Rolandelli et al., 1991). However,

Rolandelli et al. found that the auditory component is important independent of visual input. Older children process auditorially more and understand better, but both younger and older children did better with narration. Rolandelli et al. (1991) concluded that "auditory attention contributes, both uniquely and interactively with visual attention, to children's processing of television" (p. 120).

Inconsistencies in findings of children's relative abilities in these areas may be due to the fact that specific visual information may be relatively easier to remember, but deriving meaning from complex visual sequences or scenes may be harder for young children than deriving it from verbal descriptions (Hoffner et al., 1988). As some films and many programs for children are essentially nonverbal (mostly action/adventure), however, with little dialogue, young children may have difficulty interpreting their content (Hoffner et al., 1988). Moreover, they may remember those programs without having been able to derive complex meaning from them. Young children also may lack adequate language skills to describe the meaning they get from complex visual material.

Formal Features

The levels of comprehension of which children are capable are not a function solely of viewer age and maturity or developmental level, however; they are also influenced by specific characteristics of the television content. Features such as pace, for example, may affect not only attention but also may influence comprehension and in unexpected directions at times. Fast pace may actually interfere with comprehension, as fast-paced shows are harder for children to integrate than slower paced ones (Wright et al., 1984). In addition, format of the show (e.g., story vs. magazine) appears to be more important than fast pace; and high-continuity programs such as stories result in increased attention, better comprehension, and better recall than shows with low continuity such as a magazine format (Wright et al., 1984).

Hayes and Kelly (1984) suggested that the formal features of radio or television such as sound effects and zooms may serve as "punctuation" and may influence attention to particular aspects. If these are clear and consistent, comprehension and recall might be facilitated; if shifts are not marked by perceptually salient features, however, comprehension might be negatively affected. In either case, young children attend primarily to certain aspects of the television experience; to the extent that other aspects are ignored, their understanding is distorted and limited.

Realism of Content

Much of the literature suggests that realism in television content and children's ability to distinguish real from fantasy material are important factors in their comprehension of television information and in television's effects on them. Young children have difficulty distinguishing television content from real-world experience and may overgeneralize. They first attribute equal reality to everything they see. They are high on the *Magic Window* dimension, the degree to which the belief is held that television content accurately and literally represents real life (Potter, 1986, 1988). First-grade children in one study (Van Evra, 1984), for example, did not see television as a separate world. They appeared to be sufficiently egocentric as to assume that whatever happens in their own family is also what occurs more generally in other families both in real life and on television.

There is some disagreement in the literature on the age at which children can distinguish reality from fantasy, but in general, there is a negative relation between age and perceived realism over the elementary years (Rubin, 1986a). By age 5 or 6, children have a rough sense of what is realistic and what is not. Their major continuing task, however, a more complex one, is to see how much something that looks real is actually staged (Gardner & Krasny Brown, 1984).

Children show a huge increase at age 4 or 5 in their ability to understand the differences between appearance and reality, and by age 4, most children can see what is real (Adler, 1991). Before that, they believe that what they see is real. Therefore, things that look scary arouse fear in preschoolers, whereas for older school-age children who can discriminate better between what can and cannot occur, there is more fear in response to things that actually could happen regardless of appearance (Cantor & Sparks, 1984). Thus, one would expect younger children to be more frightened by ghosts, monsters, and other imaginary creatures that they see on television. Older children might well be frightened by such events as a kidnapping, which they perceive as an actual possibility even though the perpetrators of the crime may have conveyed the threat calmly and subtly. Younger children would likely miss the more subtle danger. Conversely, coverage of real-life events such as the 9/11 attacks that are highly perceptually salient would be attended to but likely poorly comprehended by young viewers. Young children's difficulty distinguishing real information from fantasy material may cause further distortion and poor comprehension of television messages. As with attention, comprehension is increasingly influenced by the prior experience and knowledge that a child brings to the situation.

Even adults blur the line between fantasy and reality when comedians play themselves in other programs, or real people such as newscasters have cameo roles on sitcoms, or celebrities play other celebrities, or sitcom characters make reference to real people. This makes the material part real and part unreal with a mix of celebrities, images, entertaining news, and "newsy" entertainment (Lacey, 1993). The advent of a wide range of "reality shows" further blurs the line and contributes to the difficulty that some adults have in separating fact from fiction or in deciding what is realistic or "normal."

Methodological Issues

Methodological weaknesses can result in inaccurate conclusions from the data. The important difference between linguistic competence and linguistic performance, for example, is very relevant in this context. Young children's relatively poor performance on many tasks may well be due in some cases to their inability to express their mastery of a concept or an idea rather than to their inability to understand it. Or, in the case of lengthy programs, they may have difficulty remembering particular components. When Pingree et al. (1984) used stimuli that were short and simple and a method designed to maximize children's ability to communicate, for example, the results were quite different. When 3- and 5-year-olds in that study were asked to reconstruct an 8-minute television program with dolls to avoid reliance on verbal performance, their children's versions were not as rich as those of adults, but they did not have a qualitatively different meaning.

RETENTION

If it is important to ascertain which variables affect a child's attention to and comprehension of television content, it is even more essential to consider what factors lead to retention of that material, as one might assume that what is not remembered has little long-term effect. Discerning the most significant variables in this process is not as easy as it may appear at first glance. Retention is related not only to a child's age and level of cognitive development, but also to features and characteristics of the television information, to methods of measuring retention, and to interactions among many variables.

Mediating Variables

The mediating factors and intervening mental processes involved in the memory of television messages are still a source of some controversy. Some (e.g., Reeves & Thorson, 1986) have considered memory to be mediated by the processes of attention and mental effort, and these processes are determined by both the structure of the message and the processing strategies of the viewer.

Formal Features.   Formal features such as pace and continuity influence recall and recognition. Shows with a slower pace and greater continuity tend to be remembered better than high-paced shows (Wright et al., 1984). As high continuity is associated with better recall, one would expect poorer recall in young children who are unable to integrate material to increase its continuity. In addition, Singer and Singer (1983) argued that the very rapid pace of television may minimize chances for reflection and effective storage and retrieval, although the salience of the information affects recall positively (Kellermann, 1985).

Campbell, Wright, and Huston (1987) found better recall and recognition scores among kindergartners for easy versions of messages about nutrition and poorer scores for difficult ones, with only slight variation in attention as a function of difficulty. Participants were given a child form and an adult form, and each form had three levels of difficulty. Campbell et al. (1987) concluded that formal features influence the level of processing independent of content and that formal features probably signal appeal and comprehensibility that affect attention, processing, comprehension, and recall.

Developmental Differences. Developmental level is, again, a very significant determinant of the differences that have been reported. Verbal encoding of auditory input appears to lead to the best recall, but such encoding is an age-related skill that is not available to young children who rely more heavily on visual input and hence show poorer recall of auditory information.

When fourth and sixth graders in one study (Walma van der Molen & Van der Voort, 2000) were presented with news in four modalities—television form, a bare print version, print supplemented with photographs, and an audio version—the television version was remembered better than any of the others. According to Walma van der Molen and Van der Voort, this finding supports the dual-coding hypothesis, which says that redundant television pictures provide additional mnemonic support and, hence, better retention. This becomes especially important given the exposure to such news stories and images as were replayed hundreds of times following the 9/11 attacks. This coverage was likely to be misunderstood or distorted by young children, but the images would be remembered for a long time.

Effective learners process information in a smoothly integrated process that involves visual recognition and verbal encoding, but older children process linguistic presentations more easily, encode them more efficiently, and remember them better. Meadowcroft and Reeves (1989) found that 5- to 8-year-old children with advanced story schema skills showed less processing effort, better memory for central content, and better attention/memory coordination. Beentjes and Van der Voort (1993) found that television stories led to more influential learning than print. Print stories were recalled as well as television stories when immediate retention was tested, but retention of television stories on delayed tests was superior to that for print.

One very significant age-related difference in the viewing experience between adults and children noted by Winn (1985) is in the background of actual experiences that they can bring to bear on their viewing. According to Winn, adults have a vast number of experiences, fantasies, and relationships that can be used to transform the television material into something that they need. The experiences of young children, on the other hand, are limited; televiewing for them is more of a primary activity. Children's real experiences even may stir memories of television content rather than the reverse, as is the case for adults (Winn, 1985).

Recognition Versus Recall

The suggestion from the literature that young children remember little of what they see depends in part on the measures used to assess their retention. Young children typically perform better on recognition tasks than on tests of recall, and many researchers have reported significantly better recall of television content by older children. If both kinds of measures are not included, younger children who focus on visual input are penalized by the typical open-ended, verbal recall measures. If recognition of material they had viewed was measured as opposed to recall, one would expect their performance to improve. Hayes and Kelly (1984), in fact, did find better retention of visual material when a recognition measure was used rather than a recall measure.

Young children are less able than older children to encode the information verbally, but they might well recognize it as familiar. Therefore, when various comparisons are made and when age is important, one should look carefully at the measures used; it may well be that a recall task was used, whereas television's advantage, especially for younger children, lies in its visual components, which are more important in recognition. Cullingsford (1984) noted that recall is voluntary and recognition is not; he claimed that children recall little of television but recognize a lot because television includes much repetition and familiarity.

Motivation for Viewing

Motivation for viewing television also affects recall, although there is no simple one-to-one relation between motivation and recall (Kellermann, 1985). According to Kellermann, watching television to relax leads to different mental activities than watching it to seek some specific information. Children may approach television programs with an attitude of not feeling it necessary to remember; that is, they approach it differently than if they thought it was significant (Cullingsford, 1984). The amount remembered, according to Cullingsford, is inversely related to the amount watched because those who watch more pay less close attention and do not try to remember. Moreover, Kellermann (1985) noted that motivation interacts with attention to determine what message is received, and the structure of the message affects how the information is encoded and retrieved.

LINGUISTIC AND HOLISTIC ASPECTS

Research indicates that not only do certain specific features and forms of television affect attention and comprehension, but verbal encoding and storage is essential to efficient processing of information and to recall of that material. For the most part, however, visual and auditory features have not been broken down further or separated into other groupings. Yet doing so can help to pinpoint more specifically which specific factors make a significant difference and how and why they do.

Auditory and visual aspects of television stimuli can be distinguished and refined further, for example, on the basis of their linguistic and / or sequential features as compared with their more holistic and spatial ones. Terms such as *linguistic* and *sequential* can be used to connote stimuli that are largely objective and informational, that rely heavily on language, verbal encoding, and logical thought or reasoning; and that are usually thought to be processed largely in the left hemisphere. The terms *holistic* and *spatial*, on the other hand, can be used to connote those stimuli that are not encoded verbally; that are reacted to as wholes; that are more dependent on images, moods, and impressions than on information; and that are usually thought to be processed largely in the right hemisphere. Thus, one can broaden and refine opportunities to understand children's television experience by conceptualizing expanded stimuli groups: visual–linguistic, visual–holistic, auditory–linguistic, and auditory–holistic.

Distinctions such as these can be helpful in explaining some of the rather paradoxical and seemingly contradictory findings that sometimes emerge. Moreover, as is seen in the following paragraphs, linguistic and holistic features of the stimuli interact with the viewer's age, gender, cognitive level, and experience.

Most research to date has focused largely either on what an individual did, such as using visual recognition or verbal encoding (i.e., the kind of processing the individual engaged in), or on specific aspects of the television stimulus itself such as the modality involved (visual or auditory) or the formal features employed. Clearly, however, all manner of interactions occur among various aspects of both the stimuli and the viewer's processing. For example, one cannot verbally encode visual–holistic information unless labels are applied. Similarly, long printed messages are not visual in the same way or with the same effect as are more salient visual stimuli such as animation. The grouping of all visual techniques together and all auditory techniques together and the consequent reporting of children's attention to visual features or auditory features of the television presentation, then, masks important differences.

Furthermore, analytic or sequential processing is more common with verbally encoded stimuli, and global or holistic processing is more common with salient, holistic stimuli, but each type of processing can be applied to other stimuli. One can, for example, cast a critical, analytic eye on holistic content, although one is not likely to do so automatically. These variations are indicated in Fig. 3.1.

Stimuli and Processing Interactions

There appear to be two similar and parallel but quite different issues involved that are significant to an understanding of children's comprehension of television and of its impact on them. One focuses on the TV content and one on viewer processing characteristics. First, a distinction can be made between linguistic and holistic characteristics of the television input within each of the visual and auditory modalities. Second, there is the differentiation between largely analytic and largely global processing of the material. The first distinction has to do more with the television stimuli presented and the second with differences in the viewer's processing of that information.

The interaction of the television stimulus characteristics, then, with the types of processing leads to four very broad categories of processing activity: visual–ho-

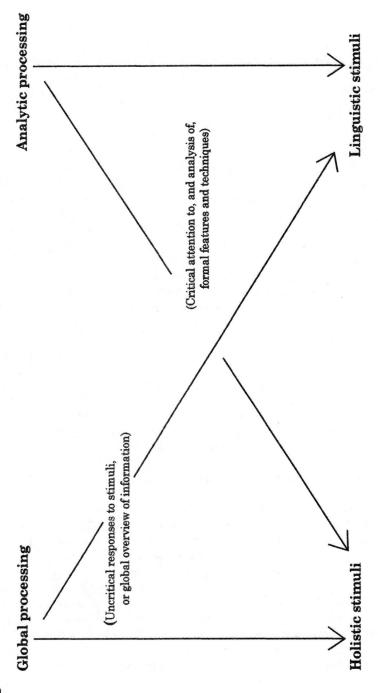

Global processing

Analytic processing

(Uncritical responses to stimuli,
or global overview of information)

(Critical attention to, and analysis of,
formal features and techniques)

Holistic stimuli

Linguistic stimuli

FIG. 3.1. Interactions of processing style and type of stimuli. Older and more mature children can use all four combinations; younger ones rely largely on holistic processing of any of the data. Even among older children, however, reactions may vary at different times and with different content.

listic (viewing much TV salience), visual–analytic or sequential (as in reading either from text print or TV), auditory–holistic (attending to salient auditory messages), and auditory–analytic or sequential (listening to verbal presentations, explanations, and dialogue). These categories are depicted graphically in Fig. 3.2.

Although this characterization is admittedly oversimplified, this conceptualization can contribute to an understanding of children's television experience. Clarification of many of the complex, interesting, and at times contradictory findings reported in the literature might well be enhanced by a consideration of such distinctions.

Differentiation of types of visual or auditory stimuli (linguistic vs. holistic) or of the type of analysis required by the child, including processing differences (analytic or global), and varying levels in the capacity for such analyses by different gender and age groups have not been reported. Young children, for example, are better able to process holistic aspects of both visual and auditory information.

The less efficient holistic processing that young children use is also the kind of processing that television relies on to a large extent. It often emphasizes quick overviews of material with less depth of processing or analysis of content and less reflection because of the quick pace and content changes. The growing ability of older children to use verbal encoding and more analytic approaches to cognitive information, then, also means that they can pay less attention or view less and still derive as much meaning as younger children who view more; older children are more efficient viewers.

Younger viewers are less able to distinguish relevant from irrelevant information and have fewer schemata and less complex codes to use to process what they see. This makes their viewing experience quite different from that of older children in terms of what content they understand and retain. When confronted with auditory stimuli, there is often little verbal encoding done by young children whose language skills are less well developed; they likely do not understand or retain the information conveyed through adult narration or conversation (linguistic) as well as they understand and retain that conveyed by sound effects (holistic).

One could hypothesize, then, that among young children, adult dramas might be poorly understood when compared with comprehension of cartoons not only because of the content and the less well developed cognitive capacity of younger children but also because of the mode of transmission or format. Adult dramas rely heavily on verbal interaction and conversation, and they are much less dependent on the perceptually salient features that are a mainstay of cartoons.

Although the content of these programs is very different, the form in which that content is presented also varies significantly and further affects its comprehensibility to children and, hence, their preferences and levels of attention.

This conceptualization of the interplay between specific stimulus characteristics and processing strategies raises some interesting questions and possibilities. The reported fragmentation in comprehension that has been attributed to young children's difficulty integrating information temporally (Anderson & Collins,

MODE OF PROCESSING		
	Analytic	Holistic
Visual	**(1) Linguistic stimuli** (e.g., reading print in text or on television)	**(2) Holistic stimuli** (e.g., viewing logos, animation, scene changes)
Auditory	**(3) Linguistic stimuli** (e.g., listening to explanations or dialogue)	**(4) Holistic stimuli** (e.g., attending to jingles, slogans)

FIG. 3.2.   Summary chart of types of stimuli and modes of processing and their interaction. *Note.* Younger children rely primarily on (2) and (4); older children can use (1) and (3) more effectively as they gain experience with the medium and as they develop generally more mature cognitive abilities and strategies.

1988), for example, may be due in part to the difficulty they have integrating linguistic and holistic components of that information. Moreover, important age–gender interactions in the relative importance of these perceptual components are likely as well and would affect further the impact of the child's viewing experience and the kind of content information that is derived from it.

Analytic and holistic processing differences also interact with cognitive style. According to Smith and Kemler Nelson (1988), analytic processing is associated with controlled and effortful cognitive processes, whereas holistic processing is associated with a more automatic kind of processing. One might ask further whether similar differences exist between normal children's processing of television information and their processing of print. As linguistic stimuli are likely to be perceived as more difficult and requiring more complex processing than holistic input, learning to make the distinction between them may facilitate learning for children. They might become better able to adapt their level of effort to the demands of a specific task or type of material.

Differences in Retention

A further question that needs to be addressed concerns how all of these factors interact with different measures of memory. Holistic stimuli, for example, whether auditory or visual, would be expected to be more highly related to recognition and linguistic or sequential material, whether visually or auditorially presented, to be more highly related to recall. As the linguistic or sequential material requires a higher level of processing and more extensive verbal encoding, recall is more effi- cient with older children who are more capable of such encoding. The recogni- tion scores of young children who rely more heavily on holistic aspects of television input are higher than their recall scores; and their retention of holistic stimuli is higher than their retention of linguistic, verbal information, whether it is presented visually or auditorially.

Most reports suggest that young children's better performance on recognition tasks than on recall tasks is due to their reliance on visual stimuli. Preschoolers may in fact ignore large chunks of auditory input (Hayes & Birnbaum, 1980) be- cause it is more often linguistic and less frequently holistic. When the auditory stimuli are in fact holistic (e.g., slogans, jingles), even very young children often demonstrate their retention by repeating the slogans or jingles and in other ways revealing their recognition memory of them. Older children, on the other hand, who are increasingly able to process or deal with linguistic or sequential features, also demonstrate more accurate recall.

Thus, level of retention varies depending not only on the gender and age of the child or on the type of retention measure that is used but on the relative weighting of linguistic and holistic components in the material. Distinctions between types of visual and auditory input, as well as processing differences, also might help to clarify the bases for some of the differences that have been reported in the literature be- tween recall of information received from books and that received from film.

In addition, if age and gender differences emerge in encoding strategies and processing techniques, television's impact on these groups should also differ con- siderably. Might girls, for example, demonstrate an earlier ability to deal with or be interested in and attentive to more linguistic material such as adult dialogue and abstract material? Would they, then, perhaps be more drawn to and affected by soaps and situation comedies? Might boys, on the other hand, especially youn- ger ones, be expected to favor and respond more positively to perceptually salient and holistic material such as cartoons, other animated presentations, or shows with more action for a longer period of time? Would soaps and other adult shows perhaps have less effect on younger children or on boys at later ages because they might be less attentive to them?

Further investigation of the impact of variations in the purpose of viewing, of age differences, and of age–gender interactions, as well as the relation between specific content and kinds of processing, is needed.

SUMMARY

Which televised information is actually attended to, understood, and retained by child viewers depends on a complex interaction of factors. These include the child's developmental level, past experience with television, interest in and motivation for viewing, as well as content and format variables of the television programming. Confounding variables can lead to some misinterpretation of data. For example, children's more limited verbal expressive skills or poorer recall of lengthy segments may be mistakenly perceived as lack of understanding. Newer research suggests that younger children have a basic understanding of much television information, but it is incomplete, frequently distorted, and often largely forgotten, although highly salient visual images may be remembered for a long time.

Children are active viewers whose processing of television material becomes more efficient as they get older. Older children are less dependent on stimulus features, more able to focus on a central message, and better able to distinguish reality from fantasy. They increasingly use verbal encoding of television material that enhances their comprehension and retention, and they use their past experience when possible to interpret television content.

A linguistic–holistic distinction within areas of auditory and visual stimuli and an interactionist position can facilitate our understanding of children's processing of television information. Although the best learning comes from a smooth integration of both auditory and visual information and of linguistic and holistic components, such distinctions can be used to clarify developmental differences in attention and recall, programming preferences, advertising's impact, and other aspects of a child's television experience. Differences in processing style also interact with the characteristics of the stimuli, resulting in important differences in comprehension and retention of various components of television's messages.

DISCUSSION QUESTIONS

1. Discuss the ways in which changes in children's ability to process information affect their vulnerability to TV and other media messages.
2. How would gender differences be expected to affect children's interest in and response to various program types such as cartoons, situation comedies, news programs, or advertising?
3. Sort various advertisements into visual or auditory and linguistic or holistic categories. Which corner of the grid would likely lead to the greatest impact on children at various developmental levels?

Language, Reading, and Academic Achievement

Language, Reading, and Academic Achievement

Despite the clear significance of language in children's understanding and retention of television content, there is disagreement in the literature on the role that television plays in children's language development. Some have argued that television viewing impedes language; others have claimed that it facilitates language acquisition.

Parents and educators also have worried about the possible adverse effects of excessive television viewing on children's academic achievement as well as its impact on their desire and ability to read. Evidence has suggested that their worries may have some basis in fact, but the relation is not simple or straightforward, and many variables interact to produce the results that have emerged.

LANGUAGE DEVELOPMENT

Television as Hindrance

The accusation that television impedes language development has often been based on television's emphasis on action, short sequences, fast pace, and reliance on visual stimuli. Other qualities of television's language may be important as well. Doerken (1983) noted, for example, that television language includes much doublespeak and contradiction (e.g., dye your hair for a natural look), and slang and street language are part of many programs. Moreover, reliance on superlatives and exaggeration is the norm, which Doerken felt has an effect on cognitive structure. Doerken worried that we may program children in ways that make them less able to think about and articulate their own experience because of changes in the language itself. By narrowing word use or substituting jingles for thought, we may limit rational capacity, which is especially important for young viewers who are just starting to internalize language (Doerken, 1983).

According to Winn (1985), years and years of televiewing have adversely affected viewers' ability to develop the verbal skills that a literate society requires such as concentration and reading and writing clearly. Winn argued that it is the commitment to language as a mode of expression and not the acquisition of language that suffers with heavy television viewing.

Television as Facilitator

Rice (1983), however, challenged the notion that television interferes with a child's acquisition of language and claimed that there is a "link between the child as language learner and the child as television viewer" (p. 214). Given the well-documented ability of preschoolers to learn vocabulary incidentally, television dialogue should serve as a source of new words (Rice, 1983; Rice, Huston, Truglio, & Wright, 1990). Although programs vary greatly in their linguistic complexity and in their dependence on visual or verbal material, some formats that are appropriate for young children include simple dialogue, redundancy, visual salience, and repetitions, according to Rice (1983). Meanings are often depicted explicitly and visually, and children also are presented with a broad range of social contexts and the different language associated with them (Rice, 1983). One of the important differences between television and reading in the stimulation of language is that unlike reading, talk about television occurs along with other conversational events and other activities like playing, and *Sesame Street* was especially likely to elicit television talk (Lemish & Rice, 1986).

Rice (1984) claimed that the emphasis on television's visual aspects has been misleading because it ignores the auditory aspect, the verbal dialogue, and the important generic verbal codes that complement television's visual information. With increasing language facility generally, children can better understand television's language, and television can aid their language development (Wartella, 1986), but children need experience with the uniqueness of television's codes nonetheless (Rice, 1984).

Age is likely an important variable once again, as rapid language development occurs during the preschool years, the time when heavy viewing of educational programs is prevalent (Rice, 1984). Young children can learn about new words while viewing television and thus facilitate their language development, although 5-year-olds did appear to benefit more from the viewing situation than did 3-year-olds (Rice & Woodsmall, 1988).

Language comprehension also can be facilitated by television because it makes many of the same adjustments that mothers make to adapt language to a child's needs, including a reduced rate, short comments, recasting of key information, and many comments about present referents (Rice, 1984). Lemish and Rice (1986) likened the rich verbal interaction of the viewing context for children in the early stage of language acquisition to that experienced by them with their parents when they have books read to them. Seen thus, television is an important source of verbal stimulation and interaction.

More recent research (Naigles & Mayeux, 2001) indicated that children can learn words or vocabulary from viewing educational programming, but TV view-

ing does not facilitate the development of grammar, and there was nothing to indicate that TV could ever replace natural language input in teaching children
language. "If the environmental influences on child language acquisition were
thought of as a four-course dinner, then the place of television input is as one of
the options on the dessert plate" (Naigles & Mayeux, 2001, p. 150).

Amount of Viewing

Some have argued that the amount of viewing is the important variable and that
heavy television viewing is negatively related to language development. In one
study (Selnow & Bettinghaus, 1982), for example, there was an inverse relation between viewing time and language performance in preschool children. On the
other hand, Harrison and Williams (1986) found light viewing habits among children who had higher vocabulary scores before television was introduced. This
suggests that negative correlations between vocabulary and television viewing
might best be interpreted as an indication that children with better vocabularies
choose to watch less television rather than that television blocks or hinders their
vocabulary development (Anderson & Collins, 1988). In fact, bright and linguisti-
cally more sophisticated children tend to watch programs with more sophisticated language, whereas children with simpler language skills tend to watch more
"language-poor" programs (Selnow & Bettinghaus, 1982).

Sesame Street and Language Gains

Part of the debate over television's impact on cognitive skills generally and language skills in particular has relied on data from well-established programs like
Sesame Street to support a positive view of TV's potential impact. The results of a
2-year longitudinal study by Rice et al. (1990) offered solid evidence for the positive linguistic impact that *Sesame Street* has on young children, particularly 3- to
5-year-olds. Rice et al. (1990) studied children in naturalistic settings that provided
an especially strong test because of the possible interruptions, distractions, and
competing activities. They compared language gains after viewing *Sesame Street*
and after viewing cartoons and other programs. The data supported Rice et al.'s
(1990) hypothesis that *Sesame Street* contributed to vocabulary development, but
other viewing did not have similar effects. Moreover, those findings were independent of family size, parent education and attitudes, and gender, and much of
the learning occurred without direct intervention by parents. In fact, adults were
present less than one fourth of the time, indicating that the cognitive gains after
viewing were due to the content, not to the adult intervention by parents who encouraged children to watch as had been suggested by Winn (1985).

The vocabulary gain in the Rice et al. (1990) study was especially pronounced
for 3- to 5-year-olds who are experiencing rapid development of oral language
skills and who compose the target group for *Sesame Street*. The effect was weaker

for 5- to 7-year-olds who are learning more sophisticated vocabulary and whose interests are changing to other types of viewing. Rice et al. (1990) suggested that one reason for *Sesame Street*'s success lay in its format and techniques, which are intended to involve children, focus children's attention, use verbal and visual redundancies, and contain dialogue that resembles mother–child interactions, such as emphasis on the present and on key words and simple sentences, features not seen in other shows. Therefore, other shows are less likely to contribute to the language development of very young children (Rice et al., 1990). Although the results suggest that viewing *Sesame Street* led to vocabulary gains, Rice et al. (1990) acknowledged that the data are correlational, and more evidence is necessary to demonstrate causality.

Comstock and Scharrer (1999) noted that *Sesame Street* was seen four or more times weekly by 50% to 60% of preschool children from age 2 to 5. It attracts similar proportions of children from racially and socioeconomically varied backgrounds but is seen more often in Black households. It provides instruction that does not require adult intervention but is enhanced by adult encouragement to view and by adult conversation with children about the content. It is economical, costing from $2 to $6 per child per year, and it accounts for a bit more than half of educational programming watched by preschoolers. Advantaged viewers benefit more because of access to other resources like educational games and higher skills for media use (Comstock & Scharrer, 1999).

Parent Intervention

Although cognitive and language gains likely are not dependent solely on adult intervention, parent–child linguistic interaction is clearly important. For example, parents contribute to their children's linguistic processing when they watch television with their young children (6 to 30 months of age), take turns asking questions, label, and comment on the content, thus providing a rich combination of television dialogue, their own language, and comments about language and about television events (Rice, 1984).

When one studies the relation between amount of viewing, level of encouragement, and cognitive gains, however, one must also consider the many potential confounding variables. In a naturalistic situation, for example, parents who encourage their children to watch *Sesame Street* to improve their skills are also likely to encourage them in other ways. Surprisingly, however, Rice et al. (1990) found that encouragement to view was negatively related to vocabulary acquisition, at least as measured by the Peabody Picture Vocabulary Test (Dunn, 1965; Dunn & Dunn, 1981), despite the positive relation between actual viewing and vocabulary gain. They suggested that the negative relation between encouragement to view and vocabulary gain may have emerged because parents who encourage viewing of *Sesame Street* may encourage other viewing as well, or because parents encouraged slow language developers to watch the program because they consider *Sesame Street* to be educational. Children of parents with positive attitudes toward television in general had relatively lower vocabulary scores, perhaps because they were less likely to engage their children in nontelevision activities.

A uses and gratifications approach might suggest that children with higher scores were being encouraged to use television in a selective, instrumental way, whereas those with lower scores may have been using it more ritualistically and less selectively.

New Technologies and Language

Television is not the only technological influence on language development and language usage. New technologies have spawned many new ways to communicate, perpetuating the debate over whether technology's influence is primarily positive or negative.

The heavy reliance on e-mail with its abbreviated messages, absence of facial and other nonverbal cues, and unidirectionality is one form. Enthusiasts argue that it increases communication and language use and is highly efficient. Critics argue that it is overused, easily misinterpreted, and lacks affect and depth.

Other technologies have also affected language use. Teens, for example, have developed a whole new language to talk with their friends on computers and cell phones and have become used to instant connection. They keep in touch by "texting," a new verb, and use "vowel-starved" spelling rules as the modern version of passing notes but with the advantage of not having to be right near the person to whom you are passing a note (Anderssen, 2003). Examples are BRB for 'be right back' or ILBL8 for 'I'll be late.' Teens are fluent in this informal language, and they develop codes among friends that befuddle their parents. "Who would never [sic] know that WWJCD stands for What Would Jackie Chan Do?" (Anderssen, 2003, p. F9). They say it is habit-forming and necessitates rereading school papers to fix all of the Us and Rs. Instant and text messaging may serve as a social equalizer because even shy individuals can have their say without having to break into a group first. However, the debate now goes on about whether this rapid and short form of writing is "dulling the brains of the text generation" (p. F9) or whether they are simply adapting the writing so that they can do it very quickly (Anderssen, 2003).

TELEVISION AND READING

Statistics from the U.S. Department of Education's National Center for Educational Statistics (NCES) showed a decline in both reading and writing achievement among students (Kaufman, 2000). The 1998 NCES report showed that fewer than 40% of students in Grades 4, 8, and 12 achieved a "proficiency" level of reading. The typical American student was not proficient in writing, showing only partial mastery of the necessary skills. Kaufman noted that the best readers are those who live in homes that value literacy and encourage children to read and who spend nonschool hours in reading and writing. The media, on the other hand, present stimuli to the child in a packaged form, a more passive experience.

Skill Acquisition and Reading Achievement

Many of the concerns about television's effects on achievement have focused more specifically on children's reading skills and on their reading habits and preferences. A study (Corteen & Williams, 1986) of a community before and after television was introduced indicated that although television does not result in the deterioration of well-established reading skills, it likely does slow the acquisition of those skills. Heavy viewing was associated with poorer reading skills, and better readers more often used the print media than poorer readers. On the other hand, studies have shown that when children watch well-constructed educational programs aimed at their age level, such as *Sesame Street,* their prereading skills at age 5 are better than children who watched little or no TV (MacBeth, 1996, as cited in National Institute on Media and the Family, 2002m; Wright et al., 2001). If they watch purely entertainment shows such as cartoons, however, they do more poorly on tests of their prereading skills (MacBeth, 1996).

Summative research by the Public Broadcasting Service (PBS) has repeatedly demonstrated that *Sesame Street* helps prepare viewers for school, and other programs like *Dragon Tales* and *Between the Lions* help with goal orientation and reading (McGinn, 2002). Wright et al. (2001) found that viewing more informative programming at age 2 and 3 predicted later higher performance on measures of receptive vocabulary, reading, math, and school readiness than for those who watched general audience programs frequently. Moreover, their patterns of early viewing of entertainment or educational and informative material tended to predict later viewing patterns. Children who watched informative television as young children tended to do the same when they were older. They used TV to complement school, whereas those who watched more entertainment TV when younger tended also to use it for entertainment and leisure when they were older (MacBeth, 1996). Others (D. R. Anderson, Huston, Schmitt, Linebarger, & Wright, 2001) found a correlation between viewing more educational programs as preschoolers and higher grades, less aggression, and more reading as high schoolers.

Again, however, these correlations cannot be interpreted as evidence of a causal direction. Children with higher grades or who read more may have chosen educational programs more frequently, or higher grades and viewing more educational programs may both have been due to a third factor such as parent involvement and attitudes. Moreover, knowing how to read is not necessary for learning through visual means such as movies and television, and wider exposure to those media means an increase in the spread of knowledge to increasingly larger groups or populations (Kaliebe & Sondheimer, 2002).

Winn (1985) described the *lazy reader,* the child who reads but does so with lower levels of concentration and involvement, and she noted a change in the kinds of books that children read. According to Winn, there is a trend toward reading "nonbooks" such as the *Guinness Book of Records* that involve a new style of reading. They are books without a sustained story or carefully sculpted arguments, and they require little focus or concentration. They can be read in short segments or scanned, and they require no "getting into" (Winn, 1985) and are exemplified by the many books and magazines such as *People* magazine that are based on TV and music stars.

A current craze sweeping Japan and Korea and moving to North America is the growth of *manga* or "graphic novel-based black-and-white comics" (Considine, 2003, p. R3), which are wildly popular with teenage girls. They include female high school heroines who travel through time and find lost treasures, a futuristic fantasy about personal computers evolving into lifelike robots or "persocoms" that people can fall in love with, and a heroine who spends her time fighting villains (Considine, 2003). Most of the manga are targeted at specific groups such as early teen boys or adolescent girls, with the core group between 12 and 17 years. They include manga about fashion, sex, romance, future worlds, cooking, and all kinds of sport. Even some government informational material is published in manga form. Once titles become popular, according to Considine, they are collected into volumes and sold in bookstores like graphic novels. The stories are highly visual and much is left unsaid, which leads to greater emotional involvement of the reader. The highly visual style is attractive to young readers who are used to the fast pace and quick cuts of video games and music videos, and their popularity in North America is expected to grow quickly (Considine, 2003).

Displacement Effect

Many have argued that television has a negative influence on achievement because television viewing displaces time that children could spend reading. According to Beentjes and Van der Voort (1988), TV might also have a more indirect effect, such as displacing activities that facilitate general cognitive development, or it might weaken concentration abilities or persistence, although there was no direct evidence that television causes attentional difficulties with reading material. The fact that watching television does not require a lot of cognitive effort may make continuing to concentrate more difficult rather than easier (Kubey & Csikszentmihalyi, 1990). Over time, Kubey and Csikszentmihalyi suggested, people may miss being challenged and involved and feel worse and more passive. Kubey and Csikszentmihalyi reported that heavy viewers found their experience less rewarding and, because there was little concentration and alertness, perhaps more desensitizing.

Beentjes and Van der Voort (1988) reviewed research relating to the three main hypotheses put forward regarding television's impact on children's reading. They include television having a positive effect (facilitative effect), a negative effect (inhibition effect or displacement hypothesis), or no effect. Beentjes and Van der Voort concluded that most evidence supports the inhibition hypothesis, although the relation between reading achievement and television viewing is complex and is influenced by several conditions.

In a longitudinal study bearing on the issue of displacement and the effects of television on children's leisure-time reading, Koolstra and Van der Voort (1996) studied Dutch children who were in Grades 2 to 4 at the start of the study and surveyed them at 1-year intervals three times. They found that television viewing led to less comic book reading only from Year 2 to 3, but television viewing led to less book reading over both measurement periods. According to Koolstra and Van der Voort (1996), television's effect is due to "(a) a television-induced deterioration of attitudes toward book reading, and (b) a television-induced deterioration of children's ability to concentrate on reading" (p. 4).

Several researchers have argued that television viewing displaces primarily other forms of entertainment and media use such as movies, radio, and comic books (Anderson & Collins, 1988; Mutz, Roberts, & van Vuuren, 1993). In a study by Mutz et al. (1993) in which data were obtained before and after television was introduced in South Africa, the introduction of television affected time allocation for individuals but only for other media use. Television viewing, for example, meant less time spent on movies and listening to the radio. After a year, television viewing decreased, but there was not a return to previous levels of the displaced activities (movie and radio). When Mutz et al. separated individual and aggregate perspectives, they found that displacement continued through the first 5 years after the introduction of television, but overall, television's influence was modest, and it did not change the pattern of activities greatly, although there were slight decreases in reading, moviegoing, and listening to the radio.

Mutz et al. (1993) concluded that television led to a restructuring of leisure time, which continued even when the time spent viewing television decreased: "Displacement of time spent on some activity may likely also displace interest in that activity" (p. 71).

Simply reducing viewing time does not guarantee more reading because individuals' choices about how they spend their time are determined also by factors such as family education and attitudes, attitudes toward reading and toward television, and the time available (Anderson & Collins, 1988). Anderson and Collins argued that there is no solid evidence that television necessarily displaces activities that are more cognitively valuable than television viewing, such as reading and homework. Although some increase in reading occurs when television viewing is reduced, at least in the short term, most of the extra time that becomes available with such reduction in television time is spent on other recreational activities (Anderson & Collins, 1988). Therefore, just cutting down on TV time to try to increase time spent on reading or other activities is unlikely to work on its own.

In a study of very young children, Rideout et al. (2003) found no displacement effect for "heavy" TV users (more than 2 hours a day) who were under 3 years of age. Among 4- to 6-year-olds, however, heavy users spent less time playing outside and reading than those who were not heavy users. The authors noted that this is a correlational finding, however, and other reasons for not playing outside or reading may have led to more TV viewing.

Anderson and Collins (1988) maintained that displacement studies should look at why children spend time watching television and whether they actively choose it and should consider all of the other factors (e.g., parent education, attitudes toward reading, weather conditions, and alternatives) that are probably more important than television availability in determining the total number of "cognitively valuable activities engaged in by children" (p. 39). Anderson and Collins noted further that many other activities, including homework, are often shared with television rather than displaced by it.

Finally, Ritchie, Price, and Roberts (1987) used data from a 3-year panel study to reappraise the relation between television viewing and reading achievement and found strong negative correlations that support past findings. When they used more sophisticated analytic techniques, however, and looked at the relations over time and controlled for initial reading levels, the relations became weaker and less clear. That is, Ritchie et al.'s simple correlations supported a displacement hypothesis, but when previous levels of the dependent variables were included, relations were weaker, although in the hypothesized direction.

Changes in reading skills or time spent reading did not seem related consistently to TV viewing time, and reading nonschool content was not related to improved reading skills. Significant relations that Ritchie et al. (1987) found were mostly for older children, and it was not clear whether younger children were less affected or benefitted from more television viewing. Ritchie et al. suggested that the results could be due to a number of factors: earlier effects (before the age of their participants); subtle cumulative effects of TV viewing over time; and complex, conditional processes and interactions, such as why they watch, choice of content, and environmental characteristics, which contribute differently for different children.

After reexamining the research, Reinking and Wu (1990) concluded that regarding displacement, there is a positive relation if TV delivers strong educational content and a negative relation if TV displaces more educational activity or no effect. For example, findings might vary if parents with high SES park their children in front of the television set and low-SES parents join their children there. Reinking and Wu suggested that the study of these relations needs a more sophisticated approach than is usually used because they found that the negative relation between amount of time spent viewing TV and reading achievement was nonsignificant when relevant variables were controlled and more sophisticated data analysis was performed. Moderate television viewing does not seem to have an adverse effect on reading achievement and may even help in some populations (e.g., disadvantaged children) by giving them background information and supplanting nontelevision experience (Reinking & Wu, 1990).

Positive Effects of Television on Reading

Other researchers have gone beyond looking at potential negative effects from television viewing and have put forward a positive view of television's influence. They have suggested that although television may displace study time or affect reading habits or study skills, it also can stimulate interest in new topics, provide background material for school projects, and stimulate classroom discussions.

Wright et al. (1990), for example, reported that older children who had watched adult informative programs, whether or not they watched with parents, subsequently used print media more. That is, children who watched more demanding and informative programs also liked to read, and those who watched more child entertainment programs like cartoons or adult entertainment were less interested in reading books.

In addition, even when children view fiction, there is likely to be some information that is academically relevant, although it can be either accurate or inaccurate (Anderson & Collins, 1988), and television can be used to increase literacy if the right kinds of TV are watched (Bianculli, 1994). Bianculli spoke of "teleliteracy" and insisted that TV and books can exist alongside each other and can supplement each other. Pertinent TV content, for example, can be used to supplement classroom material because it stimulates interest in new topical areas. According to Bianculli, some barriers make it seem as though television and literature are mutually exclusive, but TV's accessibility and popularity mean it is a primary conveyor of information, including literature, and media studies are now included in many classrooms. Because television exposes children to so much so fast—music, sports, literature, and so on—its potential for use outweighs its potential for abuse (Bianculli, 1994).

J. L. Singer and Singer (1998) found that TV programming can play a significant part in providing opportunities for children for the acquisition of school readiness skills, but it must be followed up in some way by adults, for example, in games, lesson plans, curricular guidelines, and so forth to enhance the show's impact. The use of real people as well as fantasy characters on shows is very important rather than dependence on cartoons or animation.

New Technologies

The use of new technologies to provide effective learning experiences for children has also grown. "Living Books" for computers in which children can click on characters or objects and bring them to life with sounds and images and movement, adds to the fun of reading them (Hodges, 1996). It makes reading a highly interactive medium for learning (*Adventures in Learning*, 1992) and could increase motivation in children who are having difficulties. These and other programs allow children to have words pronounced repeatedly, go back to favorite or troublesome words or concepts, and generally add to children's reading experience by bringing highly salient and entertaining elements into it.

Educational software allows children to develop and strengthen their phonics skills by presenting material in novel and interesting ways and allowing them to practice at their own skill level and at their own pace. It also has the advantage of presenting auditory and visual stimuli simultaneously. Voice recognition software for children experiencing serious problems with written expression allows them to express their creative ideas and imaginative stories without the encumbrance of writing.

TELEVISION AND ACADEMIC ACHIEVEMENT

Many children spend more time in front of a TV set than in school. Morgan (1993) argued that the large amount of time spent viewing TV, coupled with the relatively low intellectual demands of most programs, have led parents and educators to worry that TV viewing can lead to the following problems:

1. Cognitive passivity with less effort expended on more demanding school work.
2. Less creativity and imagination.
3. Shorter attention spans with lower interest in less entertaining material.
4. Less perseverance and increased impulsivity with restlessness in class.
5. Visual processing skills that are not compatible with block print-based skills necessary for success in school.
6. Increased apathy about school performance.

According to Morgan (1993), however, although the potential for negative influence is huge, the research literature is less clear. The research falls into two general categories: (a) studies, mostly experimental, that look at cognitive and psychological mechanisms by which TV viewing could affect academic performance; and (b) studies, mostly surveys, that explore whether TV viewing and academic achievement are related systematically, which have produced conflicting results from the start (Morgan, 1993).

The large California Assessment Program (CAP, 1980) in the early 1980s revealed a general inverse relation between amount of viewing and achievement. Heavy viewers of television scored lower on tests of reading, written expression, and math than did students who viewed little or no television. This was true for different socioeconomic levels and at both elementary and high school levels, although the relation was more pronounced for 12th graders. There were no significant gender differences. This negative relation between achievement scores and heavy television viewing held regardless of the amount of time spent doing homework or reading for pleasure, and the sharpest decline in achievement scores appeared in those participants who viewed more than 6 hours daily. Not surprisingly, students who read the most and watched the least amount of television earned the highest test scores (CAP, 1980).

An interesting socioeconomic interaction was apparent, however. Although achievement declined in all socioeconomic levels for students watching more than 5 or 6 hours, those children at the lower socioeconomic level who watched up to 3 hours a day actually improved in achievement. Viewing more than that, however, was associated with lower achievement. Although heavy television viewing did affect school achievement, then, the effect was most pronounced for more socially advantaged students (Fetler, 1984).

According to Fetler (1984), the difference in effect between the socioeconomic levels may be a function of the fact that television is less stimulating intellectually than many of the alternatives and resources available in affluent homes where many books, magazines, and materials are routinely provided. In less affluent homes, on the other hand, television is more stimulating and educational than what is readily available and might well lead to some academic improvement.

Others (Beentjes & Van der Voort, 1988; Comstock & Paik, 1991) have also reported that the inverse relation between reading achievement and television viewing was greater among heavy viewers, children from higher socioeconomic backgrounds, children of higher ability, and viewing of mostly light entertainment content (comedy, cartoons, action, and adventure).

Neuman's (1988) analysis of data from eight states revealed little difference in reading, comprehension, vocabulary, or study skills scores with amount of viewing in the majority of children who watched for 2 to 4 hours a day. Over that, however, negative effects emerged and became increasingly harmful. As this was a correlation, however, it may reflect other differences in the characteristics of heavy and moderate viewers or in parental expectations and supervision as well as parent example, and use of better measures than just the number of hours might yield stronger relations (Neuman, 1988). Parents who watch more entertainment programs with their children may be encouraging more indiscriminate viewing and discouraging reading as an alternative activity (Wright et al., 1990). Finally, television viewing serves different needs and gratifications than sports, leisure reading, or time with friends, and viewing time decreases as children get older because of more social activities and greater school demands (Neuman, 1988).

Comstock and Paik (1991) cited studies that confirmed the CAP outcomes regarding television viewing and academic achievement. A CAP follow-up study in 1986 showed a similar phenomenon beyond basic skills to include an inverse relation between amount of television viewed and achievement in history, social science, and science (CAP, 1988). As to whether television viewing is cause or effect in this inverse relation, Comstock and Paik (1991) observed the following:

The inverse associations between socioeconomic status and reading, and between mental ability and reading, the turning away from television toward print with the passage from childhood to the teenage years, and the special population that apparently makes up young people who are very light viewers lead us to believe that young people who are able and especially those who are highly efficient at reading will come to watch less television. Thus, some of the negative association between viewing and reading and other achievement is caused by the behavior of brighter young persons who are able or highly proficient readers. (p. 134)

Comstock and Paik (1991) concluded further that children of lower intellectual ability, those who are in greater conflict with parents or peers, those in whose homes television is more central, and those who see no other activity as more rewarding or necessary watch more television. All of those factors, however, are ones that would usually be associated with lower achievement because they interfere with skill acquisition and task completion and because parents in whose homes television is more central are less apt to emphasize reading, homework, and achievement. At all ages, there is a negative correlation between viewing television and achievement, regardless of the amount of time children spend on homework or reading for themselves (Comstock & Paik, 1991).

In an experimental study by Pool, Van der Voort, Beentjes, and Koolstra (2000) to investigate the impact of different types of background television programs on homework performance, Grade 8 students were matched for reading ability and then randomly assigned to three television conditions including a soap opera, music videos, and no TV in the background. Homework performance was impeded only when it was done with the soap opera as background.

Comstock and Scharrer (1999) argued that those who watch a lot more TV are disproportionately from groups that would be less likely to do well scholastically. Viewing is inversely related to socioeconomic level, but academic achievement is positively related to socioeconomic level. Comstock and Scharrer said there is no evidence that TV viewing negatively affects one's ability to process text, but there is some evidence that combining viewing with scholastic tasks leads to lower performance.

According to Comstock and Scharrer (1999), the question as to whether TV affects scholastic achievement is still controversial. They noted that the areas in which television was expected to enhance achievement—vocabulary, interests, visual skills, and televised interventions such as televised courses, educational programming, and increased knowledge while also entertaining—work only if they are attended to. Comstock and Scharrer concluded that for children between ages 5 and 9, TV, especially violence, may interfere with acceptance of the pace of schooling.

Comstock and Scharrer (1999) also noted that television socializes children to prefer content that is not demanding and shapes their preferences toward more trivial or banal content. They viewed Winn (1985) as visionary in her view over 25 years ago that watching large amounts of TV interfered with learning to read, with the ability to concentrate while reading, and to a preference for reading material that could be read in brief segments and with little involvement.

Children also may transfer some of the lower levels of information processing that television requires, such as chunking and encoding, to independent tasks such as problem solving that actually require higher levels of processing (Williams, 1986). They may use strategies, such as divided or partial attention, that they use with television in the school situation in which the strategies may be inappropriate (Anderson & Collins, 1988). If the strategies are inappropriate, the processing will be less effective. They may also have difficulty separating visual attention from auditory attention and may have difficulty listening if there is not visual input simultaneously (Anderson & Collins, 1988). Levine and Waite (2000) found that the amount of TV viewed was significantly associated with teacher ratings of attentional difficulties but not to ratings by parents, classroom observations, or standardized tests. The type of show did not matter and did not correlate with any attentional variable. Levine and Waite concluded that there is a clear relation between amount of TV viewing and ability to attend in school.

On the other hand, children in both age groups (8–9 and 14–15) studied by Clifford et al. (1995) considered science on television to be beneficial, appreciated the fact that important information was conveyed, and felt that science should be part of prime-time programming, not just in school programs or minority channels. However, they watched such programs less as they got older. Clifford et al. did find gender differences but in the opposite direction than conventional stereotypes would predict. Girls agreed more with positive statements and less with negative statements about science programs than boys did. Children can learn from those programs when they do watch them, but whether they do so depends a lot on what skills and knowledge they bring to the viewing situation, how information is presented, and whether they are motivated and engaged (Clifford et al., 1995).

Before and after studies are all but impossible to do now because of the ubiquity of television. Although they provide some information of historical interest, they are not very helpful currently (Morgan, 1993). Morgan noted further that although there have been studies with many variations in sample size, measures used, ages of participants, and research methods, and comparisons are difficult, and although there have been mixed findings with young children, findings for children beyond Grade 4 and into high school have been quite consistent. The majority of correlational studies demonstrate a negative association between viewing TV and academic achievement scores, but this is still a correlation. One might ask whether those with poorer marks and/or ability turn to the easier, less demanding TV viewing for information or escape, or there may be some other factor accounting for both such as low parental involvement or supervision. Morgan also noted that although the correlations tend to be fairly small, they may mask a nonlinear association such as the curvilinear one described in the CAP study (California Assessment Program, 1980, 1988) discussed earlier, or varied effects among subgroups of participants may be obscured by the smaller overall correlations. Finally, gender, race, age, socioeconomic, and other differences interact with the TV viewing and result in different relations between viewing and achievement.

TELEVISION AND OTHER SKILL DEVELOPMENT

Some have worried about television's effect on children's curiosity, imagination, and creativity as well as its influence on their verbal ability and cognitive development. Harrison and Williams (1986) found that children in a town where television was introduced for the first time earned higher creativity scores initially but 2 years later had scores similar to those of children who had grown up with television.

Valkenburg and Van der Voort (1994) concluded from their research that the evidence supports the view that TV stimulates or fosters daydreaming (stimulation hypothesis) and reduces creative imagination (reduction hypothesis), although this is a correlation, and causation cannot be inferred. Valkenburg and Van der Voort (1994) found that daydreaming and imagination overlap but are different cognitive processes. Research data suggests that TV affects them differently. It encourages daydreaming in its role as provider of information, but there was no evidence that individuals were less able to form visual images because of TV and less practice doing so. Valkenburg and Van der Voort (1994) also found no evidence that the quality of products of the imagination improves with TV viewing despite getting greater amounts of information. In fact, TV viewing may adversely affect the conditions or processes that are important for imagination such as sustained effort, reflection, and quiet (Valkenburg & Van der Voort, 1994).

Others have claimed that the growing fear of TV as a resource is not deserved and that one should use TV's potential rather than avoid it (Bianculli, 1994). According to de Groot (1994), research by J. L. Singer and Singer (1998) has demonstrated that preschool children watching *Barney and Friends,* which was beating out *Sesame Street* and *Mister Rogers* in Nielsen ratings, showed improved cognitive and attitudinal skills including better number skills, vocabulary, knowledge of shapes, colors, neighborhood locations, and manners, and the creation of positive feelings. Their findings were true of preschoolers of all cultures and races (de Groot, 1994). Regular viewing of *Sesame Street* and *Mister Rogers,* however, was also associated with improved vocabulary and greater learning as well as positive behaviors (de Groot, 1994).

Comstock and Scharrer (1999) concluded that regarding imaginative play and daydreaming, there was no support for displacement of time that would have been spent playing, but TV shapes play. Comstock and Scharrer also found no support for a decrease in daydreaming with TV or that TV increases positive daydreaming or building of fantasy, but they did find a link between kinds of daydreams and what was viewed. Watching science fiction, for example, was associated with thinking about how things work. Watching general drama, comedies, and others was associated with pleasant fantasy, and viewing violent programs was associated with aggressive daydreaming whereas viewing nonviolent programs was associated with inhibition of aggressive daydreaming. Comstock and Scharrer concluded that the evidence does not support the view that TV viewing decreases creative ability, and mental ability predicts use of print, computers, Internet, and other electronic sources of information and data banks.

SCHOOL VERSUS TELEVISION

Postman (1985) raised other concerns about television's "style of learning," which he said is, by its nature, hostile to school learning or learning from books. Postman distinguished between what he called the *television curriculum* and the *school curriculum*. He claimed that television's philosophy rests on three features, commandments whose influence can be seen in every kind of programming: no prerequisites (you can turn it on and watch anything without any background) and an undermining of the importance of sequence and continuity; no perplexity and an assumption that the viewers' contentment and satisfaction are more important outcomes than viewer growth; and no exposition in the form of reasons, discussion, or argument but rather an emphasis on storytelling. According to Postman, the school curriculum is strongly influenced and determined by the character of television.

In fact, however, many features and purposes of television and the schools have become blurred. School, once the bastion of the three Rs, now includes affective, emotional, and value-laden issues, and much effort is expended to stimulate, entertain, and hold the interest of students in unique and varied ways. Television, on the other hand, although seen largely as an entertainment activity, also can be very educational.

Children learn much about the world from their television viewing, and the study of television's techniques can be fascinating for young viewers as well as helping them to become more literate, less vulnerable viewers. Once they see how specific television effects are achieved and how various subtle messages are communicated, they can view TV more critically and understand better the television programming and advertising that they see. Critical thinking and analytic skills developed in school can be applied to the analysis and evaluation of TV content and can stimulate debate as to the reality and desirability of the values presented.

Conversely, television's inherent fascination and interest for children can be used well in the classroom. Teachers can use children's television to promote reading instruction without worrying that there will be negative side effects. For example, children can watch programs to get background information and show new words they learned from television (Reinking & Wu, 1990). Some classrooms devote time to studying movies, plays, or TV programs as part of a reading curriculum. Others have encouraged children to dissect television plots, to debate the merits of the strategies used by characters to solve problems, to identify stereotypes, and to separate fact from speculation, in other words to deconstruct television and develop more informed viewing and critical thinking skills.

Because of its strong visual component and capacity for compelling graphics, television can explain complex concepts in ways not possible in a regular classroom. Multimedia presentations can be exciting and stimulating for all learners and in fact reflect the reality of learning in the world today. Schools also can use television's intrinsic appeal to encourage discussion of important societal issues such as violence, stereotyping, and advertising. Television has much to offer academically and educationally if it is used sensibly and creatively.

Television is only one factor in a context of many other cognitive, socialization, and experiential variables, all of which interact to produce both television viewing and achievement behavior. School personnel, parents, peers, and television characters all serve as models of social behavior for children. They provide many behavioral options, both appropriate and inappropriate. Although the modeling is usually implicit rather than explicit or direct, children learn all kinds of ways to solve problems, to interact with others, to obtain what is important to them, and to "get ahead." How strong an influence, normal or deviant, each of these models has on children, however, is controversial.

Fortunately for today's students, increasingly widespread interest in media literacy is helping children to understand and evaluate the impact of the media on them and to soften the sharp, often adversarial, line between children's viewing experiences and their school experiences. The best aspects of each need to be used to capture and foster children's enthusiasm for learning and to facilitate their healthy development.

METHODOLOGICAL ISSUES

Some have criticized the methodology in studies relating television and school achievement or reading skills. Roberts, Bachen, Hornby, and Hernandez-Ramos (1984), for example, argued that typical studies of television use and school performance use amount of viewing as a critical variable despite the fact that children are poor estimators of their viewing time and despite the fact that the notion of an additive effect in which more television viewing leads to a greater effect is too simple a view of television behavior. According to Roberts et al. (1984), such a practice ignores mediating variables such as different attitudes, uses made of television or gratifications sought, and others that affect behavior. Moreover, school achievement is usually represented by test scores; however, as with television, reading is only one part of a larger pattern of attitudes, behavior, and cognition related to reading. It is not just a matter of skills but of what is read, how much is read, and family attitudes (Roberts et al., 1984).

Anderson and Collins (1988) suggested that correlations between low achievement and heavy television viewing may be a result of a third factor, namely, imitation of parents who do not have a strong interest in reading and model television viewing as an alternative leisure activity. Even if excessive television viewing interferes with school performance, however, one cannot isolate television itself as the cause because the same could be said for any other activity such as sports that occupy too much of a child's out-of-school time (Hodge & Tripp, 1986).

Finally, television viewing and other media use, school behavior, and skill development are all part of a much larger context of cognitive and social development in which multiple, complex variables and events affect children's school
performance and academic achievement as well as more general learning about
themselves and the world around them.

SUMMARY

Many feel that television can enhance children's language in various ways, particularly when parents are involved with them in the viewing situation. Programs
such as *Sesame Street* in which modifications are made to approximate parent–child verbal interactions seem most likely to facilitate vocabulary gain,
whether or not a parent is actually present. However, excessive television viewing
may interfere with the acquisition of reading, listening, and writing skills, and it
may affect reading preferences as well.

Research into the relation between television viewing and academic achievement suggests that it may be a curvilinear one, and the amount of viewing interacts
with socioeconomic level and IQ. Children, especially those from deprived or disadvantaged backgrounds who view some television, often show improved achievement. Viewing more than 5 or 6 hours a day, however, is associated with poorer
achievement in all groups. Television appears to have a more negative effect on the
achievement of socially advantaged students than on disadvantaged ones, presumably because it displaces other, more beneficial alternatives. For disadvantaged students, however, television may provide some compensatory information.

Finally, rigidly separating school learning and learning from television seems
increasingly counterproductive. Rather, the intrinsic appeal of television and its
capacity for transmitting information in complex and stimulating formats can be
used in classroom settings. Similarly, the critical thinking and analytic skills developed in school can be used to understand and evaluate television content.

DISCUSSION QUESTIONS

1. Discuss the positive and negative effects that TV viewing might have on children's reading skills and on their overall academic achievement.
2. Discuss ways in which information processing and critical thinking skills
   used in classrooms could be used to process TV content more effectively.
   What information-processing skills used with TV content might contribute
   to or interfere with classroom learning?
3. Discuss the evidence for and against a displacement effect from media use.

PART III

Social, Emotional, and Behavioral Aspects of Media Experience

CHAPTER FIVE

Violence and Aggression

Violence and Aggression

Startling statistics have been reported on the number of violent incidents on television to which children are exposed and the level of violence in the video games so many children and adolescents love. Viewers are likely to see violence in two out of three programs they watch, regardless of time of day of viewing (Smith, Nathanson, & Wilson, 2002). Assuming 2 to 4 hours of viewing a day, by the time children finish elementary school, they will have seen 8,000 murders and 100,000 other violent acts (Donnerstein, Slaby, & Eron, 1994). Sixty-one percent of TV programs have some violence, 75% show no immediate punishment, and 43% of violent scenes involve humor (Smith & Donnerstein, 1998). Donnerstein et al. (1994) maintained that the level of television violence had remained fairly constant over the past two decades, although cable television has added to it. They say most of the violence is presented without context or judgment about its acceptability, and most morning and early afternoon violence is seen by children.

In his testimony on television violence before the U.S. Senate, Kunkel (1999) reviewed the National Television Violence Study that involved more than a dozen leading researchers in independent studies at four university sites. Each one examined a different aspect of the issues that media violence raises. Unlike many earlier studies, these researchers did not simply count violent episodes or actions; they also analyzed the context within which it occurred. They asked, for example, who committed the violence, whether it was rewarded or punished, whether realistic consequences were presented, and whether it was shown graphically. They concluded that violence was widespread and some form of it was shown in 60% of all shows they sampled over a 3-year period.

Kunkel (1999) noted that if one picked a sample at random, the odds were greater than 50–50 that the program would contain violence. There was an average of 6,000 violent acts in a single week across 23 channels that included cable and broadcast networks. One in four of the programs that involved violence depicted gun use. Most of the violence was sanitized (made to look less painful than it really was) and glamorized (engaged in by attractive role models who were often justified in behaving aggressively and who often suffered no remorse, criticism, or punishment for their violence).

Music videos and video games also include significant amounts of violence. Children Now (2001) reported that 89% of video games contained violent content, half of it serious, and 79% of games rated "E" for "Everyone" also contained violence that was significant to the plot in half of them. Killing was usually seen as justified and rewarded, negative consequences of it were rarely shown, and 40% contained comic violence. In 17% of the games, violence was central, and the game could not be played without it. In many violent games, the user is obliterated if they fail to choose a correct and predetermined strategy; there are no compromises, there are sexual stereotypes, and there is little portrayal of any realistic consequences of violence (Funk & Buckman, 1996).

Discovering possible links between children's exposure to such large amounts of violence and their aggressive behavior, as well as other behavioral effects, continues to be a very important undertaking.

DEPICTIONS OF VIOLENCE

Wilson, Smith, et al. (2002) found that programming targeted at children age 12 and younger contained more prevalent and more concentrated violence than other programs. It was as likely to be glamorized as in nonchildren's programs, as well as more sanitized, and therefore more likely to trivialize violence. According to Wilson, Smith, et al., this makes it more likely that viewers will learn aggression and become desensitized from viewing such portrayals.

Wilson, Smith, et al. (2002) divided children's programs into five subgenres of violence: slapstick, superheroes, adventure/mystery, social relationships, and magazine. They found significant differences among the five groups in the amount of violence shown and in the concentration of violence. All of the programs in the slapstick category, 97% of the superhero programs, and 89% of the adventure/mystery programs included violence. Fewer than half of the programs in the social relationships category and only 17% of the programs in the magazine category, such as *Barney, Bill Nye the Science Guy,* and *Sesame Street*, contained violence, making magazine programs a "risk-free zone" for children (Wilson, Smith, et al., 2002, p. 31).

The breakdown of programming into these types of programs for a comparison of levels of violence in each type is important because very different populations would be expected to watch each of the types. In a study commissioned by *TV Guide,* cartoons were found to have the most violent scenes of the programs monitored (471 in 1 day), and one in five of all violent scenes involved a life-threatening assault, most involving guns (Disney, 1995).

The prevalence and concentration figures from the Wilson, Smith, et al. (2002) study fell between lows and highs of previous studies. According to Wilson, Smith, et al., however, their statistics are arguably the most accurate because of the size and representativeness of the programming that was included in the analysis, setting new benchmarks with which to compare future content analyses. Unlike previous studies, their analysis included cable channels devoted to children as well as major networks; it included all types of programs for children, not just cartoons; and it included full days from 6 a.m. to 11 p.m. rather than only prime time or weekend mornings.

Wilson, Smith, et al. (2002) pointed out that children's programs differ in important ways that make the risk of effect higher for children. For one, perpetrators are more likely to be anthropomorphized, which rather than making it less harmful actually increases the risk of effect because of the well-documented difficulty young children have distinguishing fantasy from reality. The second difference is that perpetrators in these shows are significantly more likely to be reinforced or rewarded for violence, and such glamorization makes it a higher risk to young children. The shows are also significantly less likely to show any serious consequences of violence.

Wilson, Smith, et al.'s (2002) findings are consistent with developmental research and social cognitive theory that has demonstrated that children who cannot distinguish fantasy and reality are more at risk from the programming, and perpetrators who are rewarded more frequently are more likely to serve as role models, as are superheros who use violence to do good, that is, who engage in justified violence.

Younger perpetrators of violence are also more likely to be depicted as attractive than are adult perpetrators (Wilson, Colvin, & Smith, 2002). They were punished less often for their aggressive behavior, there were fewer negative consequences for victims when compared with adult perpetrators, and they were featured prominently in programs targeted to children. Although the proportion of child and adolescent perpetrators was much smaller than that for adults (11% and 89%, respectively), Wilson, Colvin, et al. (2002) still documented more than 1,600 violent interactions perpetrated by individuals under 20 in an average week of American TV. Most child perpetrators were boys, with whom young boys would be more likely to identify. Given children's greater attention to same-age characters, their greater liking of them, and their greater likelihood of seeing them as role models, these findings warrant further attention.

The difference in the means of violence was also important. For younger children, there were more likely to be acts that used natural means and were less lethal, making them easier for children to duplicate or emulate. They were more likely to see less serious or intense violence, although teen perpetrators were more likely to use repeated violence against the same target and were more like adult perpetrators in that regard (Wilson, Colvin, et al., 2002). Because the analysis was based on individual behaviors rather than characters, however, characters who engaged in repeated violence were counted multiple times, which may have overrepresented them. Moreover, nonviolent characters were not coded, so the prevalence of violence among all young TV characters could not be assessed (Wilson, Colvin, et al., 2002).

When violence on broadcast, cable, and independent channels during prime time was compared and social cognitive theory used to explain it, prime-time violence was seen to have contextual features that may increase its risk for adding to harmful effects (Smith et al., 2002). These include featuring humans engaged in violence who are portrayed as attractive and who share demographic characteristics with viewers, making it easy for viewers to identify with the perpetrator, and the use of guns for realistic violence, two attention-getting factors. This creates a greater problem for children who are more likely to learn through observation, but it also is more realistic and depicts consequences, which may reduce the negative impact (Smith et al., 2002). Smith et al. concluded that violence in prime time has elements that work to both increase and decrease a tendency to learn aggressive behavior from it.

Smith et al. (2002) also found that premium cable channels had the most violence, and PBS had the least. They recommended that young viewers not watch premium cable channels during prime time. Broadcast channels, on the other hand, aired violence that increases attention and retention and may lead to more observational learning. It is likely to encourage disinhibition because there is more justified violence and less reference to pain or harm. Cable channels were less likely to promote observational learning of violence in prime time because there was more violence with punishment or harm, but they were also likely to increase disinhibition because of more humorous violence, and they were more likely to show sanitized violence that would reduce inhibitions and increase aggression. Both broadcast and cable, then, depicted violence in the most potentially harmful ways (Smith et al., 2002).

Smith et al.'s (2002) comparison of genres revealed that prime-time movies were among the most violent, although they were also more likely to show long-term consequences as well, and fewer than half of them contained the most problematic aspects just discussed. Reality shows were the most problematic. Although fewer than half of the reality shows contained violence, when they did, they had the most effect of all of the genres for several reasons. They involved humans and therefore would seem more relevant to viewers and attract attention, contributing to observational learning. They also showed justified violence with few consequences, suggesting that violence is acceptable and maybe even necessary (Smith et al., 2002). Over 90% of the movies aired during the day part of the study involved violence.

Shocking statistics on professional wrestling on TV also emerged from a year-long study at Indiana University. Professional wrestling's *Raw Is War* program on cable, viewed regularly by 5 to 6 million households (*Newsweek,* 2000, as cited in National Institute on Media and Family, 2002k), includes not only big hulks throwing each other around but hundreds of observed incidents of simulated sex acts and drug use, rude and crude behavior, and foul language with heavy marketing of related action figures, T-shirts, and other clothing marketed to children as young as 2 (National Institute on Media and the Family, 2002k).

This "entertainment" has been associated with similar behavior exhibited by children with their teachers and has led to tragic deaths after children tried to imitate wrestling holds and moves they had seen on TV (National Institute on Media and the Family, 2002k).

RESEARCH TO DATE

Correlation or Causality

Much in the current press and popular opinion assumes a causal relation between TV violence and aggression. Those who are convinced of the impact of TV violence on children's behavior insist that it is inconsistent and nonsensical to assume that advertisers' 30-second spots affect behavior change but that a half hour of gratuitous television violence will not (Spicer, 1995). Others are quick to point out that many currently middle-aged individuals who watched violence on TV and in movies as children did not become violent, and many other countries that have had TV for over 40 years have far less violence than occurs in the United States (Cuff, 1995). Moreover, most children watch these images without developmental problems with violence or aggression. Ideally, research should help determine which children might be at a higher level of risk for negative influence (Kaliebe & Sondheimer, 2002).

Most researchers do agree that there is a strong association between viewing violence and behaving aggressively, but there is still considerable disagreement about the nature and direction of that relation and its duration. Many have cited recent research covering a wide range of research methodologies to support the claim of a causal relation. Others have concluded that there is a relation, but they have stopped short of claiming a causal one. Still others say the relation has been exaggerated and decreases greatly when specific variables are controlled.

Leonard (1995), for example, claimed that the impact of television violence has been exaggerated and that ratings concerns actually have led to a decrease in network violence and the airing of mostly sitcoms. Wiegman, Kuttschreuter, and Baarda (1992) reported that the possible correlation they found between television violence and aggression almost totally disappeared when they corrected for intelligence and starting level of aggression. Wiegman et al. also noted several interesting cross-cultural gender differences. Correlations between television violence and aggression were significant for both genders in the United States and the Netherlands, only for boys in Finland, and for neither gender in Poland and Australia. When all of the countries, and an Israeli kibbutz, were included, over half of the longitudinal findings were not significant. Wiegman et al. concluded that there was almost no evidence for a causal or bidirectional relation between aggression and viewing violence. They noted that Huesmann and Eron (1986) interpreted the data differently to mean that there is significant evidence to support such a relation; but, they say, Huesmann and Eron's conclusions have been partially supported only in the United States and not in the other countries.

According to Murray (1998), there have been over 1,000 studies on television violence in the past 50 years. Murray described three broad strategies to study the prevalence (content analysis), correlations (surveys of real-world relation between viewing patterns and viewers' attitudes and behavior), and causation (experiments in the laboratory or field). Correlational studies place an emphasis on co-occurrence but not causation. Special correlational studies, on the other hand, allow "intimations of causation" (Murray, 1998, p. 387) to be derived from the fact that they were conducted over several time periods.

Many studies have been done in structured laboratory settings or playrooms where viewing violence and aggressive behavior, desensitization, or arousal were relatively contiguous, but questions remain about what happens in more naturalistic contexts and field studies. According to Murray (1998), however, laboratory and field studies join in suggesting that there is a causal link between viewing violence and increased aggressive values, attitudes, and behavior. The main classes of effects of viewing TV violence include increased aggression, desensitization and greater tolerance of higher levels of violence in society, and fearfulness ("mean world syndrome"). Murray noted that not all children are influenced or affected to the same extent, but viewing violence can lead to increased aggression. Despite all the research, however, we actually know little about how the effects are produced, and we need more research, including neurological correlates of viewing television violence (Murray, 1998).

Others (e.g., Donnerstein et al., 1994) have claimed that research shows a positive relation between exposure to TV violence and aggressive behavior over many different kinds of measures and ages, and exposure seems not only to increase violence but to decrease prosocial behavior as well. Comstock and Scharrer (1999) noted that experiments with children show effects in young viewers that also occur in everyday life and across environmental circumstances. Comstock and Scharrer concluded that portrayals can raise or lower the likelihood of aggressive behavior, depending on whether the level of inhibition is increased or decreased.

Comstock and Scharrer (1999) reviewed many field experiments and surveys that measured exposure to TV violence, aggressive or antisocial behavior, and other variables that might be involved, and a group of meta-analyses that they said provided incontestable empirical documentation of a positive relation between exposure to violence and aggressive and antisocial behavior. The pattern is the same regardless of laboratory versus surveys, simulated aggression, seriously harmful or minor behavior, or interpersonal conflict (Comstock & Scharrer, 1999).

There also appears to be increased documentation in the literature for a third-person effect (Hoffner et al., 2001), the idea that exposure to media violence poses less risk to one's self than to one's peers. Hoffner et al. (2001) observed for both perceptions of a mean world and for aggression. They found individuals less willing to admit effects on their own aggressive tendencies compared with their perceptions of a mean world. Hoffner et al. (2001) suggested that the finding emerged partly because people have more information about themselves than others to which TV effects can be attributed, and they also see noneffects on them-selves, whereas noneffects are not reported in the media. Liking and exposure to television violence moderated the third-person effect. Those who liked violence more thought it affected both self and others less, although there were also gender differences (Hoffner et al., 2001).

In another meta-analysis, Wood, Wong, and Chacere (1991) looked at the ef-fects of exposure to media violence on behavior in spontaneous social interac-tions. Wood et al. found that exposure to violence was associated with more aggressiveness with strangers, friends, and classmates when aggregate findings were examined, but the effect was not consistent across studies. There were stron-ger relations with normal than with emotionally disturbed children and in labora-tory settings over others. Wood et al. (1991) noted that the effect size is important given that the behavioral assessment occurred during natural interactions. "Expo-sure to media violence may have a small to moderate impact on a single behavior, but cumulated across multiple exposures and multiple social interactions, the im-pact may be substantial" (p. 378). Thus, the impact over a lifetime would be ex-pected to be greater than after only a few episodes. Wood et al. concluded that their analysis demonstrated a causal relation between media violence and aggres-sion, but more research is still needed on viewer selection of violent programs and the cumulative impact over time of exposure to such programs.

Various studies, then, using a range of methodological designs including meta-analyses, naturalistic and field studies, and experimental research have reported strong relations between exposure to TV content and behavior. Paik and Comstock's (1994) meta-analysis confirmed Hearold's (1986) findings of clearly positive relations between exposure to TV violence and aggressive and antisocial behavior. There were also significant positive relations between exposure to vio-lence and seriously harmful and criminal acts.

Comstock and Strasburger (1993b) cited meta-analyses covering nearly 500 studies that supported the finding of increased likelihood of aggression or antiso-cial behavior after viewing TV violence, and more recent research (e.g., Anderson & Bushman, 2001; Bushman & Huesmann, 2001; Groebel, 2001) suggests a much stronger relation, including a causal one between viewing violence on TV or play-ing with violent video games and real-life aggression.

According to Bushman and Huesmann (2001), the correlation between violence in the media and aggressive behavior is only slightly smaller than the correlation be-tween smoking and lung cancer. As with smoking, there is not a perfect correlation between the two factors, as some aggressive individuals do not watch violence, and many who view it do not become violent, but it is an important factor. Bushman and Huesmann also compared the correlation to advertising. Not everyone who views a commercial will buy the product, but if it influences 1 in 1,000, it would be considered successful. If the same logic is applied to media violence, and only 1% of viewers were affected and harmed someone, the program would have led 100,000 out of 10 million viewers to become more aggressive (Bushman & Huesmann, 2001).

C. Anderson and Bushman (2001) claimed that the vast research literature on violence on TV and in movies rests on a foundation of three study types: experimental, cross-sectional, and longitudinal research, and there is a consistency of findings within and among these three. They suggested that their General Aggression Model (GAM) is useful to explain why exposure to violent media leads to increases in aggression and violence. Acting aggressively is based on learning, activating, and applying scripts or schemas. Violent media teach how to behave aggressively, prime aggressive cognitions or scripts, increase arousal, create aggressive affect, and reduce prosocial behavior (C. Anderson & Bushman, 2001). In a review of different types of studies including longitudinal, naturalistic, and population-based studies over the past 30 years, Beresin (1999) concluded that there is compelling evidence that exposure of children to media violence is a major etiological factor in aggressive behavior.

Groebel (2001) concluded that short-term effects can be described in causal terms, but the long-term effects are better described as interactive and involve many factors and conditions. According to Groebel, children are surrounded by an environment in which both real and media events support the notion that violence is natural and often involves strong characters who are rewarded for their aggression. Children get the message that aggression is a good way to solve conflicts, it offers status, and it can be fun. Furthermore, it is universal; it can "compensate" children for frustration and problems; it provides "thrills;" and for boys, it can provide a frame of reference for attractive role models (Groebel, 2001). According to Groebel, it is not individual violent films that cause problems, it is the extent of violence that creates an aggressive media environment that increases the likelihood that children will develop a frame of reference in which aggression as a way to solve problems is more rewarding than nonaggressive means.

According to Comstock and Scharrer (1999), the question of whether TV entertainment violence affects behavior is still controversial, but recent data goes beyond formerly forceful conclusions. Moreover, Comstock and Scharrer said, the data do not support the reverse hypothesis that aggressive children simply prefer viewing violence. According to Comstock and Scharrer, three theories lead to an expectation that exposure to violence will lead to increased likelihood of aggression or antisocial behavior. These three are relevant to behavior generally and implicate TV in other behaviors as well (Comstock & Scharrer, 1999).

1. Social cognitive theory, an elaboration of social learning theory, that emphasizes learning processes (acquisition and performance), and the meaning that individuals attribute or ascribe to others. Individuals observe and interpret, taking into account setting and consequences, and they emulate behavior that is seen as appropriate and effective.

2. Neoassociationism that emphasizes storage of thoughts and images and their retrieval. Repetitive portrayals of violence lead to an increase in the num-

ber and variety of antisocial behaviors in a viewer's repertoire as well as the mental content and the number of cues related to antisocial behavior.

3. Arousal theory that emphasizes physiological involvement that can be transferred to other behavior (Comstock & Scharrer, 1999).

Social factors that moderate or enhance TV's influence include socioeconomic level, parental involvement, varied media use, reasonable discipline, and the extent to which issues and topics are discussed freely. Most susceptible, then, would be those from lower socioeconomic homes with high centrality of TV, little involvement of parents or discussion of issues, and a lot of exposure to TV violence with little to mitigate its influence (Comstock & Scharrer, 1999).

Conclusions From Research to Date

To be sure, television violence undoubtedly plays an important role in the aggressive behavior of children, and efforts to reduce the level of violence in TV programming are laudatory indeed. However, many questions remain. Why does violence have such appeal to some viewers? Why do many children not become aggressive or violent after media exposure to violence? What mediates the relation between television violence and aggressive behavior? What variables are important in this relation? Who is most vulnerable to the effects of television violence? Factors such as opportunity, control, rehearsal, perceived reality, the presence of an adult, and other factors affect a child or adolescent's behavioral response to television.

Schools, families, and peers also play important roles. Children learn how aggressive behavior is dealt with on the playground. Did teachers turn a blind eye, or did they offer a protective response? Did they seize the opportunity to teach other alternatives to handling problems? What modeling goes on there? Parents may also model aggression, and the aggressive child then learns by example. Peers can exert pressure and model behavior. The frustration of a child who is not learning well may also contribute to that child's potential for increased aggressiveness.

Different responses to violence result from variations in children's cognitive and personality development, social learning, family and situational variables, reasons for viewing and use of TV, perceived reality, exposure to real violence, amount viewed, level of identification with perpetrators, and other factors in interaction with the nature of the content viewed, such as whether the violence was punished or unpunished. Of the many interacting factors, Sawin (1990) said, "Exposure to television violence results in increases in aggressive behavior for *some* children in *some* situations, but there are insignificant or no direct instigating effects on the behavior of other children in other situations" (p. 175).

TYPES OF VIOLENCE

Part of the difficulty in arriving at definitive conclusions in this field of inquiry lies in the definitions of violence, and what is counted as violent can vary from study to study. Even asking what appears to be a simple question in fact raises very complex issues. If one hypothesizes, for example, that viewing violence on television has negative effects, many possible directions and definitions emerge. What is meant by violence on television? Is it only "gratuitous" violence, or does it include justified or "necessary" violence as, for instance, that required for self-defense? Should one include or exclude violence in aid of a good cause or violence on the news? Further, how should violence be measured? Should there be a clear indicator such as number of fights per half hour, or should one try to assess verbal violence, the violence of a mood, or violence "in the air" as in a sinister and foreboding atmosphere? Newer research has begun to address this issue more clearly by studying different types of violence.

These questions of definition are affected by variables such as age. Young children, for example, are more likely to react to fights that are clear, concrete, and perceptually salient, whereas more subtle forms of violence might elude them. The other two parts of the sample hypothesis can be just as thorny to study. Consider the same hypothesis again: Viewing violence on television has negative effects. How shall viewing be defined? Should it include everything from a quick glance to hours of viewing? Should it include only the shows that a child chooses to watch or also those selected by others? Should it include viewing time that is spent concurrently with other activities such as homework? Finally, how should negative effects be assessed? Should this include a greater tolerance for violent behavior in others as well as increased aggressive acts on the part of the viewer? Should subtle and hard to measure changes in the viewer such as increased fearfulness and distorted perceptions of the environment be included? Are the effects short- or long-term ones? What is short term, and how long is long term?

The point is clear: Definitions and issues vary from researcher to researcher and from study to study, making simple comparisons of results impossible. Thus, frequently heard statements such as "viewing violence on television has negative effects" in the absence of elaboration and greater specificity regarding definitions and populations involved are not very meaningful.

C. Anderson and Bushman (2001) defined *violent media* as those showing intentional efforts to hurt others, including real people, cartoons, and everything in between. They defined *aggression* as behavior intended to hurt someone who is motivated to avoid the harm, and they defined *violence* as extreme forms of aggression. Therefore, "all violence is aggression, but not all aggression is violence" (C. Anderson & Bushman, 2001, p. 354). Most accounts of violence restrict it largely to physical injury and do not include the frequent verbal abuse, intimidation, aggressive humor, sarcasm, or other forms of verbal aggression seen in many programs, which may also be quite upsetting to children.

Newer research points to the importance of looking not only at violence as a global concept but looking at different types of violence to help explain the relations between viewing violence or playing violent games and engaging in real-life aggression and violence. Buchanan, Gentile, Nelson, Walsh, and Hensel (2002) compared not only physical violence, which is the most frequently studied, but also relational violence. Relational aggression threatens relationships or feelings of acceptance such as excluding someone from a birthday party list or play group, insulting or putting down others, ignoring someone, spreading rumors or gossip, and others. Most research has focused on physical aggression, which tends to be more common for boys. Relational aggression is more typical of girls, and therefore, less is known of the impact of media violence on girls' aggressive behavior (Buchanan et al., 2002; Crick, 1996).

A moderate correlation exists between physical and relational forms of violence, but no study had yet compared children's violence in those forms with their media violence viewing habits (Buchanan et al., 2002). Buchanan et al. also studied differences in styles of social information processing as it related to media exposure and how exposure to media violence might relate to the development of attributions of intent. According to Buchanan et al., physically aggressive children tend to infer hostile intentions in others even in situations in which their intent is ambiguous or even benign and that processing style contributes to their aggressive behavior.

Crick and Grotpeter (1995, as cited in Buchanan et al., 2002) demonstrated that relationally aggressive children also tend to show hostile attributional biases, but the social context makes a big difference. Crick and Grotpeter showed, for example, that instrumental conflicts such as breaking a toy were provocative for physically aggressive children, whereas relational conflicts such as not being invited to a party tended to elicit responses in relationally aggressive children that were consistent with a hostile attributional bias (Buchanan et al., 2002). Social information-processing theory suggests that exposure to violent media could activate cognitive structures that would result in processing incoming information in an aggression framework, thereby perhaps leading to increased aggression (Bensley & Eenwyk, 2001 as cited in Buchanan et al., 2002).

Buchanan et al. (2002) studied third-, fourth-, and fifth-grade boys and girls and collected data from a variety of sources including peer-nomination surveys, teacher ratings of the children's aggressive and prosocial behavior, and self-report data on media habits and a measure of hostile attributional bias. They grouped the children into four groups: those high on both types of aggression, those high on physical aggression but low on relational aggression, those high on relational aggression but low on physical aggression, and those grouped as nonaggressive. Buchanan et al. found that amount of viewing and amount of time spent playing video games were related not only to exposure to violence across various media but also to a preference for violent games and both teacher and peer reports of physically aggressive behavior. "In general, children with greater exposure to violent media preferred more violent video games" (Buchanan et al., 2002, p. 5).

Children who were relationally aggressive viewed and played with more violent media than their nonaggressive counterparts. Age and gender were also important in the findings. Boys were exposed to and preferred more violence, and there was an increase with age in preference for violent media forms (Buchanan et al., 2002). There were also many significant correlations with the hostile attribution scores and various indexes of exposure to violence and violent behavior ratings. That is, children with the most exposure to violence in viewing and in play tended to assume or expect the worst in their interactions with others.

Buchanan et al. (2002) pointed to some of the questions that remain. Do some children engage in relational aggression because it is more subtle and likely to lead to fewer repercussions from adults? Do relationally aggressive children move on to more physical aggression? The findings are correlational and do not establish a causal direction, but the consistency of the findings certainly underscores differences in children's aggression related to their consumption of violent media (Buchanan et al., 2002). Buchanan et al. concluded that the seriousness of relational aggression and its potential for destructive effects is just now starting to be recognized.

INTERVENING VARIABLES

Significant developmental and gender variables, family background and attitudes, and the quality and nature of a child's other experiences as well as his or her perception of television portrayals are important factors that influence television's impact. Other factors that affect the likelihood that an individual will actually perform a specific aggressive act include arousal level of the viewer, predisposition to act aggressively, reinforcement of the behavior, the nature of the television content, and the viewing context.

In the following paragraphs, we will consider the many mediating variables that are involved in the relation between television viewing of violence and actual aggressive behavior. We will take a look at developmental variables that influence who will react aggressively as well as some of the television features that make a difference. We will also consider some proposed mechanisms by which viewing violence might be translated into actual aggressive behavior, that is, the "how" of the relation, and at some of the effects other than increased aggressiveness that viewing violence can have.

Viewer Variables

Developmental Level. The cognitive and social maturity of children at the time that they view violence is a critical variable in any relation between viewing such violence and aggressive behavior. As children's levels of comprehension of television content and their own behavioral controls are not fully developed, the potential effect of violent portrayals may be considerably stronger for children than for adults. In addition, whereas adults can distance themselves from violent television programs, young children feel very involved and see the images as real (Van der Voort, 1986). They are more likely to imitate aggression because they do not understand the consequences of that behavior as well as older children and adults do. They do not even understand that death is permanent (Cannon, 1995). These factors become especially important when one considers that children frequently watch programs that are not child oriented but rather are intended for an adult audience.

Children tend to watch more television and hence more violence during the period between ages 9 and 12, an important one for changing perception and experience (Van der Voort, 1986). As they mature over that time period, they understand more, they are less inclined to see television violence as realistic, they tend to be more detached and respond less emotionally, they are less frightened by violence, and, by the time they are 12, they are less inclined to view the violent programs negatively (Van der Voort, 1986).

Paik and Comstock (1994), on the other hand, reported a positive association between viewing violence and antisocial behavior regardless of age, from nursery school to adulthood. Preschoolers showed the highest effect size but are least capable of acting on it, although violence between preschoolers is as real to them as other violence is to adults, and long-term consequences need to be considered (Paik & Comstock, 1994).

In a survey of 1,500 middle and high school students, Chapin (2002) found that they demonstrated a third-person effect, but the effect decreased with age. It was influenced by perceived reality of violence in the media, an optimistic bias, and knowledge of violence in the real world. Chapin argued for early media literacy to prepare them for the real world.

Developmental changes in viewer perceptual and cognitive factors in the viewing situation are also important. Young children's greater reliance on perceptually salient cues, for example, and their more concrete approach to material (e.g., reacting to things that look violent), may result in very different perceptions than older children have. Age differences, then, as well as personality, experiential, and contextual ones interact with the television content to affect what is perceived as violent and what the viewer response will be.

In a study of children's moral reasoning and their perceptions of television violence (Krcmar & Cooke, 2001), two groups of children were randomly assigned to conditions in which they viewed violence that was or was not punished and violence that was or was not provoked. They were then asked for their judgment about the video clip and whether they would use aggression in a hypothetical conflict later on. Younger children judged unpunished violence as more right than punished violence, and there was no significant difference for the older ones. The older children tended to see provoked violence as more right and more justified than unprovoked violence, a finding that approached significance. This result is consistent with developmental theory, as the older children were better able to take motivations into account. The willingness to choose a violent story ending related to the experimental condition for older children but not for the younger ones. Older children who saw violence that was provoked were likely to select an aggressive story end to the hypothetical conflict. Krcmar and Cooke concluded that children's age affects their interpretation of the context for violence, and their interpretation of that context is consistent with developmental theory on moral reasoning.

Intelligence Level.   Several sets of studies have reported a negative correlation between intelligence and aggression. Wiegman et al. (1992), for example, found a significant negative relation between intelligence and both aggression and viewing of television. Children who watched a lot of aggression and who also behaved aggressively were lower in intelligence. In boys, intelligence was related to less viewing of violence and less aggressive behavior. Correlations were in the same direction for girls but were not significant. Wiegman et al. noted the important difficulties in trying to compare various studies, as some measures of intelligence in fact were measures only of academic achievement, and school achievement is a less stable factor that can be influenced by television and by aggression.

In data collected over 22 years on the relation between intellectual functioning and aggressiveness, Huesmann and colleagues (Huesmann, Eron, Lefkowitz, & Walder, 1984; Huesmann, Eron, & Yarmel, 1987) found that aggression interfered with intellectual development and predicted poorer adult intellectual achievement. They hypothesized that lower intelligence increases the likelihood of learning aggressive responses early, and then this aggressiveness makes continued intellectual development more difficult. Children who have superior analytic and language skills are more likely to imagine different viewpoints, are less likely to use force to persuade others, are more able to foresee consequences of their behavior, and have a greater range of behavioral options to violence (American Psychological Association, 1995).

Gender.   Others have found that gender differences also exist in the relation between viewing violence and aggressive behavior. Paik and Comstock (1994), for example, found a consistent positive and significant gender effect, but it was only slightly higher for males in more realistic survey studies. Levine (1995) reported that boys seem more drawn to violent shows and are more agitated by them, whereas girls are more often repelled by them and saddened.

Interactions between types of aggression and gender can help to clarify or explain some of the gender differences often reported. Lagerspetz and Bjorkqvist (1994) spoke of direct and indirect aggression. They defined *indirect aggression* as aggression in which the perpetrator stays unidentified and therefore avoids counterattack and disapproval. Examples would be spreading gossip or setting fire to someone's house. Lagerspetz and Bjorkqvist found that boys engage in more direct aggression, especially physical. Direct aggression is discouraged in girls who are then more likely to use indirect aggression, which the authors found they use extensively.

According to Lagerspetz and Bjorkqvist (1994), direct aggression, either physical or verbal, is most common in young girls. In adolescence it may shift into more indirect aggression for girls but perhaps not so in boys who develop social skills later. Lagerspetz and Bjorkqvist noted that girls' friendships and social relationships are closer and offer more opportunities to use them for the expression of indirect aggression. Lagerspetz and Bjorkqvist also found low correlations between self-ratings and peer ratings for individual aggression, and perpetrators may not admit to or even be aware of their own aggression, which might include scheming, for example, which is easier to "explain away." Girls dealt with conflicts in more peaceful ways than boys who used less mature and more direct aggressive means (like younger girls). The 11-year-old cohort was the most aggressive, especially in the use of indirect aggression (Lagerspetz & Bjorkqvist, 1994).

Crick (1996) also noted that most research has focused on overt aggression, which is more typical of boys, and has neglected relational aggression, which is more typical of girls. Moreover, more studies have looked at negative behavior than prosocial behavior. Crick's (1996) longitudinal study included measures of relational aggression, overt aggression, prosocial behavior, and social adjustment. The results indicated that individual differences in overt and relational aggression were relatively stable over time. Measures of relational aggression and prosocial behavior contributed uniquely to the prediction of future poor social adjustment. The combination of high aggression and low prosocial behavior was especially problematic.

Crick and Grotpeter (1995) demonstrated that relational aggression is a valid and distinct form of aggression and is higher for girls. Moreover, relational aggression leads to risk for future adjustment problems such as more rejection by others and higher depression, loneliness, and isolation relative to peers who were nonrelationally aggressive. Crick and Grotpeter concluded that relational aggression is distinct from overt aggression and is significantly related to gender and to social/psychological adjustment. Aggression in girls has been underestimated, according to Crick and Grotpeter, because earlier studies did not assess different forms of aggression. Crick and Grotpeter suggested that relational aggression may lead to dislike by peers, or the reverse may hold. Finally, status as controversial children, those liked by some and disliked by others, was significantly related to relational aggression in which a child would be disliked by victims and liked by others and may control peer group interactions (Crick & Grotpeter, 1995).

Initial Levels of Aggression. Children's initial levels of aggressiveness are also important factors, both in the material they choose to watch or games they choose to play and in the impact of those choices on their beliefs, attitudes, and behaviors. Some argue that not enough attention has been paid to the question of selective exposure or why viewers select some messages and programs over others (Zillmann & Bryant, 1985b). Although higher levels of viewing may lead to more aggressive behavior, it is also the case that more aggressive children select violent television more frequently (Eron, 1982; Friedrich-Cofer & Huston, 1986; Huesmann, 1986; Huesmann, Eron, et al., 1984). Their aggressive predisposition may well determine their viewing preferences as well. That is, there may be selective exposure to television violence (Zillmann & Bryant, 1985b).

Johnston (1995) used a uses and gratifications model to study adolescents' motivations for viewing graphic horror. She found that their motivations for viewing such slasher films differed and mediated the relation between violent content and affective and cognitive responses to it. Johnston also found that the motivations were related to different preferences, ideas about positive attributes of those movies, patterns of affect before and after viewing, and character identification, as well as different personality profiles. The four motivations Johnston discussed reflected very different affective and cognitive experiences in the viewers' response to violence. The motives (gore watching, thrill watching, independent watching, and problem watching) were each associated with varying levels of empathy, positive and negative affect, adventure seeking, substance abuse, and identification with victim or killer. It seems clear that such distinctions among viewers of violence would shed considerable light on the differential effects of television violence on child and adolescent viewers.

Huesmann, Eron, et al. (1984), in their oft-cited study over 22 years and with data on the aggressiveness of over 600 children and their parents, showed that children who were more aggressive at age 8 were also more aggressive at age 30. They concluded that whatever causes it, aggression is a trait that is persistent and quite constant across situations once it has been established, although it may be influenced by situational factors. In a different study, however, Huesmann (1986) found that boys who watched violence and identified with violent characters were more aggressive 2 years later no matter what their original level of aggressive behavior was. Children who identified more with characters watched more violence and vice versa. The degree of identification of the child with the television character then may be as important as the amount of viewing or exposure (Huesmann, 1986).

Viewing Variables

Perceived Reality.   Hearold's (1986) meta-analysis, based on data on over 100,000 participants and involving over 1,000 comparisons, included laboratory experiments, surveys, and field studies from both psychology and communications fields. One of Hearold's conclusions was that television realism was the most important factor, at least for older viewers. This finding raised important developmental issues, as older viewers can more easily make distinctions between real and fantasy; young ones cannot. The realism of the portrayal is also likely to affect attention because realistic portrayals may be perceived as more relevant to the viewer and thus increase the likelihood of that individual attending to and learning from them. Preschoolers' inability to distinguish real and fantasy is an important concern, as they are the ones who are most likely to be watching cartoons, including violent ones.

Some researchers have noted the strong reinforcement effect that justified violence has, a depiction of violence that is common on TV and in movies (Comstock & Strasburger, 1993b). Krcmar and Valkenburg (1999) studied 156 children between ages 6 and 12 who watched fantasy violence and realistic violence and then were evaluated regarding their moral interpretation of justified and unjustified violence. Those who watched more fantasy violence tended to see justified violence as less wrong, whereas those who watched more realistic violence tended to see justified violence as more wrong. Both used less advanced moral reasoning when discussing their judgments. Krcmar and Valkenburg explained that violence by heroes has little if any negative outcome or consequences and therefore is glorified, and it reduces or discourages empathy for the victim or perspective taking by children.

Krcmar and Valkenburg (1999) suggested that the fantasy violence and justified violence finding likely occurred because after viewing fantasy violence in programs like *Superman* and *Power Rangers Turbo*, the children admired and identified with the hero, not the villain. They saw the violence as done for the greater good, and they were more likely to agree that if it is for the greater good, violence can be good (Krcmar & Valkenburg, 1999). One meta-analysis of over 200 studies (Paik & Comstock, 1994) revealed that television violence has a stronger effect on aggression when it is depicted as justified or socially sanctioned behavior. The greatest effects, then, according to Hearold (1986), should be with a newscast of triumphant soldiers or police putting down a riot, that is, real violence that is justified and followed by reward, with no negative consequences.

Some of the news coverage of the buildup to war against Iraq made distinctions between reality and drama harder to make. For instance, a military newspaper reported that a "'glitzy, high-tech set'" (Doyle, 2003, p. R2) was being built in Qatar for military briefings to reporters and news reports about the war at a cost of almost a quarter million dollars. It was to have five 50-in. and two 70-in. plasma screens to show maps, computer images, and other information and led some to see the project as "plans to make the coming conflict a really cool war to watch on TV" (Doyle, 2003, p. R2).

We know that the violence seen daily on the news can affect viewers, but O'Keefe and Reid-Nash (1987) found no overall relation between crime shows and fear as they had found with the news, perhaps because the viewers understood clearly that news is real.

What impact do these same shows have on young viewers? Young children who have difficulty with reality–fantasy distinctions would not easily be able to make a discrimination between news and crime shows. For them, the fear-evoking characteristics of both would likely be about equal. Moreover, their inability to understand subtle dimensions of the information, political intrigue, language intricacies, and many other aspects of what they view makes their experience a very different one than that of older children and adults. In addition, as younger children cannot distinguish between news and fiction and do not understand some techniques such as replays, the endless repetition of the 9/11 footage, terrifying as it was to watch even for adults, may have led children to believe that new attacks were continuing to occur.

The realism of the violence, then, and its perceived justification, the level of identification of a child with the perpetrator, and the perceptual and cognitive skills of the viewer determine the impact of the violence.

Amount of Viewing. Although the frequency of exposure to violence is also an important factor, its role in the association with aggressive behavior is not a clear-cut one. Lynn, Hampson, and Agahi (1989) suggested that the amount of time spent watching television violence is less important in later aggression than an individual's genetic predisposition and that an individual's reaction to violence, such as the amount of enjoyment that is expressed about a violent show, is more important than the amount of violence viewed. Other studies (Singer et al., 1999) found exposure to violence and parental monitoring to be the most influential factors in explaining children's violent behavior, although the number of hours spent watching TV and a preference for violent shows were also positively related to children's violent behavior.

Family Background. Family attitudes toward aggression constitute a critical variable in television's impact on the attitudes and behavior of children and adolescents. Parental influence through the medium of modeling, punishment, and choice of discipline, as well as through general attitudes toward aggression and toward the child, is strong. Many researchers have noted the relation between parental discipline styles and aggressiveness in children. Singer and Singer (1986), for example, reported that children in high-aggression groups were more likely to have experienced power-assertive techniques, and harsh physical punishment has been associated with aggressive behavior in youth (Farrington, 1991; Pepler & Slaby, 1994; Straus, 1991; Wiegman et al., 1992). Wiegman et al. (1992) also found that parents' punishment style was related to children's aggression but not to viewing violence.

Others have noted the relation between parental attitudes toward television in general and toward violence in particular and aggressiveness in their children. Children whose parents were less concerned about television violence's effects showed a stronger preference for violence, they responded to it less emotionally, they tended to be more aggressive, and although needing them most, they were less likely to learn critical viewing skills (Van der Voort, 1986). Messaris (1986) suggested that children do not imitate television unless others have previously encouraged them, intentionally or not, to engage in the particular kind of behavior being imitated. Previous encouragement or discouragement of a behavior by parents may be the crucial factor in whether a child imitates it after viewing it on television independent of any intervention that the parent makes in the actual television experience.

Socioeconomic level may be an interactive factor here as well. Children from lower socioeconomic homes not only engaged in higher levels of viewing; they also showed more enjoyment of and approval of violence, identified more strongly with the television characters, and had lower achievement levels at school (Van der Voort, 1986). They also were often left alone with the TV as a babysitter (Scheer, 1995).

CAUSAL EXPLANATIONS

Although there is considerable agreement that an association between viewing violence and aggressive behavior exists, particularly in short-term laboratory studies, there is far less agreement on the nature of that relation or its causes. Several explanatory models have been put forward in an attempt better understand the relation.

Modeling

The relation between violence on TV and aggressive behavior has often been attributed to modeling or social learning as the mediating variable. A recent murder in California, for example, attracted attention when a 15-year-old and his 20-year-old brother allegedly killed their mother and dismembered her before dumping the body as they had seen on *The Sopranos* (Associated Press, 2003b). A particularly strong finding is the report of a significant increase in aggressive behavior, both physical and verbal, among children in a community that had no television after television was introduced to that town (Joy, Kimball, & Zabrack, 1986). Those increases, still apparent 2 years after the introduction of television, occurred not just in children who were already aggressive but for children who were low in aggression initially.

Studies with young children, such as Bandura's (1967) with the Bobo doll, have good external validity because young children do not understand experimentation and would not role play (Comstock & Paik, 1991). That validity also is enhanced, according to Comstock and Paik, by more naturalistic studies that produce similar results and by studies of communities before and after the introduction of television such as the work of Williams (1986).

On the other hand, not all children who view violence become aggressive, and a social learning or social cognitive model does not explain why some children appear to be more interested in television violence, enjoy it more, and are more affected by it. Wiegman et al. (1992), for example, found that in a naturalistic viewing situation, children view both violent and prosocial programs, so they are highly related, and discrimination between the two variables is difficult. Children who have seen a lot of prosocial models also have watched many aggressive models. According to Wiegman et al., this is important because social learning theory says modeling occurs only with a diet that is more or less pure. Wiegman et al. found no evidence that the two types of television models influenced the children's aggressive or prosocial behavior, and they could not find children who watched mostly violent content. Because of this mix, the influence of viewing violence could not be separated from other effects of viewing television.

Contextual factors such as the attractiveness of the perpetrator increase attention to media violence. Viewers are more likely to identify with and imitate attractive perpetrators than unattractive ones (Bandura, 1986). Similarity of gender, age, ethnic and social background, or other characteristics tends to increase the attractiveness and thus the identification of the viewer with the model (Smith et al., 2002).

According to Comstock and Scharrer (1999) and Comstock and Paik (1991), four factors or contingencies increase media effects and the chance of increased aggression or antisocial behavior. Whatever heightens these four factors increases the likelihood of similar behavior in the future. The first three have to do with the portrayal and the last has to do with the viewer. These include efficacy (whether the behavior is rewarded or punished), normativeness (e.g., whether it is justified, has consequences, is intentionally hurtful, etc.), pertinence (e.g., similarity between viewer and perpetrator, real-life cues, lack of humorous violence), and susceptibility (e.g., predisposition to act aggressively, pleasure, frustration, anger, lack of criticism). Factors that might facilitate effects include identification with the perpetrator, justification or reward for antisocial behavior, and cues that appear to exist in real life (Paik & Comstock, 1994).

The most important contextual factors for viewers' interpretation of what they see are portrayals of rewards and punishments and showing the consequences of violence (Smith et al., 2002; Willis & Strasburger, 1998), but these are often missing, as other studies have shown how rarely negative consequences are portrayed. Depictions of consequences remind viewers of the serious effects associated with physical aggression and activate inhibitory mechanisms such as empathy or sympathy that decrease the risk of aggressive behavior. If no negative physical or emotional consequences are shown with the violence, the inhibitory reactions may not occur, thus increasing the likelihood of aggressive behavior. Smith et al. (2002) concluded that although prime-time violence is frequent and has features or elements that would be likely to lead to observational learning, it has other features such as showing long-term consequences that would make it less likely to result in disinhibition. Therefore, viewers who have developed nonviolent scripts would be less at risk (Smith et al., 2002).

Repeated exposure to violence in the media may function as a kind of cognitive rehearsal that increases retention and strengthens and reinforces aggressive scripts (Smith et al., 2002). The possible use of violence as a reaction to some situation, then, is more readily available to the person. Behavioral reproduction or enactment depends on the individual having the skills or means to do something (Bandura, 1994). Imitation of violence by younger viewers, then, would be more likely if the violence they observed was committed by natural means such as kicking or hitting. Therefore, the type of violence depicted and whether the viewer has the skills to replicate it also affects viewer responses to the violence and the likelihood of imitation.

If a child who is very frustrated in his or her interpersonal relationships watches a good deal of violent content, for example, and if that child receives little other competing information to counter aggression as a solution, he or she well may imitate it. Another child with the same interpersonal problem who learns alternate strategies from parents or peers or who is actively discouraged from using the aggressive techniques that were observed on television may not emulate the television models.

Social cognitive theory also posits that viewing certain types of violent depictions can also weaken restraints over previously learned behavior (Bandura, 1986, 1994), a process known as disinhibition. According to Bandura (1994), people often refrain from engaging in aggressive behavior to avoid either social censure such as punishment or self-reproach such as feelings of guilt or shame. The frequency with which violence is presented in the media or the nature and content of the depiction, however, can work to weaken or disinhibit those sanctions and make the acting out of aggressive behavior more likely.

Finally, the inclusion of humor in a violent scene may influence sanctions against aggression by dehumanizing the victims, which can reduce empathic responses and have a disinhibiting effect (Bandura, 1990), or by undermining or trivializing the seriousness of violence and its consequences, which could increase the likelihood of aggression (Smith et al., 2002).

Cognitive Neoassociationist Theory

In his cognitive neoassociationist theory, Berkowitz (1986) also asserted that viewing aggression disinhibits viewers' controls on aggressive behavior. If the aggression is approved and the disinhibition increases, aggression is more likely, although the aggressive acts are not necessarily imitations of the specific acts seen on television (Berkowitz, 1986).

According to Berkowitz (1988), even neutral stimuli can evoke aggressive behavior when they are associated in one's mind with aversive conditions or events. That is, negative feelings evoke aggressive tendencies, and this process underlies the aggression that often follows frustration. Virtually any type of negative affect, even depression and sadness, can activate or trigger the anger-aggression network if the feeling is sufficiently intense, but some types of affect, such as feelings of agitation, may be more likely to prime it (Berkowitz, 1994). In addition, later comments or objects may serve as retrieval cues for aggressive thoughts that occur during the viewing of a violent program through a system of semantically related concepts (Berkowitz, 1986; Berkowitz & Rogers, 1986).

Berkowitz and Rogers (1986) also described the role of a *priming effect* or the increased likelihood that an activated concept or elements of thought associated with it will come to mind again for some time after it has been activated. Furthermore, viewing violence can prime related thoughts, resulting in a greater likelihood that other aggressive thoughts will be recalled quite automatically and involuntarily (Berkowitz & Rogers, 1986). Later comments or objects then may serve as retrieval cues for aggressive thoughts that occur during the television viewing (Berkowitz, 1986).

Script Theory

The real-life experience of children is an important determinant of television's effect as well. As most viewers have little real-life experience with violence but much exposure to it on television, most of the knowledge and scripts about violence are likely initially derived from and hence influenced by television (Williams, 1986). If only aggressive scripts are acquired during the sensitive period when children acquire a network of behavioral scripts, they can only behave aggressively (Huesmann, 1986, 1988). These processes become automatic as children develop and mature and become more resistant to change as they are rehearsed and acted on (Huesmann & Miller, 1994).

Huesmann and Eron (1986) suggested that children store aggressive solutions in memory and use them to guide their behavior. Those who watch lots of violence are more likely to develop cognitive scripts that entail violence or aggression as a solution, and they may be rehearsed in fantasy. Moreover, the more that children rehearse aggression in fantasy, the more likely they are to recall such scripts and the more aggressive their overt behavior becomes (Eron, 1982; Huesmann, 1988; Huesmann, Lagerspetz, & Eron, 1984). Individual differences in aggression after viewing violence are due to a cumulative learning process that strengthens the schemas or scripts for aggressive behavior (Huesmann, 1986). This has important implications for the effects of playing violent video games as well, which would provide further fantasy rehearsal of aggressive behaviors.

The individual most likely to engage in aggression or violent behavior "is one who has been programmed to respond in this way through previous experience and learning" (Eron, 1994, p. 9). The conditions most likely to result in learned aggression include those in which a child is reinforced for aggressive behavior, has many opportunities to observe aggression, and is the object of aggressive behavior. If children grow up in those circumstances, they see aggression as a normal and appropriate response to many situations. They then come to rehearse aggressive responses and dismiss alternative behaviors. When they face situations in which cues are similar to the original situation in which they learned violence, an aggressive or violent response is more easily triggered.

Huesmann (1988) noted that aggressive behavior usually has negative consequences including decreased popularity, poorer achievement, and parent and/or teacher intervention; for most children, these expected consequences lead to an inhibition of aggressive scripts. For some, however, negative consequences lead to more aggression (Huesmann, 1988). As aggressive behavior becomes a habit, it interferes with social and academic adjustment and leads to greater frustration and more aggressive behavior (Huesmann, 1988; Huesmann & Eron, 1986). If aggression is learned early as a problem-solving technique, it is very resistant to change (Eron, 1980, 1986; Huesmann, 1988). Finally, social-processing deficits also may interfere with creative conflict resolutions, and individuals with such deficits tend to generate fewer solutions and more aggressive ones (Geen, 1994).

Habituation and Desensitization

One of the most alarming aspects of television violence is its potential to habituate and desensitize people to violence and aggression after significant exposure over a long period of time. According to Van der Voort (1986), heavy viewers are less likely to see violence as "terrible." They enjoy and prefer violence, they are more likely to see it as justified, and they show less emotional reactivity to repeated viewing of violent programs. A decrease in physiological arousal and emotional intensity after frequent exposures to violence has also been demonstrated (Rule & Ferguson, 1986). Worries abound that perhaps children of this violent media culture will not only become more aggressive but may be slow to help victims of real-life aggression.

Kosinski's (as cited in Sohn, 1982) recounting of an experience he had while teaching is a rather disconcerting one. Video monitors were installed on both sides of a blackboard in a large classroom to which several 7- to 10-year-old children had been invited. As Kosinski sat reading them a story, he was attacked by an intruder (a prearranged event) who rushed into the room and began hitting and pushing him and arguing with him. Cameras filmed the incident and the reactions of the students. To Kosinski's dismay, most of the students rarely looked at the actual happening in the room; rather, they watched it on the television monitors, which were easier for them to see:

> Later, when we talked about it, many of the children explained that they could see the attack better on the screens. After all, they pointed out, they could see close-ups of the attacker and of me, his hand on my face, his expressions—all the details they wanted—without being frightened by "the real thing" (or by the necessity of becoming involved).... The kids were less interested in the actual assault than in what the TV cameras were doing—as if they had paid to see a film, as if the incident had been staged to entertain them! And all during the confrontation—despite my yelling, his threats, the fear that I showed—the kids did not interfere or offer to help. None of them. They sat transfixed as if the TV cameras neutralized the act of violence. And perhaps they did. By filming a brutal physical struggle from a variety of viewpoints, the cameras transformed a human conflict into an aesthetic happening, distancing the audience and allowing them an alternative to moral judgment and involvement. (as cited in Sohn, 1982, pp. 356, 359)

Much research does show callousness toward female victims, especially rape victims, after exposure to violence or sexually explicit content, with perhaps an even greater effect on younger viewers who do not have critical viewing skills or experience to negate such portrayals (Donnerstein et al., 1994). After continued exposure, then, alterations in perception and affect may carry over to real-life situations.

Genotype–Environment Correlation and Interaction Theory

Lynn et al. (1989) claimed that their genotype–environment correlation and inter-action theory takes into account two important factors not included in other ex-planatory models: (a) the genotype–environment correlation (the way parents pass on characteristics to their children through genetic and environmental means) and (b) the genotype–environment interaction (the idea that genetic pre-dispositions cause children to act differently within the same environment). The genotype–environment correlation tends to increase similarities among siblings of a family, whereas the genotype–environment interaction tends to decrease it. According to Lynn et al., such a model differentiates among passive viewers of vi-olence (children who watch with the whole family) and active viewers of violence (children who seek out violent programs). In their model, viewing of violence af-fects only those individuals who are predisposed genetically to choose aggressive TV characters as models. Lynn et al. claimed that the enjoyment of television vio-lence is the significant variable, not the amount of viewing. They believed that the results from their study of over 2,000 children in Northern Ireland were hard to explain by a sociological or social learning theory but that the theory is salvage-able if it is reformulated in terms of their genotype–environment correlation and interaction model.

OTHER EFFECTS OF VIEWING VIOLENCE

Behavioral Changes

Viewing violence on television can affect behavior in other ways than increased aggressiveness, including materialism and unlawful behavior (Hearold, 1986). Even when violence and aggressive behavior are not directly related, the effects of viewing violence may appear in the form of less civility and a decrease in affiliative and other prosocial behavior rather than more aggression (Van der Voort, 1986). According to the Committee on Public Education of the American Academy of Pediatrics (2001b), research findings indicate that violence in the media also con-tributes to various other problems including desensitization to violence, night-mares, fear, and aggressive behavior. The Committee urged pediatricians to evaluate the level of exposure to media in their patients and work toward a safer media environment.

In a poll of over 70,000 *USA Weekend* readers, 86% reported changes in their children's behavior after watching a violent show; sometimes the children be-came more detached, "spaced out," and passive (Levine, 1995). Dunn and Hughes (2001) compared "hard-to-manage" preschoolers with a normal control group matched for age, school, ethnic background, and gender to study the relation between early interest in violent fantasy and social understanding and interactions, emotional behavior, and antisocial behavior. The preschool children were given a number of cognitive tests and tasks tapping their emotional understanding. Their understanding of the emotional consequences of prosocial and antisocial behavior was then studied at age 6. The hard-to-manage group demonstrated more violent fantasy. In both groups combined, violent fantasy was related to poor performance on virtually all measures including executive control, conflicts with friends, empathic responses, language ability, antisocial behavior, anger displays, communication, and coordination of play.

Fear and Anxiety

One common reaction to television violence is fear, which has received a good deal less attention than aggression despite its importance. In one discussion (Waisglas, 1992) of television violence with 10-year-olds in a downtown Toronto fifth-grade class, virtually all of them reported having seen things on television that terrified them. They recalled nightmares, fears, and worries about parent behavior after watching abusive parents on television and fears that scary things that happened on television could happen to them (Waisglas, 1992). Children's fear reactions to TV viewing are discussed further in chapter 10.

Ridley-Johnson, Surdy, and O'Laughlin (1991) found parents to be as concerned about television contributing to fear/passivity in their adolescent children as they were about aggression-related effects. There was also a gender difference in parental concerns. Parents were as concerned about the fear-related effects for girls as for boys but more concerned about aggression-related effects among parents of boys. According to Ridley-Johnson et al., this is consistent with learning theory as well as current socialization practices because both genders can learn about aggression from TV violence. Whether those attitudes and behaviors are actually expressed, however, depends on other variables such as expectations and consequences and how the boys and girls are socialized and reinforced differently for aggressive behavior.

Nightly news tends to frighten the public, especially since 9/11. Scare tactics are used to get viewers to tune in by repeating and overemphasizing sniper killings, anthrax scares, child abductions, and other stories, tragic as they are (Children Now, 2002c). According to cultivation theory, heavy viewers are likely to develop a "mean world syndrome" in which they come to see the world as more dangerous than it is. The tendency to interrupt with "breaking news," which often involves something relatively ordinary, is "another sign that ... a powerful medium has a vested interest in disaster" (MacGregor, 2002), and it can raise anxiety levels in viewers.

There is substantial exposure of children and adolescents to news, but young people generally are less well informed or interested in public affairs than several decades ago, with some exceptions such as sports, violent events, and social issues that affect them directly (Comstock & Scharrer, 1999). Comstock and Scharrer attributed this largely to the fact that young viewers get most of their news from TV, and only prominent topics get their attention because of their striking properties, entertainment elements, or self-interest. What people learn from television is increasing apprehension about events that are unfolding with variations among individuals depending on their cognitive schema. They are more likely to comprehend and recall information when elements of the present activate cognitive schema and the new information can be incorporated into prior knowledge (Comstock & Scharrer, 1999). One might expect young children, then, who have less prior knowledge and experience to understand less well what they see and therefore, perhaps, to become more anxious or fearful. On the other hand, if disaster news, for example, is conveyed in a way that is not highly perceptually salient, young children may not attend for long periods or may not become as anxious or fearful as older children who understand what is happening.

INTERVENTION STRATEGIES

Whatever the final outcome of research on the relation between viewing violent television content and aggressive behavior, no one has argued that heavy viewing of violence is a desirable behavior or one that enhances a child's development. There is virtually no evidence to support a catharsis view in which viewing TV violence leads to a decrease in aggressive behavior by draining off a child's aggressive tendencies in fantasy. Although other variables clearly interact with the amount of violence viewed, there still appear to be strong reasons, both cognitive and behavioral, to reduce excessive amounts of violence viewing. How this might best be accomplished is less clear. Options include voluntary reductions of violence by networks, regulatory controls, enforced rating systems, technological devices for television sets, parent education and strategies, and other possibilities. These are discussed in more detail in chapter 14 on Intervention Strategies.

SUMMARY

The impact of media violence on various facets of social behavior is a critical but extraordinarily complex area of investigation. Issues of realism, salience, arousal, toy cueing, program and game preferences, strength of identification, family attitudes and behavior, habituation and desensitization, past experience, situational variables, behavioral controls, hours spent with the media and the reasons for using various media, as well as gender, age, and racial differences all interact to determine whether an individual will actually behave aggressively after being exposed to media violence. Other factors such as whether the violence is justified or provoked, rewarded or punished, harmful or humorous, and whether weapons or natural means are required to execute it further complicate the research. Discerning which individuals will react in which diverse ways adds another important component to the mix.

Media exposure to violence has frequently been associated with increased aggressive behavior, at least over the short term and in laboratory studies. Its long-term effect in naturalistic settings is less clear, although repeated exposure may serve to maintain a short-term effect. Although most researchers agree on findings of a correlation between media violence and aggressive behavior, not all agree on causal direction. Some view the relation between viewing of violence and aggression as bidirectional in which increases in aggressive behavior follow such viewing, but children predisposed to act aggressively more frequently select violent programs as well. Others have found differences between the effects of viewing violence on television and being exposed to it in video games. Different types of violence are also being studied more frequently and help to explain some of the gender differences that have emerged in the past. Developmental differences in motivation for watching TV or playing games have also been reported.

A number of theoretical explanations have been used to explain the relation between media use and aggression. In addition, studies of the impact of media violence on other facets of children's lives, such as fear and anxiety, altered social interaction, desensitization, and others are being explored more frequently.

Various technological aids and ratings systems are available to help parents control their children's television viewing and game playing, although they have some important limitations that are discussed in more detail in chapter 14. Parents need to monitor their children's media use, decrease the amount of violence they view on TV or are exposed to in games, and help them develop coping strategies to use when they are exposed to material that frightens them, including viewing real-life violence in the news.

DISCUSSION QUESTIONS

1. Discuss developmental and gender differences in children and adolescents that would help to explain their tendency to engage in either direct versus indirect aggression or physical versus relational aggression.
2. How is level of realism or perceived reality related to children's media preferences? How do developmental differences affect this relation and the impact of their media choices?
3. Discuss the relative merits of each of the theoretical causal explanations. Which one(s) seem most parsimonious and most applicable to the interpretation of data that are currently available?

CHAPTER SIX

Cultural Diversity

CHAPTER SIX

Cultural Diversity

More than 10 million children watch television between 8:00 p.m. and 9:00 p.m., the "family hour," which is the least diverse time of all prime-time programming (Children Now, 2001b). That means that children see a more homogenous world than adults who watch later in the evening. This is a concern because television can play a significant role in children's growing beliefs and attitudes about others in the world and their own role in that world. They may be more likely to develop inaccurate and unrealistic ideas about other ethnic and racial groups, gender characteristics and roles, occupational choices, and the elderly, or to perpetuate stereotypes about those groups.

MEDIA PORTRAYALS

A survey conducted for the Screen Actors Guild (Gerbner, 1998) revealed that the representation of male, but not female, African Americans on TV increased each year until their representation was actually 171% of the proportion in real life. Asian/Pacific characters were represented less than one half as often as their actual proportion in the United States, and Latino/Hispanic individuals were represented in numbers less than one third of their actual proportion in the population. The poor were virtually invisible. There was a decrease in the number of persons with disabilities, and they were still not cast in "normal" roles. Seniors were underrepresented compared to their increased proportion of the general population. There were more younger women than older ones and thus more likely young women and older men relationships. Women become more "evil" as they age and more involved with villainy of some kind. Daytime drama includes a greater proportion of White characters and female characters than prime-time programs. Finally, most crimes and violent acts were committed by "foreigners" or the mentally ill, which perpetuates damaging stereotypes (Gerbner, 1998).

There are also racial, ethnic, and gender differences in the amount of television viewing engaged in, in the use made of television and other media, and in the perceived reality.

STEREOTYPES IN THE MEDIA

Stereotypy is said to occur when a group is portrayed in a way that implies that anyone in that group has similar characteristics and attitudes or life situations (Liebert & Sprafkin, 1988). In many ways, television both reflects—and affects—our world. Many argue that the proportion of individuals and families portrayed in various groups and lifestyles on television does not accurately represent reality, and what is presented is based too heavily on stereotyped views of behavior. Of concern is the possible cumulative effect on children of repeated exposure to such "information."

Because stereotypes of any kind are based on preconceptions, television content may confirm those ideas through biased presentations and information and thus influence ideas about and attitudes toward various groups. Underrepresentation of social groups or minorities, according to Signorielli (1987), "signifies restricted scope of action, stereotyped roles, diminished life chances, and underevaluation ranging from relative neglect to symbolic annihilation" (p. 256).

Gender Stereotypes

The importance of children's attitudes about gender-role behavior is not limited to such concrete behaviors as choice of clothes to wear or toy selection; the significance of such attitudes lies in the fact that they strongly influence what opportunities children see for themselves, how they think about the world, and what they remember of what they see.

In a content analysis across six media, Signorielli (as cited in Children Now, 1997) reported that girls watch over 20 hours of TV weekly, see 20,000 ads a year, watch music videos, read magazines and newspapers, listen to CDs and radio, and play video games, making the media a very influential force. She analyzed the gender messages that adolescent girls get across all of these media, and her findings and others suggest that conflicting messages are conveyed about women, both professionally and personally. Signorielli's findings included the following:

- In TV shows and even more in movies, men are more often shown at work and talk more about work, whereas women more often talk about dating and romance, and there was more emphasis on dating than on careers or school in teen magazines.
- There are more limiting messages for girls about their potential; women are portrayed more frequently in relationship contexts and men more often in the context of a career, suggesting that careers are more significant for men.
- Positive role models were also presented in TV shows and movies in which women and girls were depicted as honest and direct, and they actively used their intelligence and acted independently to solve problems and achieve goals.

- Movies, TV shows, and commercials emphasized and commented on women's appearance and its importance in their lives far more frequently than men's, and over half of commercials aimed at female viewers used beauty as an appeal of the product.

Overall, fewer women and girls than men and boys were represented in nearly all of the media, especially in movies and music videos. Teen magazines, however, used primarily female models (Children Now, 1997).

A slight majority of the children (Children Now, 1997) said there were enough good role models for girls on TV, but many said there were too few. Older girls were less likely to think there were enough. Both genders said that crying, weakness, and concern about appearance were more likely to be associated with female TV characters, whereas sports, wanting to be a leader, or wanting to have sex were more often thought to be associated with male characters. Such qualities as problem solving, intelligence, confidence, and doing well in school, however, were equally likely to be seen in male and female TV characters (Children Now, 1997). The study also found, however, that as they get older, both boys and girls become more critical of media depictions of females, and fewer think there are enough positive female role models on TV (Children Now, 1997).

Television's presentation of women in limited and outdated roles, despite daily evidence to the contrary and the effects of such presentations on a new generation of viewers, are important areas of investigation. Despite some progress toward more equal gender representation on TV, men still appear twice as often as women (Gerbner, 1998). The domination of White males continues with males depicted more frequently, shown in higher status occupations, and more prevalent among dramatically important characters (Comstock & Scharrer, 1999). The underrepresentation of women has changed little in 50 years, especially on children's programs (Signorielli, 2001). Prime-time commercials on Spanish-language television also involved gender stereotyping similar to that in the general U.S. market, and some seemed to have simply been translated from the general market into Spanish (Fullerton & Kendrick, 2000).

Despite continuing stereotypic portrayals of women on television, there has been some progress in presenting a more balanced view. Signorielli (as cited in Children Now, 1997), for example, reported that the media breaks some gender stereotypes and reinforces others. However, in a content analysis of prime-time shows for the 30 years between 1967 and 1998, Signorielli and Bacue (1999) found that women consistently get less recognition than men. Although there were more women in the 1990s than in earlier years, they were still not shown in the same proportion as they are found in the U.S. population. There was some change in the amount of respect they were accorded. More women worked outside the home, and there was a considerable increase in the percentage of women who were shown in more prestigious occupations, but women were still younger than men.

TV's characters were still likely to be driven by formulaic scripts that have appealed to audiences in the past. This tells just part of the story of prime-time television, according to Signorielli and Bacue (1999). Factors such as race and marital status would provide more information on the respect shown prime-time characters. Lauzen, Dozier, and Hicks (2001) found greater numbers of female characters and a higher frequency of powerful language (e.g., interruptions, directives, last words) when there were female producers and writers working behind the scenes. These are important messages in the socialization of children as they turn to TV to learn about the world. The media may actually shape children's views about what it means to be a man or a woman (Signorielli, 2001).

In another study (Children Now, 1999) nearly three fourths of children sampled between ages 10 and 17 depicted males on TV as violent, and two thirds saw them as angry. These perceptions were confirmed by an analysis of how men and masculinity were portrayed on the most popular programs. Over half of the most popular shows among adolescent boys included violence, and about three fourths of males in the TV shows and movies engaged in ridiculing, lying, or aggressive acts. Many children did not consider "sensitive" to be a descriptor for TV's males, and sports commentators consistently used war-like or martial arts terms to describe the action. In other words, viewers are consistently exposed to a narrow view of masculinity, one that uses anger and violence to resolve problems (Children Now, 1999). Cartoons and advertising directed at children perpetuate stereotypes as well. Boys tend to be shown as active and aggressive or violent and girls as domestic and more concerned with appearance (Sobieraj, 1996; Thompson & Zerbinos, 1997).

The world of sports reporting appears to perpetuate considerable gender stereotypy in other ways as well. Hardin, Lynn, Walsdorf, and Hardin (2002), noting the 1996 Olympic games billing as the "gender equity Olympics," studied post-1996 editorial photographs in *Sports Illustrated for Kids*. Hardin et al. analyzed all editorial photographs over a 3-year period and found that the gender gap had widened rather than narrowed, and the photographs perpetuated gender stereotypes and differences. A similar finding emerged from a content analysis of nearly 2,400 lines of broadcast commentary about the 2000 National Collegiate Athletic Association Men's and Women's Basketball championships (Billings, Halone, & Denham, 2002). Male athletes were categorically evaluated in terms of athleticism and physical attributes, whereas female athletes were evaluated more in terms of appearance, background, and personality. Further, regardless of the gender of the commentator, men's games received significantly more commentary than women's, and male commentators monopolized the broadcast time across all games, even when female commentators were present. Finally, Tuggle, Huffman, and Rosengard (2002) examined the National Broadcasting System (NBC) 2000 Olympic coverage of women's events. They received proportionately less coverage in 2000 than in 1996, and the focus was on individual events rather than on team sports. Moreover, women who were involved in power or physical contact sports got virtually no attention, as was true of the 1996 coverage, so no progress was apparent there.

Gow (1996) looked at the Music Television Video (MTV) "Top 100 of the 90's, So Far" and found very different depictions of the two genders in the popular music videos at that time. Women were still underrepresented and their physical appearance was emphasized rather than their musical talent. Women also appeared in fewer lead roles and in a narrow range of roles. There was less emphasis on physical characteristics for men who were dominant in these videos (Gow, 1996).

Gender and racial stereotyping are also prevalent in video games. Traditional gender roles and violence were central to many of the games included in a content analysis by Dietz (1998). About 40% had female characters, and they were often depicted as sex objects. Almost 80% of the games involved violence or aggression as the object or part of a strategy, 21% of which involved violence toward women.

In a Children Now (2001a) report, female characters were seriously underrepresented in video games and accounted for only 16% of all characters in video games. They were most likely to be depicted as props or bystanders (50%). Both males and females were usually presented in stereotyped roles, with the males more often engaged in physical aggression and the females shown more often as nurturing, screaming, or dressed in revealing clothes. Almost half of the most popular video games contained negative messages about girls (Children Now, 2000). A content analysis by Beasley and Standley (2002) of 47 Nintendo® and Sony PlayStation® games, selected randomly, also revealed significant sex bias in numbers of male and female characters and in the way they were dressed. Only about 14% of the nearly 600 characters they looked at were women, and most of the female characters were dressed in clothes that exposed more skin than for the male characters. The games contained very few features that were attractive to girls.

Occupational Stereotypes

Television too frequently also portrays a distorted and stereotypic picture of occupational choice for women and reinforces traditional roles. As recently as 20 years ago, Cheney (1983) reported that television provided only five occupations for half of the women on television, including model, nurse, maid, secretary, and entertainer. Although there have been many changes in occupational opportunities as depicted on television (e.g., women lawyers, policewomen, doctors), many of these are still limited and unrealistic (e.g., mostly young and beautiful lawyers, policewomen, and doctors) and still do not reflect society realistically. Although occupational depictions have shown some change, women working outside the home are more likely to be single or formerly married (Signorielli, 2001).

Although young children may perceive television to be more realistic, by the time they are in fifth and sixth grade, children do tend to see television occupations as more stereotyped than real-life ones (Van Evra, 1984; Wroblewski & Huston, 1987). Moreover, girls who showed interest in "feminine" television occupations also watched more programs with traditional gender roles (Wroblewski & Huston, 1987).

People know all too well how narrow views of women and minority groups and their capacities severely limited occupational avenues and opportunities for self-fulfillment in the past. If children paid little attention to these television portrayals, one could dismiss them as inaccurate annoyances, but children do attend to and respond to them. They do obtain significant occupational information from television (Wroblewski & Huston, 1987).

Racial and Ethnic Stereotypes

Stereotyping of racial and ethnic minorities is also apparent on TV and in video games. Minorities are still underrepresented on television and often misrepresented as violent or generally portrayed in less desirable ways, which perpetuates racism and stereotypes (Donnerstein et al., 1994). Several Children Now (2001a, 2001b, 2002d) reports noted that half to three fourths of prime-time characters were White, and people of color appeared mostly in secondary or guest roles. In the Children Now (2001a) report, fewer than a fourth of the characters were African Americans. There were no Latina characters, few Latinos, no Native American male characters, and only three female Native Americans. Heroes tended to be White, African Americans and Latinos were athletes, and Asian and Pacific islanders tended to be wrestlers or fighters (Children Now, 2001a). African American females were generally depicted as bystanders, props, or game participants but not competitors, and they were more likely than any other group to be victims of violence. Children's programming was more diverse but still needed improvement (Children Now, 2002d). Children Now (2001a) suggested that game developers need to consider whether strong role models are presented, whether the content is meaningful to different groups, and whether it creates or uses racial or gender stereotypes.

Most research suggests that the lesser representation of non-Whites sends a message that children of color are not important. Because characters of color are nearly invisible or in negative stereotypic roles when they are shown, children of color who are heavy viewers tend to have low self-concepts and feel alienated and uninterested in activities in the broader community (Palmer, Taylor Smith, & Strawser, 1993). The effect is especially strong for Asian, Latino, and Native American children who see people who look like them even less frequently and who get a strong message that the majority culture does not respect or value them (Huntemann & Morgan, 1993).

More important than specific counts of how many Blacks or members of various ethnic groups appear on television is the way in which they are portrayed, the context of their behavior (Greenberg, 1986), and how they use television. Whites are more likely to be portrayed as crime victims than are Latinos or African Americans who are more likely to be portrayed as perpetrators and lawbreakers, and Latinos are largely absent from TV news (Dixon & Linz, 2002).

In a content analysis of crime and courtroom dramas, Tamborini, Mastro, Chory-Assad, and Huang (2000) found that Blacks and Latinos were shown in similar depictions and similar roles and attributions associated with the roles. Three fourths of the portrayals were as representatives of the court with mostly positive attributions. The groups were shown as demonstrating equal competence, knowledge, and honesty across ethnic groups. One might expect, therefore, that such depictions would favorably affect interpersonal interactions, but because the number of images was low, especially for Latinos, they may affect stereotypes in a more subversive way. Rather than helping to develop positive perceptions, they may perpetuate the idea that they are inconsequential (Tamborini, Mastro, et al., 2000).

In one study of racial differences in girls' interpretation of magazine content, Duke (2000) found that a majority of readers of the three most popular teen magazines, including *Seventeen,* were White. A significant number of non-Whites were readers as well (44%), the largest proportion of which were African American girls. Of 14 million adolescent girls between 12 and 19, estimates are that over half read *Seventeen* magazine (Duke, 2000). Most African American girls were interested in the social and entertainment aspects and portrayals of real people but not in striving for the ideal physique as portrayed or in makeup and grooming advice that seemed inappropriate for them. They tended to evaluate people on personality and character more than appearance. The evaluative statements of the White girls, however, centered more on appearance, with personality more important for less attractive girls, and they seemed unaware of bias unless asked to think about it (Duke, 2000).

The importance of the peer group for interaction with media and consolidation of identity was demonstrated in a field observation of middle school girls from varied racial and class backgrounds (Durham, 1999). The study combined participant observation and in-depth interviews to try to understand their lives and peer contacts. White upper middle class girls were the main targets of advertising and paid more attention to mass media regarding body type and beauty and they were related to experiences such as eating disorders, low self-esteem, and depression.

There is also a need for more research regarding the impact of television's content on the perceptions of the majority world by minorities, as well as on minority perceptions of and attitudes toward other minorities (Greenberg, 1986).

EFFECTS OF STEREOTYPIC PORTRAYALS

What effect do these stereotyped portrayals and misleading representations have? As we have seen, children who lack experience and information in an area and who look to television for that information are particularly vulnerable to the influence of its portrayals. If those portrayals are biased or stereotyped, viewers who depend on them are more likely to develop stereotypic attitudes.

The research generally shows a link between TV viewing and holding more stereotyped ideas about gender roles, and these relations are apparent at all ages and stages of life from preschoolers to adults. The TV images tend to perpetuate the status quo and the notion of more limited societal roles for women (Signorielli, 2001).

Some would argue, however, that a positive correlation between viewing stereotypy and exhibiting stereotypic attitudes could as easily indicate influence in the other direction, that children who hold sexist views tend to watch more television, perhaps to confirm their views. In fact, their stereotypic views develop and are perpetuated in the context of many familial, educational, interpersonal, and media experiences. Those same experiences affect their attention to, perceptions of, and interpretations of TV content.

Gunter (1985) cautioned that descriptive content analyses of stereotyped television portrayals that do not also take into account audience perceptions of portrayals and social norms, however, may not be a reliable indicator of television's potential to cultivate gender-role stereotypes. Perceptions of stereotyped content, in terms of limited choices and alternatives, for example, may be strong determinants of behavior regardless of the objective reality of the content as indicated by content analysis counts (Gunter, 1985).

DEVELOPMENTAL AND GENDER DIFFERENCES

Children's awareness of stereotyping improves with age and is learned from exposure to television and from their own direct experiences. Durkin and Judge (2002) found that when shown the same family speaking English or non-English and portrayed as antisocial or prosocial, bias was evident for 6- and 8-year-olds but not for 10-year-olds. Although 5- and 6-year-old children in one study (Augoustinos & Rosewarne, 2002) did not distinguish between knowledge of stereotypes and their own beliefs, slightly older 8- and 9-year-old children were able to acknowledge negative statements as stereotypic even when they diverged from their own personal beliefs. Augoustinos and Rosewarne concluded that young children's inability to make that distinction does not constitute prejudice as usually thought of but is an inability to separate societal stereotypes from personal judgment, an evaluation that older children are able to make.

The cognitive processing of the stereotypic television information is affected by other aspects of a child's developmental level and experiences. A child's scripts, or shared expectations, about certain situations and outcomes are also important in relation to the TV content. To the extent that TV content involves areas in which a child has had actual experience, the content is interpreted in terms of that child's existent scripts (Durkin, 1985). Television, then, is likely to confirm rather than initiate sex-role beliefs that children are learning in a broader context. Moreover, although content is largely stereotyped, some of the material is not; in that case, more frequent viewing would also mean a greater likelihood of children seeing diverse viewpoints (Durkin, 1985). Normal developmental and nontelevision factors must also be taken into account, as children tend to demonstrate more gender-typed behavior at certain ages than at others in nontelevision activities as well (Van Evra, 1984).

FAMILY BACKGROUND

There has been surprisingly little research attention paid to the influence of a child's actual family models on the impact of television's stereotypic portrayals. There are no systematic or frequent reports of differences in the effects of stereotypic portrayals on children who come from traditional and conventional homes and those who come from homes in which the family members are engaged in less stereotypic activity. One might expect, intuitively, that children from less stereotypic homes would be less susceptible to or less affected by television portrayals of stereotyped roles, that they would view stereotypic portrayals with less credulity, and that they might engage in less stereotyped behavior themselves. One would also expect the influence of family members who are more significantly related to and involved with the child to be much stronger than that of contrived and experimental or media models.

COUNTERSTEREOTYPIC PORTRAYALS

During the early 1990s, the producers of Nickelodeon® made the decision to develop shows that starred girls even though the prevailing view then was that boys would not watch shows starring girls, although girls would watch shows starring boys. Their show, *Clarissa Explains It All*, disproved that idea as the audience for the show was half boys and more than half of the fan mail came from them (Children Now, 2002d).

Exposure to nontraditional or counterstereotypic gender portrayals can make a difference, and changes in attitudes toward racial minorities also can be affected by counterstereotypic presentations. Such portrayals more accurately reflect real-world diversity. Although they alone cannot eradicate stereotypes, of course, they can help to provide a more balanced and realistic picture of the world to developing hearts and minds.

SUMMARY

The various media continue to portray a world that differs in important ways from the real world. Many groups including racial minority groups, women, and the elderly are still underrepresented. When minority groups, women, and the elderly are represented, they are still more often cast in less powerful, competitive, significant, or attractive roles than Whites, males, and/or younger characters. Thus, the media tend to perpetuate gender, racial, occupational, and age stereotypes. Children and adolescents are vulnerable to the incorporation of some of these inaccurate representations into their developing beliefs and attitudes about others and their relationships with them.

There are also important differences among various groups in how much they use the media, their media preferences, and their reasons for media use. Interactions among variables such as the nature of the content, frequency of exposure, motivation for media use, real-life experiences, and developing self-concepts have been described. They show clearly how different the media experiences of various users can be and how variable the media impact on these diverse users might also be.

DISCUSSION QUESTIONS

1. Discuss some reasons why portrayals of less diversity in the media than in real life might affect children and young adolescents more than they would affect older children and adults.
2. List programs that appear to be portraying characters in a more realistic, lifelike manner. Are there still elements of stereotypy or misrepresentation of specific groups? How could these be made more diverse and realistic?
3. Discuss what cultivation theory would predict for heavy users of media given the current level of diversity and representation in the media.

Advertising and Behavior

CHAPTER SEVEN

Advertising and Behavior

ADVERTISING'S PRESENCE

Children's advertising is big business. Teenagers between 12 and 19 spent $172 billion in 2001, or about $104 per teen per week (Teen Research Unlimited, 2002 as cited in National Institute on Media and the Family, 2002b). In 2000, children 12 and younger influenced $600 billion in spending, either directly or indirectly, and children age 4 to 12 were expected to spend about $40 billion in 2002 (McNeal, 2001, 2002, as cited in National Institute on Media and the Family, 2002b).

Television commercials have become much shorter, and more than 6,200 ads per week were aired on the three major networks—an average of 26 per hour or an average of 12 minutes per hour of commercial messages, 20% of all programming (Comstock & Scharrer, 1999). Nearly a decade ago, Centerwall (1995) estimated that an advertising decrease of just 1% would cost the television industry $250 million annually in lost revenue.

Advertising during children's programming has a federally legislated weekend ceiling of 10 to 12 minutes an hour (Comstock & Scharrer, 1999). The format for these ads includes fast pace, animation, humor, and music. According to Comstock and Scharrer, the average child between 2 and 11 will see as many commercials—60,000—as adult viewers, at least 12,500 of which have some relevance for him or her such as snacks, toys, soft drinks, or clothes. Teens watch less and would see about 27,000 commercials, but a larger number of them— 16,000—would be relevant to them (Comstock & Scharrer, 1999). Canadian children will see 200,000 TV ads between their 2nd and 12th birthdays, and 80% of food commercials on Saturday morning children's shows are for foods with low nutritional value, most of which are for high-sugar foods like cereal or candy (Media Awareness Network, 2003b).

There are different patterns of advertising across children's programming on three types of channels: broadcast networks, cable networks, and independent stations. Broadcast networks, for example, had the most advertising; cable had significantly less. Independent stations showed the most toy ads, but cable networks advertised the widest range of products (Kunkel, 1992).

According to Comstock and Scharrer (1999), three aspects of advertising are important: recognition and comprehension, specific techniques or devices (e.g., separators, disclaimers, language), and premiums. Although young children can recognize commercials and match characters with products, even Joe Camel (Fischer, Schwartz, Richards, & Goldstein, 1991), they do not understand the selling or persuasive intent of commercials, and separators and disclaimers do not help. Children do not bring the same experience or cognitive skills to their exposure to advertising, and advertising does effectively direct children's product choices. Moreover, advertising affects parent–child interactions, as advertisers also try to win the consumer dollar by appealing to children who then put pressure on parents to buy the advertised products.

In Kunkel's (1992) study, toys and breakfast foods made up over half of all ads observed, and adding sugared snacks and drinks boosted it to 74%. Healthy foods, on the other hand, were represented in only 2.8% of all advertising directed to children. Heavy viewers wanted more of the toys and ate more of the food that they saw advertised than those who watched less TV (Strasburger & Wilson, 2002). They also are exposed to hundreds more ads because of the high number of viewing hours.

It is not just television advertising that reaches children either. There are children's magazines, promotional toys, cartoon characters, logos on clothes, and promotional giveaways such as MacDonald's® Happy Meals®. From elementary to high school, students are targeted for direct advertising on free book covers, so-called educational posters in hallways, brand name foods on lunch menus and in cafeterias, reward coupons from various eateries, sides of school buses, and teaching materials that incorporate specific brands or products ("Classrooms for Sale," 1999*; "Junk-Food Marketing," 2000*; "Reading,"1998*). Advertising aimed at students and parents also appears on school Web sites (*Christian Science Monitor*, 2001*), and corporate logos adorn gyms, libraries, athletic fields, and other venues in recognition of their donations ("School Board Considers," 2000*) in addition to all of the advertising children and adolescents see as they surf the Internet. Recently, *Roxy Girl*® clothing, a favorite with girls between 8 and 12, has linked its label with preteen reading. A series of books written to be "good reading" was created in the company's headquarters as a way to promote its brand. Titled *LunaBoy, the Roxy Girl Series* ("Roxy Girl," 2003), it was the first time a fictional series grew from a clothing company.

Because children either spend or influence spending of $500 billion, they are now targeted for direct advertising rather than through their parents, and even "adult" products such as toothpaste and cars are now often paired with kid-oriented images and logos (National Institute on Media and the Family, 2002b).

---

*Cited in National Institute on Media and the Family (2002c).

Moreover, with the avoidance of advertising now possible with VCRs, commercials more and more frequently are developed to merge with nonadvertising, to be so entertaining and appealing on their own that they will be "zapproof" (Miller, 1987). However, because viewers can still zap many commercials, advertisers have begun to rely more on product placement, the placement of their products in movies and television shows, sometimes without viewers even being very aware of them. In one rather extreme example, MacGregor (2003) pointed out that the science fiction thriller *Minority Report* included strategic placement of a Lexus® car, Nokia® cellphones, Reebok® footwear, The Gap®, Burger King®, American Express®, and Oakley® sunglasses. *My Big Fat Greek Wedding* gave a nod to Windex® and *Die Another Day* sported Finlandia® vodka and Omega® watches (MacGregor, 2003).

Advertising can affect the beliefs, attitudes, and buying behavior of children and adolescents. It also can influence family relationships, self-esteem, eating habits, and behavioral decision making and choices such as whether to drink or smoke.

The means by which advertising has an impact on children and their families in both direct and indirect ways is an issue that has generated a considerable amount of research involving a wide range of variables in both cognitive and affective areas of functioning. Many studies have focused on the ability of children of various ages to distinguish television programs from commercials, their ability to understand the persuasive purpose or intent of advertising, and their ability to evaluate commercials objectively and critically. Researchers have tried to ascertain such emotional and attitudinal responses to advertising as trust, liking, believability, and desires for advertised products. Researchers have sought to determine the actual impact of advertising on parent–child relationships and on the buying behavior of both sets of viewers, although some feel that only a small number of the thousands of ads children see actually lead to requests to their parents (Fowles, 1992).

NATURE OF ADVERTISING'S APPEAL

Product Information Versus Images

The primary goal of advertising is not necessarily direct persuasion but to put awareness of a product in the viewer's conscious mind and to have him or her associate it with something good or desirable (Cheney, 1983). The aim is to create an image or impression rather than to provide information, to persuade through emotional rather than rational argument, and to associate a product with positive attitudes or things (Carpenter, 1986). Advertising has become an art form (Rutherford, 1994).

Advertisers want to shape their message to viewer needs and experiences. Commercial messages are meant to resonate with a viewer's feelings, and they trigger emotions that are then labeled for the viewer or associated with a product name (Nelson, 1987). At times viewers can be hard pressed to see any logical connections between some of the components of a commercial because of the abundance of associations and images.

The effectiveness of advertising lies in its reliance on recognition memory rather than recall. Recognition of a brand that one has seen advertised can affect a person's decision when faced with a buying choice. Recognition is easier than recall for everyone but especially so for young children, and holistic material, either visual or auditory, is more easily recognized and remembered. Hence the success of logos, jingles, slogans, and other advertising devices. Logical, critical components may have far less impact than those that make a more emotional appeal through the use of images and impressions. In one study (Macklin, 1988), for example, background music succeeded in creating a positive outlook toward a brand being advertised and affected recall of its characteristics. Rather than objectively considering a product's merit, viewers respond in less rational, more emotional ways. They may suspend rational analysis temporarily as a direct result of advertising's appeal to strong but vaguely and poorly defined needs to succeed or to belong. Viewers may respond emotionally in spite of a need to be rational because of the powerful persuasive impact of the advertisement. There is a strong emphasis on an emotional subtext and a decided underemphasis on analytic content (Rajecki et al., 1994).

In viewers of any age, then, television programming and advertising can manipulate or override analytic and logical processing of the information. This persuasive effort is often facilitated or accomplished through the use of half-truths and fallacious logic, such as reports of so-called scientific research or extensive surveys, which are used in association with highly salient images. Such a combination may make people think that they are responding rationally when in fact they are responding emotionally on the basis of the images.

Rather than conveying information about product characteristics, then, advertising offers information on lifestyles and about viewers, and ways are presented to solve discontent about one's appearance or status (Rutherford, 1988). The fact that there are increasing numbers of such ads as compared with more informational ones may mean that children and adolescents who rely on and respond more to such techniques will be even more vulnerable to advertising messages.

Television advertising helps people to support their buying decisions by providing them with some apparent logical basis for their behavior, even though on closer examination the logic does not stand up. With increasing age, people may become more aware of the weak or nonexistent logical base of an advertisement and reject the message, but the emotional side or appeal of the advertisement may still override that logical decision and lead to yielding behavior. There is frequently a lack of relation between knowledge about advertising itself and its actual impact on behavior. This seems to have occurred in Grade 7 girls in one study (Van Evra, 1984) who freely expressed negative attitudes toward advertising and verbalized their awareness of being exploited or manipulated and at the same time acknowledged that they were still very much influenced by it in their buying behavior. The impact of television advertising depends on many complex processes, and negative attitudes toward advertising do not necessarily predict behavioral effects.

Advertising can affect viewers in other ways as well. Comstock and Paik (1991) suggested, for example, that advertising can adversely affect self-esteem in three ways: (a) by portraying achievements that viewers are not capable of, (b) by portraying others as better off in some way than the viewer, and (c) by portraying individuals who are like the viewer in socially inferior roles. Conversely, the obverse occurs when portrayals show achievements that viewers are competent at, or persons like the viewer are shown as better off, or viewer roles are portrayed as superior, all of which lead to enhanced self-esteem. As Comstock and Paik pointed out, however, these would be more common for males than females given the content of most advertisements.

Celebrity Endorsement

Children's response to television commercials is also affected by the person delivering the commercial message. The mere appearance of a character with a product can significantly affect a child's evaluation of that product depending on how the child views the character. In one study (Ross et al., 1984), for example, children who watched ads in which a celebrity endorsed the product believed that the celebrity was an expert about the product (toy), and they showed an increased preference for it. The younger boys in the sample, 8- to 10-year-olds, were more reliant on the endorser's advice than the older ones, and they seemed more vulnerable to the perceptual tricks used in the ad. There was no significant difference between them in affective response or in preference, however, and there was no evidence of greater resistance on the part of the older boys. "The combination of a famous presenter with perceptually exciting and dramatic material from his 'real' world would be a powerful message for children who are prone to believe adults, aspire to emulate heroes, and are literal-minded in their interpretation of sensory information" (Ross et al., 1984, p. 187).

Celebrities whom children associate to some degree with activities represented by a toy were seen as more credible or reliable experts than those who had no such association. Moreover, "synthetic" celebrities (e.g., someone dressed as a football player but not really one) may well have the same influence, especially if live action is included (Ross et al., 1984). The practice of using live action to fill time that might have been used to view the actual product instead, however, serves no legitimate informational purpose and tends to mislead children about the product (Ross et al., 1984).

Program-Length Commercials

Some programs are populated by licensed characters that began as toys and later had programs developed around them in what are sometimes referred to as program-length commercials (Engelhardt, 1987; Kunkel, 1988). The main goal of such shows is to sell toys through the heroes of the show. Many have argued that this takes unfair advantage of children, as the practice makes separation of program and advertising less clear and harder to discern (Kunkel, 1988).

MEDIATING VARIABLES

Developmental Variables

Because the forms used in advertising vary greatly among shows, children's viewing patterns as well as age, gender, and socioeconomic differences and varying needs among viewers might well be expected to result in differing levels of impact of television advertising.

Age as an index of developmental differences is an important component in determining how able children are to deal with commercial information. Studies (Brucks, Armstrong, & Goldberg, 1988; Young, 1990) indicated clearly that children's comprehension of television advertising and its persuasive intent as well as their recall of advertising content increases with age. Young children do not have the critical viewing skills that older children and adults can use, and they are unable to understand subtle cues and messages, making them significantly more vulnerable to advertising techniques. Young (1990) noted that it takes certain skills to understand that advertising is advocative and the intent is persuasion, skills that emerge along with others in middle childhood and through early adolescence. One of these skills, for example, is knowing that a literal interpretation is not the only one or learning to "read between the lines." Young children are less able to discriminate between reality and fantasy and tend to believe more of what they see.

As they get older, children are better able to understand verbal or linguistic stimuli and become less reliant on, perhaps less attentive to, perceptually salient stimuli than they were when they were younger. At the same time, however, if they watch mainly shows directed at younger children, they are exposed to quite different types of commercials than their peers who watch more age-appropriate programming, and they may be attracted to them as well. Although little attention appears to have been paid to the relation between children's viewing patterns and their favorite programs on one hand and the attitudes of those children toward advertising on the other, it seems to be an area worthy of attention.

Thus, levels of cognitive development or maturity interact with the process of attending, and this interaction affects the reception, processing, and memory of commercial content. Cognitive ability is clearly an important component in children's level of understanding of advertising and in their subsequent responses to it. When interpreting age differences in comprehension, however, one must be careful not to confuse children's inability to express or explain something clearly with their actual level of comprehension (Levin, Petros, & Petrella, 1982).

Formal Features

Most of the special effects in children's commercials that have been reported, such as fast-cutting visual techniques and music, appear to be largely holistic and designed to create moods, images, and impressions rather than to convey accurate information about a product and its uses and benefits. Advertisers know that such features as music, repetition, jingles, slogans, visual effects, and animation command greater attention in viewers of all ages but are especially attractive to young viewers who rely most heavily on such perceptually salient cues to derive meaning or to gain information from the television input.

As young children are more likely to watch programs that include cartoons, animation, animals, and other rapid-paced and highly salient material, and as advertisers also rely frequently on similar techniques, young children may have considerable difficulty distinguishing programs from commercials. Even when they are able to discern differences between programs and ads, young children still show very limited knowledge of the commercials and their purpose. Now, with elaborate and sophisticated computer technology and editing techniques such as "morphing," there can be endless mutations of toys into live-action characters, movie scenes, and back to toys again. This confuses young children even further, and some ads even fool most adults (Saunders, 1996).

Advertising's "Information"

Unlike other advertising media in which there is more augmentation in print, TV ads are frequently multidimensional in appeal:

> Television commercials are visual anecdotes enhanced by voice and music. They have become remarkably brief. Argumentation has been largely abandoned in favor of an emotionally satisfying exposure to the product or brand name. Music not only often advances the theme but also has become a cue aiding the viewer in the recall of what is to be presented. This anticipatory aspect is a key element in television advertising not ordinarily present in advertising in other media, and increases the likelihood that viewers will recognize the product or brand name. Commercials are not perused; they are experienced in real time with scant opportunity for reflection or examination. (Comstock & Scharrer, 1999, p. 23)

According to Comstock and Scharrer (1999), television advertising invites "peripheral processing" in which viewers react quickly and emotionally to the message, either favorably or unfavorably, without a lot of rational thought or consideration of alternatives and counterarguments as one would use in "central processing." Even those who are predisposed to try to process such appeals centrally usually process them in a peripheral way.

A further difference in advertising from other forms of more "balanced" presentations in education and other media areas is due to advertising's presentation of only the positive aspects with virtually no attention to the negative (Young, 1990). In addition, the interests of the advertiser are not the same as those of the one receiving the message, the child. Some studies have shown increased cynical and negative attitudes toward advertising with more experience, but not all children become cynical and advertisers can reestablish credibility by creating new types of ads (Young, 1990).

Most television commercials involve a relative lack of solid or objective product information such as material, price, or performance and much more reliance on appearance, image, or fun. A theme of fun/happiness was involved in just over one fourth of the ads in Kunkel's (1992) study and appeared predominantly in commercials for fast foods. Taste/flavor/smell and product performance each accounted for an additional 18%. Those three themes, then, accounted for nearly two thirds of all advertising. Least frequently used as a principal strategy to advertise products were quality of materials, safety, and peer status.

Both live action and animation, used frequently in advertising directed at children, are highly visual, largely holistic techniques, which often are used to convey an image of fun or action rather than to provide information about the actual characteristics or virtues of a product. Studies have documented the importance of nonverbal elements in advertising that may have an influence either in the information they provide, in the way information is processed, or in the way affect is used or induced (Edell, 1988).

Premiums are also an important determinant of children's response to advertising (Comstock & Paik, 1991; Kunkel, 1992). Kunkel (1992) reported that premiums appeared in 10% of ads, whereas contests were reported in only 3%. Children recalled premium offers more than the attributes of a product, and they were more important to younger children in choosing a product (Comstock & Paik, 1991). The younger children also recalled attributes less well than older viewers (Comstock & Paik, 1991). Not only would an attractive image or impression of a toy be expected to influence buying behavior more strongly, but products that are less attractively presented command less attention and hence would be remembered less well.

About half of the commercials that Kunkel (1992) looked at included at least one disclaimer, and almost 10% had two or more (e.g., "parts sold separately," "some assembly required," "get your parents' permission"). Half were conveyed by auditory messages only, and about one third were conveyed visually only despite research showing that children's understanding is greatest when both visual and auditory information is presented.

The form of presentation for such disclaimers as "batteries not included" or "parts sold separately" or "some assembly required" determine how salient such messages are for a viewer. Qualifiers and disclaimers would rarely, if ever, be presented in a highly salient manner as, for instance, with a catchy jingle. Because they tend to be the "small print" of the commercials, they command far less attention. In fact, they may go largely unnoticed, something the advertiser may hope for, as an unassembled product or one without batteries would be far less attractive to potential buyers.

Gender Differences

Gender differences in responses to advertising may be related to the degree of gender-role stereotyping of a child, the interaction of that stereotyping with the particular advertisement, the willingness to admit persuasibility, the cognitive levels of processing of commercial information, and the different information-processing styles of males and females. Gender differences do emerge in older children regarding the reported impact of the commercials on buying behavior, however negatively the commercials are viewed by both genders (Van Evra, 1984).

One recent study demonstrated gender differences in adolescents' processing and analysis of advertising messages. When 578 9th and 12th graders were exposed to eight alcohol-related messages, boys were more persuaded by individualistic messages and girls more by the collective public service announcements (Andsager, Austin, & Pinkleton, 2002). In another study (Slater et al., 1997), female teens responded less favorably to beer ads and sports content in ads but positive responses that were given were associated with present and planned alcohol use among both genders. As Slater et al. pointed out, however, this was not a random sample. Participants were self-selecting and for one season's viewing only, although the study did include a broad cross section of behavioral and academic types and a wide range of programs and ads. Slater et al. suggested that if ads were targeted at females, they might be as receptive and vulnerable to their influence as males.

Even the formal features (e.g., pace, sound effects) of television can be selected and used to enhance stereotypic content, and they may come to have connotative meaning as when masculine and feminine content is presented with different forms. An example of this synthesis of form and content occurs when an ad for tissues or deodorant, aimed at women, is presented with soft lights, hazy and muted colors, and a filmy, slow-paced voice-over as opposed to an action packed, loud beer commercial directed at men.

Gender differences in the commercials themselves also should be investigated further to determine whether advertisers actually take into account age and gender differences in the processing of commercial information. Do advertisers, for example, use more highly perceptually salient and image-oriented advertising for some target groups and more logical, authoritative content for others? Do these variations make a difference? Answers to such questions would shed light not only on advertising's effectiveness with different groups but also on differences in the cognitive processing of television advertising by children of both genders and at different ages.

Viewer Needs

Advertising effectiveness also depends to some extent on why viewers are watching television. If they have a need for a specific product, such as when they are feeling miserable with a cold, they likely will be more receptive to messages about cold remedies than they would be when they are feeling fine. Even if they are feeling well when they view a particular ad repeatedly, they are more likely to remember it later when they do have a need for that type of product (Van Evra, 1995).

Simply viewing a few commercials, then, is not likely to have a pervasive effect in real life in the face of other experiences and a long history of other messages, but frequent repetitions over a long period of time may have a significant impact in various areas.

STEREOTYPES IN ADVERTISING

Advertising still tends to perpetuate gender and racial stereotypes. Women, for example, are still presented more frequently as silly, helpless, dependent, passive, weak, lacking in competence, or competent mainly in trivial roles. Exceptions are some of the larger-than-life female heroines.

To be fair, commercials do exist that portray competent women or women as successful business types. Despite some improvements, however, these are still rather few and far between, and the demographics in advertising do not reflect accurately women's actual presence in the real work world. Moreover, women are much more likely to be shown to be puzzled by consumer choices to be made, to seek advice, often from a man, and to speak in irritating and whiny voices. As recently as the late 1980s, men's voices were heard in over 85% of television commercials (Ambrose, 1991). The heavy imbalance in the number of male versus female voice-overs and males in authority or expert roles continues despite an absence of data to demonstrate their greater effectiveness in such roles (Canadian Advertising Foundation, 1987).

Racial stereotypes also appear in advertising. Li-Vollmer (2002) found that Asians, Latinos, and Native Americans were significantly underrepresented, whereas the proportion of Whites and African Americans was higher than in real life. Moreover, the types of roles they were cast in revealed more racial bias. Whites were the only ones shown in high-status roles, and compared with minority groups, Whites were significantly more likely to be depicted as spokespersons and problem solvers.

Cotrane and Messineo (2000) also found that characters in ads were more prominent and more authoritative if they were White or male. Cotrane and Messineo's study coded the content for the presence or absence of passive–emotional or active–instrumental interaction styles. The passive–emotional styles included such characteristics as being a follower, deferential and submissive, dependent and insecure and indecisive, passive, and emotional. The active–instrumental style included characteristics such as being a leader, being directive, dominant, and authoritative, and having respect, status, independence, and autonomy.

Women and Whites were disproportionately depicted in family settings and in cross-sex interactions. White women were generally seen as sex objects and men as powerful. African American men were depicted as aggressive and African American women as unimportant or inconsequential. Cotrane and Messineo (2000) concluded that these differences contribute to the maintenance of subtle prejudice against African Americans by exaggerating the differences and denying positive emotions.

CRITICAL VIEWING OF ADVERTISING

Even young children can be taught to discriminate between factual information about a product and persuasive advertising techniques. Peterson and Lewis (1988), for example, studied children ages 6 to 10 in an after-school day-care center who learned to discriminate information and advertising techniques after being shown ads that were relevant to the day's learning module. Learning modules included information (factual content of the commercials) or advertising tricks or persuasive techniques. A control group did not show the same learning.

However, although children as young as 9 and 10 can be led to be more critical of advertising, they may not spontaneously retrieve their knowledge while viewing TV. Children that age need more than a critical or skeptical attitude toward advertising; they need more knowledge about how advertising works and cues to use that knowledge (Brucks, Armstrong, & Goldberg, 1988). Simple cues will work; schools could teach about advertising, and parents could provide cues regarding watching advertisements carefully (Brucks et al., 1988). Parents can also help their children become more aware of "weasel words" in advertising that are used to trick or deceive them (Media Awareness Network, 2003g). These are words that mean less than they seem to such as *studies have shown,* or *new ... fantastic ... super,* or *nutritious.*

"ADVERTISING" CAMPAIGNS IN OTHER AREAS

Although much of the research on advertising's effects has been done in relation to buying behavior, advertising also can affect other behaviors than product purchase patterns. Some do not consider this to be advertising, but rather promotion or public action campaigning. Nonetheless, many of the techniques that serve advertisers well can convey other messages effectively as well.

Advertising has been used to discourage smoking, drinking and driving, shoplifting, use of drugs, and other behaviors and to promote sound nutritional practices. The number of such ads in television and print media is strong testimony to the perceived effectiveness of such advertising. The actual impact on behavior of this use of advertising, however, is inconsistent. Changing knowledge about a topic is far easier than changing behavior in that area. Information about quitting smoking is a case in point. Most smokers know about the dangers of smoking; actually quitting is much more difficult.

For actual behavior change to occur, viewers must see the relevance of the messages, and alternative behaviors must be modeled. Roser (1990) found, for example, that attention to messages could affect recall but did not affect attitudes or behavior directly because they were influenced by viewer perceptions of relevance. It seems unlikely, then, that children's behavior would change unless they saw the messages being delivered as providing significant and relevant information (Van Evra, 1995). As with other aspects of media use, complex interactions exist that operate to influence behavior, and consumer behavior is no exception.

SUMMARY

Advertising's influence on children's behavior is not as straightforward as one might expect or as advertisers might hope. As children grow older, they develop an increasing awareness of how advertising works, but it still influences their buying behavior. Young children are more vulnerable to the perceptual salience of most commercials and do not have the cognitive capacity to evaluate them critically. They have more difficulty than older children distinguishing commercials from programs, and they do not view commercials as selectively as older children do. Moreover, advertisers' use of premiums, contests, animation, and other appealing tactics make actual product attributes more difficult for children to discern or evaluate.

Most ads rely on holistic stimuli to command attention and create moods and images rather than providing solid information about a product, and many stereotypes are still apparent in advertising content. Advertising also can affect children's interactions with their parents and their self-esteem. However, children can be taught to view advertising more critically and thereby reduce their vulnerability to its persuasive tactics.

Advertising's techniques have been used to modify other behaviors such as smoking, shoplifting, impaired driving, and nutritional habits. The effectiveness of these programs is not clear because actual behavior change is determined by a very complex interactive network of variables. Conveying information is easier than effecting actual behavior change, but these advertising campaigns undoubtedly make a positive contribution.

DISCUSSION QUESTIONS

1. Discuss the important role that developmental level plays in children's comprehension of and vulnerability to advertising.
2. Design an educational program about advertising for children and adolescents. What are the most important points that you would like to get across to them?
3. Discuss your own reactions to advertising and how ads may affect your own decision making and product choices. How and why might the effect be even stronger for children and young adolescents?

Television and the Family

Television and the Family

The context in which children view television and use other media and their inter-action with family members or lack thereof also moderates media impact in im-portant ways. Media use can become a social activity with other family members. It can also become a more isolating experience in which children and adolescents view TV, play video games, or surf the Internet alone in their rooms. Kaliebe and Sondheimer (2002) pointed out that with a dominant media culture, the family barrier between children and society will become more porous, and preserving customs and group identities will become increasingly difficult.

TELEVISION AND OTHER FAMILY ACTIVITIES

Media use has often been criticized for undermining important aspects of family life by displacing other important family activities such as talking and interacting together, children playing with their siblings, and others. Some (e.g., Winn, 1985) have argued that although television has kept family members from dispersing, it dominates their time together and can destroy the qualities that distinguish one family from another such as unique activities, games, and rituals. Winn felt that despite the fact that families still do special things together, television diminishes their ordinary daily life together because it is a regular, scheduled, and rather mechanized daily activity. Children certainly tend to model their parents' viewing patterns. Higher estimates by children of how much their parents watch was asso-ciated with higher reports of their own viewing (Henning & Vorderer, 2001).

Robinson (1990) maintained that television has taken time away from "function-ally equivalent" (p. 108) activities such as reading fiction and movie attendance as well as from nonmedia activities such as gardening or sleeping and most important, has been associated with decreased social interaction outside the family. "Family life has evolved into watching sitcom families. Public life is something that happens on the other side of the glass. The talk show has replaced the neighbors we no longer see because we are at home watching talk shows" (Feldman, 1994, p. 29).

According to Robinson (1990), television viewing is associated with a less active lifestyle, and there is little support for the idea that viewing television together increases family cohesion or discourse. According to Kubey (1990), family television viewing is less challenging and less activating than family time in other activities, and heavy viewers in his study felt significantly less activated when they were participating in non-TV family activities. Kubey (1999) suggested that clearly some family members would benefit from engaging in more direct interaction and in more creative and active pursuits. It is especially problematic when some family members, such as children, have to compete with television for parental attention (Kubey, 1990).

Others claim that television has become an important way to bring family members together in an era when demands on them differ significantly from those of pretelevision times. Even though viewing levels drop off in adolescence, television viewing is still a common activity and offers the opportunity for shared experiences with other family members. Rather than be associated with poor family relations, TV viewing may indicate a preference for spending time with family and may even increase a family's togetherness (D. Brown & Bryant, 1990; Kubey & Csikszentmihalyi, 1990).

Now that so many families have two parents working outside of the home, both parents are often tired and more families prefer to stay home for entertainment than to go out (Lull, 1988a). Watching television or renting videos or DVDs rather than going to a movie can be a very comfortable and economical entertainment experience for a family. Moreover, television is often a background to other family activities.

TELEVISION MODELS OF FAMILIES

The way in which members of a family perceive what families should be like and what is appropriate and desirable behavior may be influenced by television's portrayals of families (D. Brown & Bryant, 1990). D. Brown and Bryant noted that children who watch many families on television tend to believe that those families are supportive and show concern for each other. If they watch those shows with their parents and discuss the content with them, they are more likely to have positive views about families (D. Brown & Bryant, 1990). They are also likely to see greater variety in the makeup of families including single-parent families, blended families, and same-sex relationships.

Domestic comedies, unlike other dramas, generally show a traditional family model with families managing their relations and conflict quite effectively (Douglas, 1996). Parents are generally portrayed as providing appropriate models for the children in the family, and implicit rules are as prevalent as explicit attempts to influence activity. There are generally positive and cohesive family relationships, although children in families are shown more negatively and in less satisfying relationships. Relationships between and among siblings were evaluated as less effective than ones involving adults, and there was more conflict and less support among sib-lings. According to Douglas, the results are consistent with real family life. "These results are significant, in part, because domestic comedy often is seen as real and is especially likely to influence family cognition" (Douglas, 1996, p. 696).

In addition, however, Douglas and Olson (1996) found that children's experi-ence on television seems to have deteriorated over time. The general environ-ment of modern families was rated as more conflictful and less cohesive, and parents were less able to socialize their children or manage daily life effectively. Siblings were seen to be more hostile, less cohesive, and less effectively socialized. Douglas and Owen suggested that television families appear to behave in ways viewers understand and can relate to, but more study is needed of how much viewers integrate family life on television into their own lives.

Elkind (1993) suggested that the media contribute to a perception that postmodern adolescents are sophisticated rather than immature, and they may in fact be more so than previous views of immaturity allowed. According to Elkind, this perception changes the views of parents, schools, and other institutions re-garding their roles, but this "liberation of parents" has not seen the development of new agencies to provide guidance and protection needed by children and ado-lescents. It has instead led to an abrogation of social responsibility toward them to set standards, provide models, and establish necessary limits (Elkind, 1993).

COVIEWING WITH PARENTS

Benefits of Coviewing

The viewing context, especially whether children watch alone or with friends, sib-lings, or parents, greatly affects TV's impact. Direct parental communication and discussion help to shape children's perceptions of families in the real world, which then are used to assess the realism of the television world (Austin, Roberts, & Nass, 1990). Parent coviewing also can provide children with a role model for ap-propriate television viewing behavior (Anderson & Collins, 1988). Coviewing with adults can enhance children's understanding of television content if the par-ents offer comments about it during and after viewing a program, and they can re-inforce content children learn during educational programs (Wright et al., 1990).

One of the significant aspects of the viewing context lies in its role as a source of alternate information. If parents watch television with their children, they can provide other views to supplement, alter, modify, or refute information that their children are receiving from TV. Adult intervention and discussion about television can enhance its impact because such comments and discussion make the viewing experience an informational session in which parents can offer alternative and per-haps competing information. They may, of course, still provide alternate infor-mation even if they are not coviewing; but it comes to the children in other contexts, then, and perhaps has less direct association or immediate relevance for the child. Moreover, if the information does not come in other contexts, television serves as the major source of that knowledge.

Messaris (1986) reported that parents were very involved in their children's learning from television and said that children rely on their parents or other household adults to construct a picture of the world from television in three ways. First, the child needs to learn to distinguish one program type from another (e.g., fantasy vs. documentaries) and to distinguish the difference between television content and reality. Cognitive developmental level and parent intervention both play a part in this learning.

Second, when parents judge the accuracy of a program's portrayal and engage in frequent discussion with their children, they play an important role in their children's use of television to explore the real world and to evaluate the accuracy of its portrayals of both negative and positive situations and events. According to Messaris (1986), conversations with mothers help to decrease the unrealistic expectations in overly positive or exciting portrayals. In addition, parents were protective regarding negative information or events, although they usually confirmed the accuracy of the information. Parents also used those conversations to try to strengthen their own families, such as by playing down differences that are threatening or playing up ones that were to their advantage.

The third way that parents and sometimes siblings interact is to supplement the information that the child receives from television by providing "background" information when the child is confronted with unfamiliar material. Messaris (1986) found this to be a very common television experience mentioned by 80% of the mothers he interviewed. Information was either such that all of the children would acquire it as they grew up or it was "specialized" information such as scientific information or information about specific ethnic or occupational groups.

Not all families are as actively involved as this in their children's viewing, however, or as selective in their own viewing, and they are modeling TV viewing behavior just as they model other behaviors. If they watch hours and hours of television, have few other interests or activities, and tend to see TV personalities and content as realistic, their children are much more likely to do the same. The children, however, are still developing attitudes and beliefs about the world, and they need more help distinguishing what is real from what is fantasy and learning about TV's potential impact.

As Anderson and Collins (1988) pointed out, the effects of coviewing may not be directly related to the time spent together with the television. It likely has more to do with actual comments and explanatory behavior of the mother, such as making a comment as she enters or leaves the room (Anderson & Collins, 1988), or with the degree of control exerted by parents. Moreover, worry about the effect of a single program ignores the usual viewing situation in which several programs are viewed over a single viewing session, providing a variety of messages that dilute any single portrayal (Gunter, McAleer, & Clifford, 1991).

Parental mediation during viewing can sometimes have an adverse effect on children's experience as well (Desmond, Singer, & Singer, 1990). For example, if calling attention to the screen is a characteristic mediation activity, but a parent does so during a violent scene with a "look at that" comment, the child's attention is heightened, and the parent may be conveying tacit approval of the content. At the very least, the parent in that situation is heightening the salience of that scene, which the child may then be viewing out of context, and the meaning and significance of the action may or may not be understood by the child.

Levels of Coviewing and Monitoring

Despite frequent reports on the importance of parental coviewing, monitoring, and limiting of children's television and video game use, however, recent research consistently shows that relatively few parents are as highly involved as the ones Messaris (1986) reported on or actually mediate or monitor their children's viewing. In the Kaiser Family Foundation study cited earlier (Rideout et al., 1999), over 60% of children over 8 said there were no rules for viewing. According to diaries by parents, 95% of children over 7 viewed TV without their parents, and 80% of the time parents were doing something else while their 2- to 7-year-old children were watching TV. Moreover, nearly half (44%) of children and adolescents watched something different, most often MTV, when they were by themselves than when they were with their parents (Children Now, 1995).

The fact that parents are often unwilling or unable to limit their children's viewing may be due to the failure of "expert" warnings to really resonate with parents, too little time or energy of parents to monitor their children, or the pervasive and overwhelming influence of the media (Kaliebe & Sondheimer, 2002). The number of children with TVs, video games, and other media in their bedrooms makes monitoring even more difficult.

Age and developmental level of the child are especially important in this context. In one study of over three hundred 3- to 5-year-olds (St. Peters, Fitch, Huston, Wright, & Eakins, 1991), the majority of children's programs were watched without parents, and coviewing declined with age. Children of parents who encouraged television viewing watched more child informative programs. In another study (Dorr, Kovaric, & Doubleday, 1989), coviewing occurred least often with younger children who need parental mediation the most, and the coviewing appeared to be motivated by similar interests or preferences rather than to mediate children's viewing experience.

The relatively low incidence of adult mediation is rather troubling given the strong research evidence that confirms its importance. Lawrence and Wozniak (1989) urged more research on the verbal interactions among family members while watching television and on which interactions enhance learning. The best situation occurs when parents watch with their children, talk about programs with them, and help their children relate the TV content to their own lives (Lawrence & Wozniak, 1989).

Parental Mediation and Commentary

Simply coviewing with an adult is not enough, however. Comments from parents affect what the child learns and retains from TV viewing. Parents can help their children to comprehend what they see by directly mediating the child's TV experience. They can help them learn to distinguish fiction from news and documentaries or from real life and to understand and resist advertising's messages. They can compare their own values and beliefs with those being depicted on television. They can counter stereotypic information, and they can elaborate on topics raised on television but not explained. "Children who dwell in such a positive atmosphere of family communication are less fearful of being harmed, less aggressive, and more willing to wait patiently than are children from families who simply comment on televisions' [sic] array of people and events" (Desmond et al., 1990, p. 304).

Nathanson (1999) delineated three types of parental mediation: active (talking with children about TV), restrictive (rules about viewing), and coviewing (simply viewing with the child). This study included mediation in the home and reported by parents. According to Nathanson (1999), most studies have been experimental and have focused on the first type, but it is not clear how this affects influence outside the home. We need to know more about how the various types affect children's response.

Nathanson (1999) found that parental mediation and restriction were negatively related to children's TV-induced aggressive tendencies regardless of whether they were heavy viewers or not, which further underscores the importance of such mediation. Simply coviewing was positively associated with those TV-induced tendencies, although not with general aggression. Nathanson (1999) also noted that the results for restrictive mediation were curvilinear, suggesting that high restriction could conceivably backfire. Active mediation, then, using reasoning and talking with the child about TV may be the best, which is consistent with child development research findings on the greater effectiveness of talking and reasoning with children as a general method of discipline. Nathanson (1999) found no mediation related to the instrumental use of violence on TV, that is, to learn.

Finally, Nathanson (2001) noted the importance of peers versus parents in the mediation process. Nathanson (2001) found peer mediation to be more frequent than parent mediation in adolescence. Peer mediation promoted more positive orientation toward antisocial behavior on TV, which can lead to more aggressive behavior and may reflect shared interests. Peer discussion of antisocial TV was related to aggression of adolescents, although there were gender differences. Parents' mediation, then, can inhibit negative effects, whereas peer mediation tends to enhance or facilitate negative outcomes. One of the limitations of the study, however, was that it was based on retrospective reports of college students recollecting their behavior and attitudes in high school (Nathanson, 2001).

COVIEWING WITH SIBLINGS

Although coviewing with parents has been found to be an important mediating variable in children's television experience, coviewing with siblings is the most common viewing context (Lawrence & Wozniak, 1989; Wright et al., 1990). Wright et al. (1990) found that only children viewed a lot of child-informative programs, whereas when children viewed with siblings, the pattern of viewing depended on the age of the siblings. Children with older siblings stopped watching child-informative programs fairly young and watched more entertainment programs and comedies, more often without adults present. Children with younger siblings viewed child-informative programs for longer and usually with an adult present. In one study (Pinon, Huston, & Wright, 1989), for example, the presence of younger siblings increased viewing of *Sesame Street*, and the presence of older ones decreased it.

In other research, Wilson and Weiss (1993) gave two versions of a scene to preschoolers. One was a normal scene, and one was a dream that included a prologue and epilogue to convey that it was a dream. Coviewing produced both positive and negative results. Those preschoolers who were coviewing with an older sibling showed less ability to recognize the special effects and the dream; they also were less aroused emotionally and liked the program more than those viewing alone. Those watching alone, on the other hand, were more likely to recall the dream in later story reconstruction. Wilson and Weiss suggested that coviewing did not appear to improve comprehension perhaps because older siblings did not interact much or help the younger ones regarding the dream. The young children also attended less when coviewing than when viewing alone, perhaps because they were distracted by the presence and conversation of their older siblings, making it harder for them to process the story. Coviewing did lead to less fear, perhaps because the distraction may have reduced negative emotions (Wilson & Weiss, 1993) or perhaps because they felt safer than if they had been viewing alone.

In a study by Hoffner and Haefner (1997), children from Grades 1 to 6 described how they had comforted someone who had been frightened and how they would comfort a hypothetical friend of varying age and gender. They also gave a self-report on an empathy measure. The results indicated that empathy and comforting were positively associated, and comforting increased with grade level but only in the hypothetical situation. About half of the girls and a third of the boys reported that they had tried to comfort a coviewer who was frightened. Moreover, even young ones adjusted their strategies to the intensity of the other's response. Emotions were important in the real situation, and less frightened children offered higher level messages to their frightened coviewers (Hoffner & Haefner, 1997).

FAMILIES AND PERCEIVED REALITY

Other research has demonstrated the impact of family communication on children's perception of the reality of television content. Dorr, Kovaric, and

Doubleday (1990) studied 460 Grade 2, 6, and 10 children to explore the relation between children's viewing of television families and their perception of typical real-life families. Children between 6 and 16 felt that roughly half of all American families are like television families, especially in the realm of emotions. The way in which television families resolve emotional problems was perceived to be the most realistic of all of the content tested. Therefore, how a program deals with common problems of "growing up" would likely have a strong effect on the viewing audience: Healthy portrayals could positively affect family dynamics, and unrealistic portrayals might cause some difficulty (Dorr et al., 1990).

In their field study of 627 third, sixth, and ninth graders and 486 of their parents, Austin et al. (1990) found that communication within families helped to develop real-world perceptions of families that were then used to assess the realism of the television world. According to Austin (1990) et al., there are "several contexts in which children evaluate a television family's reality: against *other* families (perceived realism), against their *own* families (perceived similarity), and as a possible object for aspiration (identification) ... [and] Perceived realism predicts perceived similarity, which in turn predicts identification" (p. 547).

Once children settle on TV and real-life perceptions, they can compare them and develop constructs about reality that are based on all of their experience, both in real life and with the media (Austin et al., 1990).

Berry (1998), for example, pointed out that African Americans are a heterogeneous group and TV messages compete with those of their families. According to Berry, African Americans watch more television than their White counterparts. Therefore, they spend more hours looking at and learning from both positive and negative images of Black life, and social learning theory would predict that they learn from the TV models. To minimize the complexity of studying families, in particular portrayals of African American families, we need to find the crucial factors that lead a child to identify with or reject portrayals of Black family life (Berry, 1998).

Children's perceptions of the similarity between the real world and that of TV are influenced by their parents' perceptions of that similarity and by conversations the children have with their parents about television. When there was a mismatch between the two in one study (Austin et al., 1990), there was a decrease in perceived realism. The family proved to be a reliable information source about the world, including media, and was a help in developing strategies to analyze the media world. TV was a secondary information source, with actual experience and communication with others a more dominant socialization force. Moreover, active communication, especially about TV content, increased parents' effect on their children's TV interpretation (Austin et al., 1990).

IMPACT OF VCRS AND DVDS

With the rapid increase in the number of VCRs and DVDs, questions about their impact on family viewing patterns and family interactions is important as well. Using longitudinal and cross-sectional data from adolescents, Morgan, Alexander, Shanahan, and Harris (1990) found that VCRs primarily augment and extend a family's pattern of viewing, and VCRs can be a symptom or a cause of family conflicts. According to Morgan et al., adolescents see VCRs as an essential part of television, so their use of a VCR was usually predicted by the pattern of their use of television. Familial conflicts about television were a good predictor of conflicts with the VCR, especially among siblings. There was a strong relation between the frequency of adolescents' use of VCRs and the frequency of arguments with parents and siblings and not just over the VCR. Morgan et al. concluded that a VCR can play multiple roles in a household, and it can be used to avoid conflict in the family or it can be a source of arguments.

More research findings on VCR use, DVDs, and other technologies and their impact on children and adolescents are discussed in chapters 11 through13.

SUMMARY

The context for television viewing is a very significant component in children's television experience. Those children who receive parental comment, input, and supplementary information and interaction have a very different experience of television viewing than those who view alone or with less involved parents. Despite the frequent repetition of the need for parental involvement in and monitoring of their children's media experience, surprisingly few parents appear to be very involved.

It appears from the research that if parents simply coview in ritualistic viewing, they model TV viewing as an activity and accord it more importance, especially as they are likely to engage in heavier viewing. If, on the other hand, the coviewing involves active mediation in the form of talking about and discussing the content on one hand, and restricting amounts of viewing and what is viewed on the other, TV's negative impact can be significantly reduced, and its positive contribution to the child or adolescent's development can be facilitated.

Such differences in the viewing context play an important role in determining the strength and nature of television's impact. Families differ in their attitudes toward and use of the media, particularly television, which in turn influences their children's understanding and attitudes, perceived reality, conflicts over television and VCR use, and, ultimately, the impact of television on children and adolescents. Coviewing with siblings, the most common context, and with peers also affect children's exposure to and response to different kinds of television content.

DISCUSSION QUESTIONS

1. Discuss differences in the viewing situation for young children of viewing alone, viewing with a brother or sister or a peer, or viewing with parents. When and with whom would the child be most vulnerable to media influence?
2. Discuss the relative strength and influence of various models in a child's or adolescent's environment, including TV models, siblings, peers, and parents.
3. Discuss specific ways in which parents could counter undesirable TV messages with their own views and beliefs.

CHAPTER NINE

Health-Related Issues

Health-Related Issues

The nature and extent of media impact on the healthy and unhealthy lifestyle choices of children and adolescents depends on many factors besides their media use. Media can play a big role, however, especially in the areas of sexual behavior; use and abuse of drugs, alcohol, and tobacco; nutrition; and body image. Current research trends in these areas are discussed in this chapter.

USE OF MASS MEDIA

Use of the mass media for health education can have positive and negative effects. The media can promote reduced smoking and alcohol use, healthier eating, safe sexual practices, good medical routines, and other healthy practices. They also can raise anxiety about health issues such as AIDS or, more recently, SARS and West Nile virus. Messages tend to focus on individual responsibility for healthy or unhealthy practices and stress medical cures over prevention, and there is a tendency to try to make complex problems simpler (Brown & Walsh-Childers, 1994). According to Brown and Walsh-Childers, messages embedded in entertainment content such as movies, "edutainment," may work better than public service announcements (PSAs) because their format (music and drama) is more likely to get and hold audience attention, they are more likely to reach appropriate audiences, and they allow for development of more complex and persuasive messages. They can also have unintended negative effects, however, such as portraying models engaged in unhealthy behaviors like smoking that viewers may then imitate.

Brown and Walsh-Childers (1994) cautioned, however, about assuming causal direction in any relations between use of TV, music, or other entertainment media and health behaviors. Factors such as peer group, commitment to school, or mainstream values may be factors in a correlation between media use and unhealthy behavior. Brown and Walsh-Childers noted the suggestion from Canadian and Swedish studies, for example, that those who are not doing well in school turn to nonmainstream groups as a different source of self-esteem. As not all adolescents see the same things in music videos or other TV content, the link between entertainment media and healthy or unhealthy behavior may be more complex than some suggest, and there is a need to go beyond content analysis to see how media use actually affects individual decisions and public policy development (Brown & Walsh-Childers, 1994).

SEXUAL BEHAVIOR

Television and Movies

According to Steele (2002), adolescents look to movies and TV for information about how the world is and how they should act as adults. They see the movies as a good source of information about life and the dilemmas they will likely face as adults. Steele calls movies *agenda setters* for teens that tell them what issues are important and how to think about them.

There is no doubt that sexual messages on TV and in movies have increased over the last 20 years, both in talk about sex and in the number and explicitness of the portrayals. Kunkel, Cope, and Colvin (1996) found that only a fourth of 1996 shows included no sexual content, and an average hour included about 8½ interactions that could be considered talk or behavior involving sex. Sexual messages in 1996 were 118% more frequent than in 1986 and 270% more frequent than in 1976. Most of the talk about sex was intended to be humorous, and 84% involved flirting and kissing. Implied or explicit intercourse was involved in 3% of all of the behavior related to sex (Kunkel et al., 1996).

More recent data from studies by Kunkel et al. (2001, 2003) done for the Kaiser Family Foundation revealed that nearly two thirds of TV shows in the 1999/2000 season included sexual content. Kunkel et al. (2001) found that movies, sitcoms, and soap operas had the most sexual content (80%–89%), whereas reality shows had the least (27%). The biggest increase in sexual content was in situation comedies, which went from 56% to 84% of all episodes. There also were increasing numbers of teen characters involved in sexual intercourse, and 16% of all scenes involving intercourse were between characters who had just met (Kunkel et al., 2001). New data revealed that the percentage of programs that had sexual content decreased from 2 years earlier, but the number of scenes with sexual content increased (Kunkel et al., 2003).

The range of sexual behavior is also broader and a far cry from the separate beds shown in 1950s sitcoms and movies (Brown, 2003). Brown (2003) noted that content that was once considered too risqué or even pornographic is now "de rigueur" on late-night TV and even on some prime-time television. Talk about sex is much more common than portrayals of sexual behavior, but portrayals of sexual behavior, including sexual intercourse, have increased significantly (Kunkel et al., 2003). Approximately 14% of shows in the Kunkel et al. (2003) study depicted or strongly implied sexual intercourse, up from 10% 2 years earlier (Kunkel et al., 2001).

In a content analysis of 12 prime-time television shows most preferred by children and adolescents, Ward (1995) looked at all interactions for three episodes of each show and coded all relevant statements. Discussions about sexuality were very common. An average of almost one third of interactions and over one half for some episodes included verbal reference to sexual issues. There were more messages about the male role than female role and more messages emphasizing a recreational orientation over a procreational one. Cope-Farrar and Kunkel (2002) reported an even higher amount of sexual content. Of the top 15 shows watched by teens, talk about sex and sexual behavior was common. There was sexual talk and/or some kind of sexual behavior in 82% of the programs that were coded.

Sex and the City, a program that was awarded for its honest portrayal of sexuality, is watched regularly by 93,000 teenage girls, ages 12 to 17, who are attracted to the main characters' glamour and power (Hepola, 2003). Although some parents forbid their adolescent daughters to watch the show, others watch with them and then discuss the content openly (Hepola, 2003).

Messages across TV genres such as soaps, music videos, and prime-time shows appear to be quite consistent. Many popular shows include talk about sex and sexual behavior, generally without negative consequences, risks, or responsibility (Brown & Keller, 2000; Cope-Farrar & Kunkel, 2002; Huston, Wartella, & Donnerstein, 1998; Kunkel et al., 1996; Sutton, Brown, Wilson, & Klein, 2002). Although 8 out of 10 of the shows in the Cope-Farrar and Kunkel (2002) study involved sexual talk and/or behavior, clear positive or negative consequences were rarely shown. When consequences were shown, they were most often positive. Seven percent of the programs in their study, 1 in 15, depicted or implied sexual intercourse, again with few suggestions or depictions of risks or responsibility (Cope-Farrar & Kunkel, 2002). Kunkel et al. (2001) noted that although only 10% of all shows with sexual content included messages about safe sex and the risks and responsibility involved in sexual behavior, programs that involved teenagers in sexual behavior included more of those messages. Nevertheless, popular culture depicts sexual behavior in terms of "the 'invisible' three Cs: No commitment, no contraception, no consequences" (Sutton et al., 2002, p. 27).

Such discrepancies between TV versions and real-life experiences make healthy decision making difficult (Brown & Keller, 2000). This is especially important because many researchers have found that most adolescents rely heavily on the media, including TV and magazines, for information about sexual behavior and contraception (Brown & Keller, 2000; Elber, 2002; Kaiser Family Foundation, 2002b; Sutton et al., 2002) along with information from peers and parents.

The situation may be improving somewhat, however. In the Kunkel et al. (2003) study on sexual content in the media for the 2001/2002 season, the percentage of shows that depicted or implied sexual intercourse had risen, especially for the top 20 shows for adolescent viewers in which 1 in 5 programs included in the study either implied or showed intercourse. Eighty-three percent of the sample of programs viewed most frequently by teens had some sexual content, 80% included talk about sex, and half showed some sexual behavior, far more than for the rest of television (Kunkel et al., 2003). There also had been a corresponding increase in the amount of content about risks and responsibilities of sexual behavior in programs depicting advanced sexual situations.

Given the findings that adolescents rely heavily on TV for information about sex, findings of a more realistic and balanced depiction are welcome. The presence or absence of negative consequences in portrayals of sexual behavior or smoking or any other risky behavior is important, especially when rewards are portrayed for such behaviors. Social learning and social cognitive theory would predict that seeing a behavior rewarded and/or not punished would increase the likelihood of it being imitated.

Music Videos

Music videos introduce young viewers to the most undesirable elements of the "grown-up" world, including abuse of women, sexism, racism, and bigotry (Hattemer & Showers, 1995a); casual sex, violence (especially against women), weapons, and drug use; and negative messages about marriage, family, and work. In one study, three fourths of the music videos that told a story involved sexual images, and half involved violence, usually against women (Committee on Public Education, 2001). Music videos are discussed at greater length in chapter 13.

Magazines

According to Walsh-Childers, Gotthoffer, and Lepre (2002), magazines have significantly increased the space used for nonhealth-related sex topics and decreased space for focus on sexual health. There is more balance in teen magazines, although they have increased the amount on nonhealth-related sex topics even more than women's magazines have, but sexual health issues are mentioned fairly often in nonhealth-related topics (Walsh-Childers et al., 2002). *Seventeen* magazine had a circulation of over 2.4 million in 1997 and a "pass-along" readership of 8 million or 53% of the magazine market for teens (Walsh-Childers et al., 2002). Walsh-Childers et al. noted that *Seventeen* is very commercial and reinforces norms of heterosexuality and being attractive to the opposite sex, whereas "zines" offer alternative experiences.

Internet

Some, mostly boys, got sexual information from the Internet, and although a less common information source, that could change (Sutton et al., 2002). A small proportion of adolescent girls create their own home pages on the Web where sexual discussions are carried out and writing—including journals, poetry, essays, and biographical information—is shared along with pictures, music, and favorite links on the Web (Stern, 2002). Sexuality plays a major role, and they say things they could have said or have said before but now to a much larger audience (Stern, 2002).

Effects of Sexual Content in the Media

According to Sutton et al. (2002), age and gender differences predicted media choices for obtaining sexual information, but racial and socioeconomic differences did not. Girls tended to get more information about contraception from magazines than boys did, and magazines ranked higher for girls than parents for such information. Children in Grades 5 to 8 more often used multiple media for sex education; therefore, school programs at that early age are important to counter media messages (Sutton et al., 2002).

The research literature, however, does not sufficiently address the effects of exposure to so much media sexual content on the knowledge, beliefs, behaviors, or intentions of the children and adolescents who view it (Gruber & Grube, 2000; Huston et al., 1998). A few experimental studies have demonstrated potential for changing viewer knowledge and attitudes, and correlational studies revealed some evidence, although weak, that viewing is related to sexual beliefs and behavior, but the viewing measures were unsatisfactory (Huston et al., 1998). Huston et al. (1998) also noted that other factors such as interest, level of comprehension, perceived reality, and parental mediation affect the impact of those messages. Cognitive style, personality characteristics, and family communication styles further mediate the types of media sought by individuals and media impact (Malamuth & Impett, 2001). Those watching large numbers of these shows and/or looking to these shows for information rather than entertainment would appear to be more at risk for influence given the theoretical overview discussed in chapter 1. Moreover, social learning and social cognitive theory would predict that modeling of these behaviors would be more likely to occur if viewers were similar to or admired the individuals being portrayed.

One Kaiser Family Foundation (2002b) survey reported that nearly three fourths of teens think that sex portrayals on TV affect others their age and their behavior "somewhat" or "a lot," but fewer than one fourth think it affects their own behavior in another instance of a third-person effect. Many said that they learned useful things from TV about sexual decision making, such as how to talk with someone about safe sex or how to say no in uncomfortable situations, but few could cite actual TV role models for their decision making. TV also stimulated talk with their parents about sexual issues they had seen on TV, and they clearly were paying attention to what they saw.

After reporting on gender and ethnic differences in viewing choices and developmental differences in ability to understand and interpret sexual content, Gruber and Grube (2000) concluded that simple exposure does not lead to the denial of other information that viewers have from school, families, religion, or other adults. This again confirms the importance of having a broad range of sources of information as well as the importance of parental input. Simple exposure does not lead to simple imitation. Level of comprehension, purpose for viewing, perceived realism, reinforcement value, parental involvement, and other factors determine the effect of such portrayals on children and adolescents.

Several groups, including the Henry J. Kaiser Family Foundation, the National Campaign to Prevent Teen Pregnancy, and Advocates for Youth have been working with movie and TV script writers, music producers, and magazine editors to try to encourage more responsible and balanced content (Brown & Keller, 2000). In addition, various Web sites have been developed to try to convey more comprehensive and accurate sexual information (Brown & Keller, 2000).

Messages about sexual health in entertainment programming can have a positive effect on viewers. The Media Project, a nonprofit advisory group that partners Advocates for Youth and the Henry J. Kaiser Family Foundation, has helped to change and shape television's handling of sexual topics, especially those involving adolescents (Elber, 2002). The Project Director, Robin Smalley, noted Hollywood's role as "sex-education counselor" for many children and noted that although writers say their job is to entertain, in fact they also educate. Their impact has been documented, for example, in the tripling of viewers with knowledge about AIDS after an *ER* episode that focused on it (Elber, 2002). Smalley said the best they could do was to help writers develop programs that encourage or inspire parents to talk with their children, and 70% of parents with children under 18 in one Kaiser Family Foundation study said they had talked with their children about a sexual issue because of a television show (Elber, 2002).

DRUG AND ALCOHOL USE

Prevalence and Nature of Messages

The alcohol industry spends about $2 billion a year on all media advertising (Strasburger & Donnerstein, 1999). Although hard liquor advertising was banned on radio in 1936 and on television in 1948, the ban was broken in 1996, and most of the increased advertising was on cable channels (National Institute on Media and the Family, 2002a). In the winter of 2002, however, NBC said it would accept hard liquor ads for programs airing after 9 p.m. A poll conducted by the Center for Science in the Public Interest (2001, as cited in National Institute on Media and the Family, 2002a) revealed that nearly 70% of respondents opposed this policy change and agreed that it posed a danger to young people who would be exposed to alcohol. NBC acquiesced to this public pressure and canceled its plans in March 2002 (National Institute on Media and the Family, 2002a).

Less direct advertising of alcohol continues unabated, however. The Federal Trade Commission (1999, as cited in National Institute on Media and the Family, 2002a) reported, for example, that alcohol was included in 233 movies, including some PG and PG–13 movies, and 181 television series in 1997 to 1998 as well as over 100 Internet sites, many of which reach and appeal to children and teens.

Results from one study (Goldstein, Sobel, & Newman, 1999) revealed that more than two thirds of G rated animated children's films released between 1937 and 1997 (and all of the films between 1996 and 1997) included tobacco or alcohol use in their plots with no clear messages about negative long-term effects associated with this use. Over half of the films that were reviewed included one or more incidents of tobacco use; half portrayed alcohol use, and good characters used both as often as bad characters. Roberts, Henriksen, and Christenson (1999, as cited in Strasburger, 2001) also found that tobacco, alcohol, and drugs were very common in movies preferred by children and adolescents, but they were much less common in popular music.

In a content analyses of 276 programs, Mathios, Avery, Bisogni, and Shanahan (1998) studied the incidence of alcohol use in prime-time television and the personality characteristics of the individuals using it. Mathios et al. found that alcoholic drinks were the most frequent food or beverage portrayed, and that applied to all characters, including adolescents. When adolescents were involved in alcohol incidents, they were more likely to be depicted drinking than were adults, but they were also portrayed as having more negative personality characteristics. Adults who used alcohol were more often shown as having positive personality qualities such as being smart and/or powerful (Mathios et al., 1998).

Effects of Messages

What effect, if any, do these portrayals have on child and adolescent viewers? Studies have shown that television advertising does influence attitudes about drinking, and young people report more positive feelings about drinking and about how likely they are to drink after viewing such ads (Austin & Meili, 1994; Grube & Wallack, 1994). Over half of students from Grades 5 to 12 in one report said that alcohol advertising did encourage them to drink (American Academy of Pediatrics, 2001a).

In one study (Gentile, Walsh, Bloomgren, Atti, & Norman, 2001, as cited in National Institute on Media and the Family, 2002a), beer ads significantly predicted adolescents' knowledge of beer brands, preferences, and brand loyalty as well as drinking behavior. In another study (Grube & Wallack, 1994), awareness of beer advertising was associated with more positive beliefs about alcohol use, greater knowledge of brands and slogans, and increased planning to drink as an adult. This led Grube and Wallack to conclude that alcohol advertising may indeed predispose children toward drinking. Grube and Wallack's data were collected with structured interviews in the home and self-administered questionnaires, however, so bias, selective recall, or other factors may have affected the results. In addition, these were correlational, not experimental findings, so causality cannot be established. Individuals, for example, who already had greater knowledge and positive

ideas about alcohol use and planned to drink as adults may have been more attentive to and aware of the advertising.

Gruber and Grube (2000) concluded from their literature review that simple
exposure to advertising for alcohol does not affect its use but rather the effects depend on how much individuals exposed to the ads like them and attend to them.
Gruber and Grube also reported, however, that statistical modeling revealed that
attention to such advertising increases drinking by adolescents, but the reverse is
not true. Drinking does not affect their attention to the advertising.

Parental involvement and mediation are again seen as important in moderat-
ing the potential influence of portrayals of alcohol use in the media including
prime-time TV, sports events, music videos, and talk shows. The effects of such exposure were largely indirect and positive through intervening beliefs and expectations, although parental input can counter the appeal and perceived realism of
such messages (Austin, Pinkleton, & Fujioka, 1999). One study (Borzekowski,
1996) of 900 eighth and ninth graders did demonstrate, however, that antialcohol
messages embedded within popular shows could have an influence, as the participants were more receptive to those messages and showed high levels of interest,
knowledge, and credibility.

TOBACCO USE

Prevalence and Nature of Media Messages

Although cigarette advertising was banned from TV and radio in 1969, ads in the
print media, sponsorship of musical and sporting events, logos on clothing, and
other advertising venues went up (National Institute on Media and the Family,
2002d). In addition, smoking on TV is widespread despite bans on television advertising of tobacco and is associated with young people starting to smoke
(Gidwani, Sobol, DeJong, Perrin, & Gortmaker, 2002). Although it is illegal to sell
tobacco to children under 18, more than 974 million packs of cigarettes and 26
million containers of spit tobacco were sold illegally to children under 18, and tobacco companies took in $1.26 billion in sales and $221 million in profit each year
from those illegal sales (Carnegie Report on Adolescents, 1995, as cited in National Institute on Media and the Family, 2002d).

The National Institute on Media and the Family (2002d) described the direct
advertising aimed to enhance teens' self-esteem by appealing to their desire to be
accepted and "cool," and their desire for rebellion. The Surgeon General's conclu-
sion was the same:

> Cigarette advertising uses images rather than information to portray the attractive-
> ness and function of smoking. Human models and cartoon characters in cigarette
> advertising convey independence, healthfulness, adventure-seeking, and youthful
> activities—themes correlated with psychosocial factors that appeal to young peo-
> ple. (Annas, 1996, p. 7)

Impact of Messages

The preponderance of evidence indicates that advertising tends to encourage young people to smoke, even though the definitive causal chain has not yet been established. In a survey (Schooler, Feighery, & Flora, 1996) to explore the relation between exposure to cigarette advertising and smoking behavior, 88% of 571 seventh graders reported such exposure, largely in magazine advertising, billboards, and at events or stores. A fourth of them owned promotional products. The likelihood of trying smoking was more than two times higher among those with the promotional products and nearly three times greater for those who had received promotional mailings. Seeing ads in magazines increased this by 21%, and seeing tobacco promoted in stores increased it by nearly 40% (Schooler et al., 1996).

Even preschoolers recognize brands in advertising. In a frequently cited study (Fischer et al., 1991), children as young as 3 to 6 showed high levels of logo recognition including not only a Disney channel logo, which one might expect, but also Old Joe, the cartoon character used to promote Camel® cigarettes. The rate of recognition increased with age. Over 90% of 6-year-olds correctly matched Old Joe's picture with a picture of a cigarette, and even a third of 3-year-olds could do so. Fischer et al. concluded that their study confirms that even very young children see, understand, and remember ads to which they have been exposed.

Antismoking efforts and advertising have grown rapidly over the last few years in response to these findings, but do they make a difference? One study (cited in Children Now, 2002a) revealed that television advertisements could have a significant impact on teens' decisions to start smoking. In a survey, nearly 2 years after the 1998 start of Florida's antitobacco media campaign, those 12- to 20-year-olds who were exposed to ads describing the tobacco industry's strategies to popularize smoking and who could describe the ads were less likely to start smoking. That effect increased as the number of ads viewed rose (Children Now, 2002a). Those teens who could describe one of the ads in detail were 27% less likely to be smoking at follow-up, and the near 40% who could describe four or more ads were almost 70% more likely to remain nonsmokers. Those who could not describe any of the ads accurately were more likely to say that the ads had no influence on their smoking (Children Now, 2002a).

Programs have also been established in schools to try to prevent children from smoking. In one study (Flynn, Worden, Secker-Walker, Badger, Geller, & Costanza, 1992), one group of students received a school program plus media interventions to enhance the school smoking prevention programs. Another group received only the school programs. All 5,458 students were surveyed in Grades 4, 5, and 6 and followed up annually for 4 years. Those students in the media plus school group reported significant reductions in smoking, and there were consistent effects on mediating variables that were targeted. Cigarettes per week decreased 41%, "smoking yesterday" decreased by a third, and "smoking in the past week" decreased by 35%, but there were no changes in the use of substances that were not targeted by the intervention. Flynn et al. concluded that such mass media interventions can prevent smoking when they are targeted at high-risk groups and share objectives with school programs.

BODY IMAGE AND EATING DISORDERS

Television stars and other media characters as well as women appearing in advertisements are most often portrayed as attractive and very thin, so thin that they are sometimes referred to as anorexic. At the same time, children and adolescents reportedly spend fewer hours being active and more hours using media. They are bombarded with ads for junk food and fattening snacks, but obesity is far less common among TV characters than in the general population (Bar-on, 2000). Study of the effect of these contradictory messages and portrayals on children and adolescents' developing body image, self-esteem, physical health, and susceptibility to eating disorders is an important area of research.

Body Image

Based on social cognitive theory, Hofschire and Greenberg (2002) predicted that adolescent viewers would learn from models who were reinforced for their behavior. Hofschire and Greenberg found a significant relation between media exposure and idealization of certain characteristics, body dissatisfaction, and dieting and exercise. There was a significant association between the amount of television viewed and a preference for thinner bodies and smaller body measurements. Boys were more influenced by music videos: The more they watched, the more preference they showed for thin bodies, maybe because music videos have a less athletic focus (Hofschire & Greenberg, 2002). A desire to look like celebrities and to identify with them was associated with body dissatisfaction. Boys were less influenced, but those boys who did identify with celebrities expressed more body dissatisfaction and exercised more. Watching more and identifying with characters was associated with dissatisfaction, acceptance of stereotyped body ideals, and more involvement with diet and exercise, correlations that were stronger for girls. Girls were more likely to diet to improve their bodies, whereas boys were more likely to exercise to build more muscular bodies (Hofschire & Greenberg, 2002).

Tiggemann, Gardiner, and Slater (2000) coded discussions among adolescents for themes and found that the media exerted the strongest pressure to be thin, although peers and the fashion industry also exerted pressure. Tiggemann et al. also found that the teenage girls they studied were quite sophisticated in their realization of media effects and body image in developing their own self-image. Compared with assumptions in some of the quantitative research, these girls said they would like to be thinner, but this did not necessarily mean they were dissatisfied with their own bodies. Their "meta-awareness" and understanding of media pressures may help them resist such forces. They clearly understood that media images were manipulated and unrealistic. They said they would feel more confident if they were thinner, but they also knew that losing weight does not usually make women happier. Clothes in this study were a big issue, however. Even if they could resist media pressure and feel good about their bodies, they were challenged by clothes that did not fit or that looked very different than they did on the models (Tiggemann et al., 2000).

The peer group also needs to be taken into account in any interventions or in media literacy programs, as it is seen as "a training ground where girls learned to use the mass media to acquire the skills of ideal femininity, but it was also a place where rejection of these norms could sometimes be voiced" (Durham, 1999, p. 212).

Obesity

Television has long been associated by many with inactivity, overeating, weight gain, and passivity. Current data suggest that obesity has increased at an alarming rate and with it the incidence of Type II diabetes in children. Other health risks have grown as well. Obesity also predisposes children and adolescents to such medical problems as hypertension, sleep apnea, and liver disorders (McCool, 2003). The incidence of obesity in children quadrupled between 1982 and 1994, from 4% to 16% (Squires, 1998, as cited in National Institute on Media and the Family, 2002n).

Dennison, Barbara, Erb, Tara, and Jenkins (2002) studied the amount of time children spent viewing TV or video and whether they had a TV set in their bedroom. They looked for the prevalence of a body mass index (BMI) above the 85th percentile after controlling for possible confounding variables. Dennison et al. found that viewing times were higher for Black and Hispanic children than for White children, and viewing times increased with age. The nearly 40% of children who had a TV set in their rooms were more likely to be overweight and to spend about 4½ hours more per week watching television and video than children without a set in their rooms. Because most children are watching TV by age 2, efforts to limit their viewing and to keep TVs and videos out of their bedrooms need to start before then (Dennison et al., 2002).

Other studies have reported lower hipbone density in preschool girls who watched more television (Janz et al., 2001) and significantly lower than resting metabolic rates for 8- to 12-year-olds (Klesges, Shelton, & Klesges, 1993). The incidence of obesity was highest in those children who watched TV for 4 or more hours a day and lowest in those who watched 1 hour or less (Crespo et al., 2001, as cited in National Institute on Media and the Family, 2002n).

The direct involvement of television and video games in the obesity problem was demonstrated further in an experimental study of two sets of third and fourth graders (Robinson, 1999). One group was taught how to decrease the time they spent playing games or watching TV to a 7-hour limit per week, freeing up 14 hours for other activities. Another group did not receive such instruction and continued their usual TV and game patterns. The results show that the first group demonstrated significantly reduced obesity measures such as body mass as well as significant decreases in television viewing. The second group had higher obesity measures. The only difference between the two was the amount of time spent watching television or playing video games. The groups did not differ on amount of intake of high-fat food, moderate to vigorous physical activity, or cardio-respiratory levels of fitness (Robinson, 1999).

Anorexia and Bulimia

In a study by Harrison (2000), exposure to thin-ideal TV content did not predict eating disorders but exposure to fat character content predicted bulimia for females and body dissatisfaction for 6th-grade males. Reading magazine articles with thin ideals was positively correlated with eating disorder symptoms for females (increasing anorexia for 6th, 9th, and 12th graders and bulimia for 9th and 12th graders) but not for males. Exposure to sports magazines increased body dissatisfaction for only 12th-grade females. Harrison (2000) controlled for selective exposure and overall exposure and found a greater impact on females than males.

Some important racial differences have also emerged in the research literature. Botta (2000), for example, found that African American girls responded differently than European and American girls to thin images. There were some similarities too, however, that suggested that the gap between them in the development of eating disorders is narrowing. Botta said that individuals compare themselves and others to perceived realistic, attainable goals. Botta linked viewing, attitudes, and behavior that can lead to eating disorders. According to Botta, most thin-ideal persons are White. As more thin Blacks pervade the media, the African Americans develop thin ideals even if they do not identify with the White culture.

Blacks in Botta's (2000) study watched more TV, but higher viewing was related to eating disorders in Whites but not Blacks. Body image differences were based more on comparisons made than on the amount viewed. Both Black and White adolescents wanted to be thin, but African Americans were more satisfied with their bodies. Botta (2000) suggested a "latent mainstreaming effect" (p. 155), which mainstreams African Americans toward thin ideals. This was not due to heavy viewing, however, but was most true for those who "buy into" thin ideals. TV affects some more than others, and viewer perception and response mediates its influence. Botta·concluded that her findings confirm a social comparison theory's prediction that individuals turn to TV for images to emulate.

In a content analysis of prime-time situation comedy characters, Fouts and Burggraf (1999) examined body weights and comments that characters received from others because of their weight or their own comments about their weight or dieting. Female characters with below average weight were overrepresented compared to the general population; those with above average weight were underrepresented. The below average female characters received significantly more positive comments from males, and characters who were dieting gave themselves more verbal punishment for their weight and shape. Fouts and Burggraf noted that the thin female is clearly and frequently presented to child and adolescent observers, and it contributes to the internalization of thin as ideal, which may increase the risk for some young viewers for eating disorders. Fouts and Burggraf also observed low self-esteem in dieters and positive comments from males to them, suggesting that young male viewers may pressure females toward thinness with their comments.

SUMMARY

Children and adolescents are bathed in media stimulation and diverse content that can affect the health-related choices and decisions they make either in a healthy or unhealthy direction. A good deal of research has been directed to the study of media impact on sexual behavior, drug and alcohol use, smoking, nutrition and body image, and eating disorders. The media can be used positively such as in antismoking campaigns, public education about diseases such as AIDS or SARS, or to portray diverse personality and body types. On the negative side, it can provide unhealthy models who smoke, drink excessively, engage in risky sexual behavior, or starve themselves to stay pencil thin. Whether these messages have a significant impact depends on viewer need and past experience, reasons for viewing, consequences that are portrayed for the model such as rewards or social gains versus illness and isolation, and other factors. Racial differences have also emerged in the seriousness with which specific material is viewed and even which aspects of the message are most salient. Ongoing efforts to increase the number of positive messages and decrease the unhealthy ones will be necessary if there is to be a positive media effect on children's and adolescents' decision making and choices and on their physical, social, and emotional development.

DISCUSSION QUESTIONS

1. Discuss whether healthy messages (e.g., not smoking, responsible sexual behavior, self-acceptance regarding body image) would likely be more effective as stand-alone messages such as PSAs or as integral parts of plot lines in regular programs.
2. Discuss how social cognitive, cultivation, and uses and gratifications perspectives would predict or explain possible negative effects of unhealthy models and messages.
3. Discuss which racial, age, and gender differences appear to be most important in whether or not the media have a strong positive or negative effect.

CHAPTER TEN

Social/Emotional Issues

Social/Emotional Issues

In addition to aggressive behavior, stereotypes, and health-related choices and decisions, TV also has the potential to affect many areas of social/emotional functioning in children and adolescents. These other possible effects are discussed in the following sections.

FEAR AND ANXIETY

Compared to the amount of research on TV violence and aggression, much less has been written about the fear and anxiety that children can experience following TV viewing. Some researchers, however, notably Cantor and her colleagues (Cantor, 1994, 2001; Cantor & Nathanson, 1996; Valkenburg, Cantor, & Peeters, 2000), have studied this area extensively. Both experiments and surveys have been done to study developmental differences in children's fears and means of coping. The surveys can focus on children's exposure to and reactions to very frightening media coverage in a naturalistic setting; experiments, although more rigorously controlled, can only use relatively mild stimuli for ethical reasons (Cantor, 2001).

According to Cantor (1994), research indicates that a substantial number of viewers report fright while viewing and intense reactions and emotional disturbances that last after the viewing exposure. A random national survey in the Netherlands revealed that almost a third of children between ages 7 and 12 reported that they had been frightened by TV in the preceding year (Valkenburg, Cantor, & Peeters, 2000). Another survey of children in grades 3 to 8 (M. I. Singer, Slovak, Frierson, & York, 1998) demonstrated a positive correlation between number of hours of TV viewing and the prevalence of such symptoms as depression, anxiety, and posttraumatic stress.

There are important developmental differences, however, in how children react to potentially threatening or frightening television programming. Age is an important variable because there are age differences in the types of stimuli that produce fear. Increasing age does not lead to less susceptibility, but there is a change in what upsets children. Although older children are more mature cognitively, they may be more upset by some things (Cantor, 1994, 2001). Young children are more fearful of perceptually salient stimuli, either real or fantasy, whereas older children are more frightened by events with a higher likelihood of actually occurring. With adolescence, these include more abstract and psychological threats as well as physical harm (Cantor, 1994). Boehm (2003) said that exposure to some of the frightening events and images on television may inadvertently lead children to be "virtual victims" (p. 1) with symptoms ranging from separation anxiety to nightmares or other fears. It can also start to create a view that the world is a dangerous and cruel place with consequent feelings of vulnerability and anxiety (Boehm, 2003).

Cantor and Nathanson (1996), for example, surveyed parents of children in kindergarten and Grades 2, 4, and 6. Over a third reported that their children were upset or frightened by a TV news story. The percentage increased with age as the tendency to be frightened by nonreal content decreased. These results were consistent with research findings that younger children get as upset by unreal things as by things that could happen because they cannot easily distinguish fantasy and reality. Older children, on the other hand, tend to be more often frightened of things that could actually happen to them, and fear after exposure to news stories increased with age. The greatest increase in fright responses was between kindergarten and Grade 2 (Cantor & Nathanson, 1996). The proximity of story events made more of a difference for 10- and 11-year-olds than for 6- and 7-year-olds in one study (Smith & Wilson, 2000). The older children were more frightened by stories about local crime and perceived themselves to be more vulnerable personally (Smith & Wilson, 2000).

There are also developmental differences in coping strategies (Cantor, 1994; Wilson, Hoffner, & Cantor, 1987). Wilson et al. (1987) studied the cognitive strategies of three age groups: 3 to 5, 6 to 7, and 9 to 11. Cognitive strategies to deal with fear from the media, such as "tell yourself it's not real," increased with age. Noncognitive ones, such as playing with a toy, eating or drinking, or hugging a blanket, which may distract children from a scary program or provide physical comfort, were more effective for younger children and decreased with age. Sitting near parents was popular with all age groups, and avoidance of looking at frightening stimuli such as by covering one's face was not popular at any age. Younger children, then, use more noncognitive strategies such as holding onto a toy, whereas older children use more cognitive strategies such as thinking about the stimuli differently or focusing on the unreality of them (Cantor, 1994).

Gender differences also exist both in the amount of fear shown and in the coping strategies used (Cantor, 2001; Hoffner, 1995; Valkenburg et al., 2000) that may reflect different socialization pressures for the two groups. In Valkenburg et al.'s (2000) study of 7- to 12-year-old Dutch children, although 31% of them said they had been frightened by television during the previous year, both their fears and their means of coping with their fears varied with age and gender. Some aspects of socialization may affect which coping strategies viewers use, and coping strategies such as avoidance or interpersonal comfort were used more by girls than boys in one study (Hoffner, 1995), although both used cognitive coping strategies more equally.

Decision makers in the media share some of the responsibility for spreading fear and anxiety among viewers. According to the American Academy of Child and Adolescent Psychiatry (AACAP, 2002), several changes in how news is reported have increased the potential for child viewers to experience negative effects. Changes include news reporting 24 hours a day on both TV and Internet sites, broadcasts of live events as they are unfolding in real time such as the 9/11 attacks or war coverage, increased reporting of details from the private lives of well-known public figures and role models, pressure and competition to get news to the public, and detailed and repetitive coverage of natural disasters and violence. The AACAP noted the proclivity of children and adolescents to imitate what they see and hear in the news in "copy cat" events. Moreover, the choice of content to air does not always reflect actual trends. For example, despite a decrease in crime statistics, news reporting of crime has increased 240%, and local news shows use as much as 30% of their air time on detailed crime reports (AACAP, 2002).

Many feel that the practice of many newscasters to follow the "if it bleeds, it leads" (Lowry, 2002, p. 1) directive leads to an overemphasis on murder and violence, child abductions, and other threats. This fuels a tendency for viewers to overestimate their likelihood of becoming a victim (Lowry, 2002), consistent with the mean world syndrome that cultivation theory predicts. Lowry pointed out that this approach to news coupled with the growing number of crime shows means that viewers may well be more likely to anticipate harm from a stranger approaching on a dark street.

After the horrific events of 9/11, parents wondered how to help their children cope with what they were seeing and hearing on television. The National Institute on Media and the Family (2002e) urged parents to monitor what their children watch to make sure the messages are appropriate for their age and maturation level and to talk with them about their concerns and anxiety. In addition, the AACAP (2002) suggested that parents should reassure their young children and should look for signs that the news may have triggered anxiety such as fears, bedwetting, crying, or sleeplessness.

A series of public service messages prepared by Sesame Workshop was specifically developed to alleviate children's and parents' anxiety in the event of war (Beatty, 2003). PBS also suggested that member stations should provide a "safe zone" for children by extending preschool programming, not mentioning war, and reminding parents to maintain normal routines during stressful and uncertain times. Other programming provided reassuring information for older children, explored related issues, and addressed frequently asked questions (Beatty, 2003).

SOCIAL RELATIONSHIPS

Heavy television viewing can also be related to the quality of a child's social interaction as either a cause or effect. Children with peer problems may tend to rely more on TV for activity and "companionship." Conversely, children who spend a lot of time with television and other media have less time to engage in social relationships with peers. Kubey and Csikszentmihalyi (1990) noted that heavy viewers tended to experience solitude more negatively, and they could avoid those feelings while viewing.

Specific program content can affect the social interaction and toy play of preschoolers as well. In one study (Argenta, Stoneman, & Brody, 1986), because of the rapid visual and auditory sequences, cartoons were attended to most, with consequent decreased social interaction. Although *Sesame Street* was visually attended to less than cartoons, it elicited the most verbal imitation and seemed to encourage social interaction and active play with toys, especially for boys. Situation comedies were visually attended to least and were also the least favorite program. They involved social behavior that was similar to that occurring during *Sesame Street* because both programs allowed children to divide their activity among the television, toys, and peers and to remain active and involved. Only the cartoons led to them being mesmerized and stopping other interaction or involvement.

Some viewers become attached to media figures because they seem real, and the viewers come to believe in the actors as the actual characters (Caughey, 1986). Viewers may identify with characters on the screen or live vicariously through their heroes. In fact, viewers may become involved with media figures even after the set is turned off, as when they become "fans." The media figures then can influence goals, values, and attitudes and thus have a significant influence on social behavior (Caughey, 1986). The appeal of the reality shows that have multiplied so quickly may be due in part to viewers' identification with them and vicarious experience of adventure through them.

PROSOCIAL BEHAVIOR

Although much has been written about television's negative impact, it clearly can be a positive force as well. It can stimulate imagination as long as the child does not depend on it for imaginative activity (Singer & Singer, 1986), and it can be used to increase creativity and tolerance (Rosenkoetter, Huston, & Wright, 1990). It can teach prosocial behavior (de Groot, 1994; Forge & Phemister, 1987, Potts, Huston, & Wright, 1986; Rushton, 1988), and it can move extraordinary numbers of people to act charitably, as has been demonstrated by many telethons, "aid" concerts, and other television initiatives. It can dramatize historical events, entertain, and inform. It can facilitate the location of missing children, and it can be used to strengthen family ties and values. It can provide role models for children and teach coping skills as well as reverse negative images and stereotypes (Hattemer & Showers, 1995b; Liebert & Sprafkin, 1988).

Studies in both laboratory and naturalistic settings have demonstrated that television can lead to increased generosity, cooperation, adherence to rules, delay of gratification, friendliness, and decreased fear (Rushton, 1988). Research also has shown that children learned nurturance and sympathy from watching *Mister Rogers* and persistence on tasks (de Groot, 1994). Even prosocial cartoons elicited more prosocial behavior in preschoolers than neutral ones (Forge & Phemister, 1987). Some suggest, however, that prosocial programming is more effective with children who lack family, church, or school models and teaching (Hattemer & Showers, 1995b).

Fred Rogers, who died in 2003, exemplified prosocial television in the popular *Mister Rogers' Neighborhood*. He was genuine, nurturing, and spoke directly to the needs and concerns of young children. He taught them about self-control, consideration and cooperation, tolerance, imagination, and self-control (Higgins, 2003). Unlike many shows and movies for children that are as enjoyable for adults as for children, *Mister Rogers* did not try to pull in adult viewers with more adult references or jokes or other commentary. Rather, he treated children with respect and gave them his complete attention, which led to their seeming to be calmer and happier watching him than other shows (Salutin, 2003).

The potential for prosocial effects from commercial television may be even greater because it reaches a much larger audience (Sprafkin et al., 1992). In a study of children's understanding of moral lessons that were included in regular TV programming, Rosenkoetter (1999) found that the majority of children in first, third, and fifth grades understood moral lessons in a *Cosby Show* episode, and many of the first- and third-grade children also could identify a moral lesson in a *Full House* episode. In addition, viewing prosocial situation comedies was positively correlated with frequency of prosocial behavior, especially in those children who showed understanding of the lessons in the sitcoms. Rosenkoetter suggested that might be a function of their parents' emphasis on prosocial videos, but because many parents do not regulate their children's viewing, this area needs more research.

Other studies have given less reason for optimism about the efficacy of prosocial content in increasing prosocial behavior. Wiegman et al. (1992), for example, in their longitudinal study of the impact of both aggressive and prosocial models on children's behavior, found no significant positive correlations between viewing prosocial behavior on television and prosocial behavior in children. Interestingly, however, there was a strong correlation between viewing violence and viewing prosocial behavior; that is, the children who saw many aggressive models also saw many prosocial models because they were heavy viewers.

In their recent study of very young children, Rideout et al. (2003) reported that about 80% of the parents said that their children under 6 years of age imitated both positive and aggressive behavior they saw on television. However, they copied many more prosocial behaviors than aggressive ones (87% vs. 47% among 4- to 6-year-olds). Boys in that age group imitated more aggressive behaviors than girls did, but it wasn't clear whether they watched more violent content or were just more likely to copy it (Rideout et al., 2003).

The inclusion of prosocial content in children's programming and advertising is an important administrative decision. Prosocial behavior or positive characteristics can be included in commercials as well as programs, and new possibilities for increased prosocial program delivery exist because of the increase in cable channels with their greater ability to provide special programming for narrower target audiences (Johnston & Ettema, 1986).

It is clearly necessary to produce attractive prosocial programs, however, if children are to choose them over other ones. Television, then, can be used to strengthen values such as cooperation, family stability, gender equality, nonviolence, and other positive behaviors in the same way that it can undermine them (Lefrancois, 1992).

OTHER EFFECTS

Problem Solving

Television also may affect children's ideas about problem solving. Selnow (1986), for example, suggested that television viewing may be related to children's perceptions of problem resolution just as it is seen to be related to other beliefs such as ideas about violence or the elderly. According to Selnow, heavy viewers see much repetition in problems that are introduced and then solved rather promptly according to a few set patterns. Selnow said that the content of the problems and solutions did not matter; it is the rules underlying story lines that did. Therefore, according to Selnow, it may be the ease and speed and predictability of TV solutions that lead to concern for children who expect the same in the real world. It is important to ask whether expectations about TV's solutions influence the perceptual framework the child uses to evaluate real-life events, predict activities, and judge success or failure, especially if they see their own lives falling short of TV's ideal (Selnow, 1986).

Daydreaming

Valkenburg and Van der Voort (1995) found that watching nonviolent programs led to a more positive and less aggressive daydreaming style, whereas watching violent dramatic programs led to a more aggressive/heroic, less positive style. That is, children daydreamed more frequently about themes consistent with frequently watched television content. Valkenburg and Van der Voort (1995) also found that the children's daydreaming had no long-term influence on their viewing behavior, and the content stimulated certain kinds of daydreaming but reduced others.

Leisure Time

Kubey and Csikszentmihalyi (1990) warned that heavy viewing may so acclimate viewers to rapid changes and continual sights and sounds that they may become dependent on them and less able to fill leisure time without them. The causal direction for this is hard to pin down: Heavy viewing might lead to an inability to tolerate unstructured time, but discomfort with unstructured time may lead the person to watch a large amount of television. Furthermore, the condensation of time that occurs on television and in films may make the normal speed of one's own life seem slow compared to the experience of people living before the advent of TV, perhaps leading to impatience and an increasing desire to keep going faster (Kubey & Csikszentmihalyi, 1990).

Behavioral Controls

In one study (Singer, Singer, & Rapacynski, 1984), children who spent more time watching television, especially violent programs, were less likely to show the self-restraint necessary to sit quietly for a few minutes, and heavy television viewing in elementary children was correlated with later aggression, restlessness, and belief in a "scary" world (Desmond et al., 1990; Singer et al., 1984). Some heavy viewers in the Desmond et al. (1990) study watched more than 7 hours daily, and their restlessness and aggression scores were the highest in the sample. The researchers recommended no more than 1 hour a day for preschoolers and no more than 2 hours a day for children in the early elementary years.

Contentedness

Most children in the Rideout et al. (1999) study reported being fairly content in a number of areas of their life including the friends they had, happiness at school, and getting along with parents. However, children who were high users of the media, who spent more than 10½ hours a day using media, scored significantly lower on a contentedness index than other children (Rideout et al., 1999). Even when other factors such as income, race, age, and family makeup were controlled, high use of media was strongly correlated with indicators of discontent such as not getting along with parents, getting into trouble, or unhappiness at school. This is correlational data, however, and causation cannot be inferred. Children who are less content in other areas of their lives might well choose to watch more television or play more video games.

Positive Effects

Gunter et al. (1991) emphasized the positive effects that television can confer. Gunter et al. noted that it can encourage reading and other activities, give insight into possible coping strategies, give information about all kinds of topics from gardening to health, discuss new developments in science and technology, and give news updates. Its effects depend on how children use it. Fowles (1992), in a chapter titled "Television is Good for Children," noted that preschoolers learn vocabulary, general knowledge about how things work, nonverbal information (e.g., how to treat pets, how to shake hands, how close to stand next to someone), and real-world information that is lacking in their lives such as when a child living on a farm learns about taxi behavior. Moreover, according to Fowles, children like to watch cartoons because they can behave aggressively vicariously without re-percussions—it helps them cut tensions—and evidence that they stir children up is weak. In the short term, television leads to decreased pressure and relaxation, as with adults, but long-term effects are still not known (Fowles, 1992). *Barney and Friends* has also fostered a sense of secure attachment in child viewers (J. L. Singer & Singer, 1998).

EXCEPTIONAL CHILDREN

Although the viewing experience of normal children of all ages has been studied extensively, a relatively small number of studies have focused on exceptional children (Abelman, 1990; Sprafkin et al., 1992). The work that has been done has consistently demonstrated that children with learning, behavioral, and emotional disorders have even greater problems than other children in distinguishing fantasy and reality (Gadow, Sprafkin, Kelly, & Ficarrotto, 1988; Sprafkin et al., 1992; Sprafkin, Gadow, & Dussault, 1986), in understanding TV content, and in the linguistic processing of the material. Moreover, these children are likely to view greater amounts of television (Sprafkin & Gadow, 1986; Sprafkin et al., 1992), to have poorer social skills and fewer social contacts and experiences that would provide information to counter television's messages, and to have fewer coviewing experiences with parents or other adults (Sprafkin & Gadow, 1986; Sprafkin et al., 1992). For all of these reasons, they are more vulnerable to television's influence in their lives.

Viewing Patterns. According to Sprafkin et al. (1992), TV has the unique potential to educate children who have fewer social skills, who do not learn well with traditional methods, who need frequent repetition to learn, and who have attentional problems. For gifted children, TV can supplement classroom learning with access to new and exciting topics. On the other hand, exceptional children are at risk for viewing greater amounts of TV and for being more attracted to and reactive to adult or violent programs (Sprafkin et al., 1992), and gifted children may be intellectually ready for some content, but they may not be socially or emotionally ready. Sprafkin et al. (1992) reported that gifted children generally viewed less television than other children except at preschool age and adolescence when they watched more. Curiosity and enthusiasm may lead them to watch more adult programs as preschoolers, and in adolescence, they watch more than average children perhaps for social/emotional reasons such as isolation (Sprafkin et al., 1992).

Of all the exceptional groups, Sprafkin et al. (1992) considered mentally retarded, emotionally disturbed (ED), and learning disabled (LD) children to be the most vulnerable, as they are more at risk for heavy viewing and for adverse reactions to some content. The special education group (a) viewed significantly more TV than controls, (b) watched more soaps and sitcoms than controls, and (c) watched more crime shows and were twice as likely to say that they often pretended to be their favorite character. According to the researchers, special education groups were higher in overall exposure to TV, perhaps because viewing may substitute for real interactions, characters may provide social acceptance—especially for the ED group—caretakers may allow more TV viewing to preserve quiet time, and television viewing is stress free. The LD children performed more poorly on the TV knowledge measure and showed less critical attitudes (Sprafkin et al., 1992).

Viewing and Psychological Disturbances. Heavy viewing may also indicate the presence of anxiety, depression, and violent behaviors in children. M. I. Singer et al. (1998) studied 2,245 elementary and middle or junior high school students, two thirds of whom watched television for 3 hours or more a day. M. I. Singer et al. (1998) used a scale that assesses posttraumatic abuse symptoms in children, including anxiety, dissociation, anger, posttraumatic stress, depression, and sexual concerns. More heavy viewers, those who watched more than 6 hours a day, scored in the clinical range for trauma symptoms than did lighter viewers. Girls were high in all areas and boys more in the clinical range for anxiety, anger, and dissociation. Heavy viewers and children who preferred action and fighting shows also showed higher levels of violent behavior, although this relation is an association, not a causal one.

Grimes and Bergen (2001) argued that none of the usual reasons put forth to support a causal link between violent TV and psychological abnormalities in otherwise normal children warrant confidence in such a relation, nor is there convincing empirical evidence. According to Griffiths (1991), game players have little uniformity of personality, and there has been little research into whether playing these games is a social or a nonsocial activity. Nonetheless, playing video games can use up a lot of time, and it is clear that some individuals do show a dependency on them. Furthermore, users may spend inordinate amounts of time with games because of poor peer or parental relationships (Griffiths, 1991).

Uses of Television. Findings on the relation between reading time or reading skills and time spent watching television is inconsistent (Ritchie et al., 1987), and some viewing behavior may be a result rather than a cause of poor academic performance. Children's use of television may be due in part to frustrating experiences, specifically with print, such that poor readers may turn to television for learning more than for entertainment. Such children may use television to obtain information that they cannot get from reading. For those children, television viewing may have more of a negative impact because they may take television content more seriously in their effort to seek information and learn from it.

Aggressive Behavior. Exceptional children may substitute television for actual socialization activities and try to solve interpersonal problems with aggressive behavior they have seen on television or that was engaged in by their favorite characters (Sprafkin & Gadow, 1986). Low IQ exacerbates the effect because children with lower IQs tend to watch more television, and the violent/aggressive solutions may seem like easy ones (Huesmann, 1986).

Some research has found ED children to be more attracted to crime/adult content, to significantly more often name crime shows as favorites, to identify less with nonaggressive characters, and to show higher aggressiveness (Sprafkin & Gadow, 1986; Sprafkin, Watkins, & Gadow, 1990). They also watched cartoons for significantly more hours unlike older children in regular classes who showed less interest in cartoons than younger ones. In a different study (Gadow, Sprafkin, & Ficarrotto, 1987), preschool ED children showed reactivity to both aggressive and control cartoons. Some reacted adversely, some did not; but many kinds of content appeared to have the potential ability to increase antisocial behavior (Gadow, Sprafkin, & Ficarrotto, 1987). Moreover, those children may be more likely to view others' intentions as antisocial and more likely, then, to respond aggressively (Sprafkin et al., 1992).

Perceived Reality. Although ED and LD children differ in the nature of their social problems and interactions, they share the misperception of television's reality, and this may be due to the fact that both groups are likely to engage in fewer social interactions of a type that would lead to a more realistic view of the world (Gadow et al., 1988).

Children with learning disabilities are even less able to make a distinction between fantasy and reality, even with control for IQ (Gadow et al., 1988). Using the Perception of Reality on Television measure developed by Sprafkin, Gadow, et al. (1986) to test perceptions of reality without reliance on reading ability, Sprafkin et al. (1992) found that ED and LD children were less likely to understand that an actor's role does not continue off the screen. Those children saw TV portrayals of unrealistic situations as representative of the real world. Gifted children saw television as the least realistic, whereas children with disabilities lacked the skills necessary to determine whether content is real or not, for example, in assessing how plausible a situation is. They watched more and tended to see the fiction as real (Sprafkin et al., 1992).

Sprafkin, Gadow, et al. (1986) compared school-identified ED children with normal children. ED children also scored significantly lower on a measure of perceived television reality, the *Videotest*, even when IQ was controlled, indicating their lesser ability to distinguish between fantasy and reality on television. They were more likely to consider television programs and commercials to be accurate portrayals of the real world, more like younger children do. Sprafkin, Gadow, et al. (1986) suggested further that given the relation between perceived realism and aggressive behavior and the ED child's more likely perception of aggression as real, ED children might show greater behavioral reaction to TV aggression than their normal counterparts. They might also be expected to want advertised products. *Videotest* scores correlated highly with achievement and IQ scores. Sprafkin, Gadow, et al. (1986) urged consideration of the usefulness of a school-based curriculum to teach such children how to make the distinction between reality and fantasy more easily both in programs and in advertising.

In a parallel study with LD children, also using the Stony Brook *Videotest,* Gadow et al. (1988) obtained similar results. The LD students who were severely handicapped and in self-contained classes in a special school were more likely to think that television programming reflected real life. They also were less knowledgeable about the use of special effects and more likely to believe in the veracity of TV commercials. This was true for both genders and for all three age groups (7, 9, and 11 years old), although they did improve with age just as their non-LD counterparts did. Gadow et al. (1988) noted further that social skills deficits of many LD children may be compounded by misperceptions of television's reality.

Gadow et al. (1988) suggested that the LD children's poorer performance in relation to peers, even when IQ was controlled, may reflect their more basic information processing deficits and a more general misperception or poor understanding of reality. Gadow et al.'s (1988) findings, however, pertained to a particular population with very severe learning problems who may be in even more need of instruction in viewing skills.

There is a need for tailor-made programs for exceptional children, according to Sprafkin et al. (1992). In 1990, Sprafkin et al. compared the viewing habits of ED and LD elementary school children using the Curriculum for Enhancing Social Skills Through Media Awareness (CESSMA; Sprafkin, Watkins, & Gadow, 1986). CESSMA is a viewing skills curriculum that leads to improved perception of reality versus fantasy, knowledge of special effects, and accuracy or truth of advertising. Sprafkin et al. (1990) obtained especially strong results in the area of knowledge of TV. ED children who received the skills curriculum identified less with aggressive characters, but there was no effect of the curriculum on attitudes toward television or habits of viewing either in amount of viewing or in program choices. Sprafkin et al. (1990) concluded that most studies show that simply viewing is associated with higher levels of antisocial behavior regardless of content, so a television literacy curriculum should include lessons on both nonaggressive and aggressive content. TV literacy also can be adapted to be a truly stimulating aspect of education for the gifted (Abelman, 1987).

Video Games. Although video games have also not been shown to be related directly or causally to psychopathology (Kestenbaum & Weinstein, 1985; McClure & Mears, 1986), the fact remains that exceptional children's poorer social skills, usually lower academic achievement, weaker behavioral controls, and poorer discrimination between fantasy and reality make their heavy use of aggressive video games cause for concern. ED children who play violent video games for hours, for whom the line between fantasy and reality is blurred, who have few alternative and satisfying activities, and who experience little parental mediation or control of their viewing and game-playing activity would appear to be at highest risk for seeing violence as appropriate and realistic and for acting out aggressively.

Computer and video games, now much more realistic and more violent than earlier ones, offer opportunities for learning just as television does, but their active or interactive dimension may intensify a game's impact. The implications of pervasive preferences for violent media and the level of risk of play habits need to be examined (Funk & Buckman, 1996). Much more research is needed.

Instructional Use of Television. Interestingly, although these groups are the most vulnerable, they also stand to gain the most from instructional use of television, but little research has been done on the use of the media in teaching exceptional children (Sprafkin et al., 1992). Technology can be used in innovative ways to help exceptional children, however. Irvin et al. (1992), for example, used video and computer technology to develop a videodisc assessment program for measuring children's social skills and for sociometric assessment. Irvin et al. pointed to it as an example of technology contributing to better assessment of children with handicaps. It allowed Irvin et al. to assess children's perceptions and social knowledge directly without having to rely on others' reports. They could present computer-based video portrayals of various situations and interactions, which do not require high levels of language or reading, and sequence items to simulate real life.

Television can certainly also be used to educate others about various disorders and exceptional children's experience of them, both directly via documentaries or specific educational programming or by including characters with specific disorders in regular programming. This in turn could lead to greater acceptance of them, more empathic responses to them, and greater efforts to meet their special needs.

HIGH-RISK CHILDREN

Although the data are fairly clear about television's impact on normal children and on children with clear and significant behavioral or emotional difficulties, virtually no work has been done on those children who have not yet been clearly identified as having such problems but who do appear to be at some risk for developing them: those children who show more behavioral or emotional signals or who stand out for teachers as somewhat problematic in the classroom. Even though they have not been identified specifically as behavioral, learning, or emotionally troubled youngsters, they have weaker behavioral controls, fewer satisfactory social relationships, more inappropriate verbal or motoric expressions, and some academic difficulties or underachievement. They are the "gray area" children who are at risk for more serious difficulties; they are also children who might be expected to be more strongly influenced by television in the same direction as those who already have clear problems. High-risk children may even be especially vulnerable because they are not in special classes or a treatment program, and they may be watching more television or playing more games in unsupervised contexts with virtually no mediation or intervention involved in their media experience.

As previous research (e.g., Hearold, 1986; Potter, 1986) has demonstrated a clear relation between perceived reality and television's impact, one would expect that at-risk children are also more vulnerable to television's influence. Hence, important measures should be introduced to prevent further, more serious behavioral and emotional difficulties from developing, such as imitating violent or antisocial behavior that they observe frequently in various media. The importance of early intervention lies in its ability to reach high-risk children before television has had as great an impact as it might otherwise have.

If these children at risk for emotional and behavioral problems tend to react to and interpret television content in the same way as LD and ED children do, important steps could be taken to prevent the undesirable effects that their media use is likely to have. They would be the ones who would most benefit from critical viewing skills training, reduced viewing time, and greater selectivity in program choices before more serious problems develop.

SUMMARY

Although a huge proportion of the work done on media's effects on children and adolescents has focused on violence, advertising, stereotyping, and school performance, TV also has the potential to affect many other areas of social/emotional functioning. Children and adolescents are affected by media exposure in many ways other than increased aggression. A large proportion of children experience fear and anxiety, stress, nightmares, reduced concentration, and poor school performance. There are important age and gender differences in what children fear most and in the strategies they use to cope with their fears. Coverage of real-life events such as the 9/11 attacks can evoke significant anxiety that varies with the developmental level and cognitive skills of the children who view it. TV viewing and other media use can also affect social interactions, empathic responses, prosocial behavior, problem-solving ability, contentedness, use of leisure time, and other aspects of children's lives.

Children with learning, behavioral, and emotional disorders tend to view larger amounts of television, perceive television content as more realistic, and have poorer social skills and fewer social contacts and experiences that would provide information to counter television's messages. Therefore, they would be more vulnerable to television's influence in their lives. Exceptional children may also use television viewing to avoid academic or other problems, to get information that they cannot get from print, and as a substitute for other social interactions. Because they perceive more television content to be realistic, they also may come to see violence and aggression as realistic solutions to problems. Children at risk for these disorders also often have poorer social skills and fewer satisfactory relationships, weaker controls, and other difficulties and are also vulnerable to media influence. Their viewing needs to be monitored carefully to avoid undue influence of television in their already troubled lives.

DISCUSSION QUESTIONS

1. Discuss which types of shows would likely lead to the greatest fear responses in children and why.
2. How do children's information-processing skills affect their levels of fear and anxiety? What mitigating factors might reduce these effects?
3. Discuss the relevant differences between normal and exceptional children that contribute to their greater or lesser vulnerability to media messages.

PART IV

Other Technologies

CHAPTER ELEVEN

New Technologies and Computer Usage

New Technologies and Computer Usage

The explosion in technological options available to children and adolescents over the past few years is truly remarkable. A large proportion of children and teens carry pagers and cell phones. They communicate with their friends via e-mail and join chat rooms on the Web. They enjoy DVD and CD players and do much of their homework on computers. They have quickly come to depend on the efficiency and portability of most devices and are often more knowledgeable about them than their parents and completely at ease in their use. New technological developments can influence the impact of the media on children and adolescents in both direct and indirect ways. Not only has media content changed, but children's access to it has changed quickly too, and important questions have arisen almost as fast.

How do all of these developments in technology affect children? What influences do technological advances have on children's developmental processes? How has the nature of the information to which they are exposed actually changed? What effect do the new technologies have on families? How do families with access to the proliferating choices differ from those without such access?

In this section, we will survey the range of technological options and the varied content now available to children and adolescents. We will explore the ways in which they use those options; how technology is used for informational purposes and for entertainment; and what impact their choices have on their developing knowledge, attitudes, and behavior.

NEW TECHNOLOGIES

Mayer (1994) reminded us that the phrase, "new media" is relative—even the printing press was a new medium once—but the term usually includes VCRs, computers, car phones, CDs, fax and answering machines, e-mail, satellite dishes, cable TV, and interactive television that are used for the development, storage, and transmission of information and that have transformed traditional media. They make distance all but irrelevant and free television from the restrictions of broadcast schedules (Williams, Phillips, & Lum, 1985). New technologies mean access to more channels and more different kinds of programs on cable, some considered to be positive (e.g., educational), some negative (e.g., graphic violence). Choice in itself, however, does not guarantee quality, and many of the channels offer significant amounts of repetition and commercialism (Feldman, 1994).

The greatest changes over the last few years, made possible by the growth and application of digital technology, have been in the way technology can be used and combined or integrated and in its portability. There are TVs hooked up to cable, VCRs and DVDs, computer games and stand-alone video games, and the Internet, which can be reached through a computer, cable, various wireless devices, and cell phones. The National Institute on Media and the Family (2002h) summarized the changes and possibilities succinctly:

> Digital TV sets the stage for a more interactive use of television. The viewer will have much more control over what they watch and how they watch it. Television will become a place to do shopping, play games, e-mail friends, and select movies to watch. They will be able to view interactive programs where one can switch from a program to an Internet web site that presents more information about what is being watched. The viewer can click on an alternative video stream, music or commentary about a particular subject or interest. The potential for commercial use is unlimited. Viewers will be able to buy any item they see in a program by merely clicking on it, viewing purchasing information, and buying it.
>
> Wireless communication will bring the world of information to users no matter where they are. Cell phone use, exploding over the last few years, now connects to the Internet. Thus besides being able to place a call, the user can e-mail or search the Internet. The ramifications of this instantaneous information access is only beginning to be felt, for commercial, business, and personal use. (p. 3)

COMPUTER USE

Although many children have ample access to computers, they spend a relatively small amount of time each day using them. TV still dominates the time children spend with media, although they would prefer computers over TV if forced to choose (Rideout et al., 1999). Rideout et al. found that about 40% of children between 2 and 18 use a computer, including a fourth of the 2- to 7-year-olds and about half of children 8 or older. Almost a third of students will use a computer in a classroom, and 1 in 10 children has computer Internet access from their own rooms. Fewer than 10% spend more than an hour a day using computers for fun, and only 3% are online for more than an hour (Rideout et al., 1999).

According to Rideout et al. (1999), children 8 and older who use computers use them for an average of more than an hour and half a day. Of these, a fourth of the time is spent playing games, a fourth doing schoolwork, and about a third on the Internet either to chat, surf online, or send e-mail. Children also still read for fun too, although this drops off sharply in adolescence. In a typical week, children spend about 19 hours viewing TV, 10 hours listening to music, 5 hours reading for fun, and more than 2 hours in video game playing (Rideout et al., 1999). Most children in the Rideout et al. study did not make a huge distinction between computers and television in terms of whether their use was for entertainment or information and educational purposes. About 50% indicated that they use TV and computers primarily for entertainment, and 20% to 25% use TV and computers to learn interesting things. Only 10% to 15% use them just to kill time (Rideout et al., 1999). Nonetheless, the impact of their media use may vary depending on their reason for using them as uses and gratification theory would predict.

Even infants are being swept into the computer vortex. From software such as *Jumpstart Baby* for babies 9 to 24 months old to *My First Mouse Pad* for those 6 months and over, claims are made for a sharper brain and a competitive edge over others (Nolen, 2000). Programs for infants as young as 6 to 9 months typically involve nursery rhymes, colors, shapes, and animal sounds (Paik, 2001). Nolen (2000) cited a 1999 poll in which a fourth of the 10,000 parents polled said their children had started using a computer by the age of 2. The so-called lapware, because the baby has to be on someone's lap to use it, is built on rapidly evolving technology such as touch-sensitive screens and voice activation that attract the interest of these young users (Nolen, 2000). Some researchers claim that the use of such programs causes changes in the activity levels and electrical patterns of brain function, although the interpretation of that is unclear, and to replace the real experience of sights, smells, and sounds with a computer screen may seriously impair brain function and development (Nolen, 2000).

Given the appeals and promises to parents that software for infants and toddlers can accelerate or enhance brain function and intelligence, parents need to remember that certain maturational levels are necessary for children to benefit and perform on their own. Just as parents cannot toilet train a child at 2 months of age, so too they cannot make the brain function in different ways regardless of maturational level. Extra stimulation, variety, and novelty are solid developmental goals, but computer time should be limited to allow a child time and opportunity for all of the real-life interactions, exploration, discoveries, sensations, and experiences that go into healthy development.

Computers are also hugely popular in toys. Sixty percent of Fisher-Price® new toys in 2000 had a computer chip in them, up from under 10% 3 years before (Nolen, 2000). Some parents say children like them more than TV because they control them and they can play games or "paint."

Subrahmanyam, Greenfield, Kraut, and Gross (2001) found that computers were used more by teens than by younger children or adults. They were used more by boys than girls, more by Whites than by Black or Hispanic children, and more by children in homes with higher parental education and income (Subrahmanyam, Greenfield, et al., 2001). Subrahmanyam, Greenfield, et al. (2001) noted that children still watch TV more than they use computers, although computer users watch less TV. Subrahmanyam, Greenfield, et al. (2001) concluded that moderate use does not affect children's social skills and activities negatively and may even help them maintain communication and sustain relationships.

According to Salomon (1990), the qualities of computer use that may affect children's cognitive functioning include (a) interactivity, which involves a very different quality to a child's engagement; (b) intellectual guidance and dynamic feedback, what Salomon (1990) called an "intellectual partner"; (c) multiplicity of symbol systems for presentation and manipulation of information; and (d) the supplanting of users' memories in which viewers don't have to remember so much to carry out a task.

The varied uses and impact of the new technologies are discussed in detail in chapters 12 and 13. Two of the major aspects of the new technologies that are important from a developmental point of view are the greater access to information they provide and the interactivity that is possible.

ACCESS TO INFORMATION

For many children, VCRs, DVDs, cable, home videos, and computers, particularly the Internet, have significantly increased their access to adult information. With the flick of a switch, at least in the absence of direct parental control, children can open a window onto everything from old movies to sexually explicit and pornographic material. They have significantly greater access to programs intended for an adult audience. Moreover, they have access to information unavailable even to many adults not so long ago. Because of this increased access, children are privy, at a very much younger age, to many adult behaviors that were unknown to previous generations of children at that age. Their greater access to adult information, however, does not bring with it a complete or adult understanding of that information. Their ability to process and react to what they see is still constrained by many of the developmental factors they bring to the viewing situation that have been discussed throughout the preceding chapters, such as developmental level, intelligence, gender, range of experiences, socioeconomic level, perceived reality, and motivation for viewing.

Children who are watching material intended for adults may still be having considerable difficulty sorting out real information from fantasy material; they may not be cognizant of some of the formal features of television, and hence, they may find flashbacks, dream sequences, and other dramatic techniques confusing and incomprehensible. They may still be unable to grasp subtle messages or "morals to the story," and hence, they may overreact to salient but irrelevant or inappropriate aspects of a program. The accessibility of adult information to child viewers, then, clearly has important developmental and behavioral implications.

INTERACTIVITY

Two-way interactive television, computers, and video games provide new technological experience for children and adolescents, and these media have implications for the learning styles and developing feelings of mastery of the children and adolescents who use them. The interactive component of the new technology is important from the point of view of the child as a learner. Research (e.g., Crain, 1992) has told us clearly that children's learning is facilitated significantly by active involvement; seeing, trying out, actually doing, that is, active learning, is the most effective type. The more interactive quality of computer games makes them different from simply viewing TV, at least in those respects.

Feldman (1994) worried that with increasingly complex games, more extensive menus for entertainment and sports, access to data banks, and other technological advances, "knowledge and power per se will become increasingly defined as highly individual experiences" (p. 29), and electronic activity will replace real-life experience to a much greater degree.

DIFFERENTIAL ACCESS

Although the expanding media and technological choices are likely to continue and even to increase, some writers worry about the differential access of various population groups to these choices. Sprafkin et al. (1992), for example, noted the problem with access and the unavailability of the new technologies to lower SES families. According to Sprafkin et al. (1992), children with disabilities are likely to have less access, and gifted children are likely to have more, which may well create inequities and greater distances among the various populations. The "old media" traditional network television programming, on the other hand, was equally available to all who owned a set (Webster, 1989).

In a study involving nearly 30,000 students from over 1,100 Canadian schools, Statistics Canada (StatsCan) reported unequal access between students from homes with higher and lower SES ("Unequal Access," 2003). Eighty-eight percent of 15-year-olds, almost 9 out of 10, had access to a computer at home, and 75% used one. However, children from families with lower incomes were less likely to have access to a computer at home, although the adults had access at work, Internet cafes, and libraries. The StatsCan study also reported that students who had access used them regularly to get information from the Web, do word processing, use e-mail and instant messaging, and play games. Half used them every day, and 20% used them a few times per week. Thirteen percent did not use them at all ("Unequal Access," 2003).

Many are concerned that children who do not have access to these technological tools will not be able to keep pace academically with changing demands and expectations. Borzekowski and Rickert (2001) noted that although public locations for Internet access such as libraries and schools means that individuals can gain information from the Internet regardless of education and income, the "digital divide" along income lines is still apparent.

Unequal access to or different uses of the new technology by different population segments raises the possibility of serious social ramifications, of a division between information-rich and information-poor individuals (Wright, 1986). Imagine the huge advantage of a child working on a school assignment at home with a computer, CD-ROM, encyclopedia on disk, and access to the Internet compared with another child who has the same assignment but no computer and access only to school texts, a few resources at home, and the public library, with perhaps limited access to a computer in a public place like the library.

There is differential access in other ways and between other groups as well. StatsCan reported that a gender gap still exists in computer competency ("Gender Gap," 2003). Female students reported less competency in computer skills. Although almost all participants, both male and female (97%), reported having used a computer in the year prior to the survey done in 2000 by the new Data Research Centre, 38% of males reported excellent computer skills. Only 17% of females did. Males used computers more frequently (57% of males reported daily use compared to 45% of females), and they reported using them in more ways than female respondents ("Gender Gap," 2003).

Differences between children in urban and rural areas also emerged in the StatsCan study ("Gender Gap," 2003). Although most children from both types of environment (96%) said they had used a computer in the 12 months before the survey, children from rural homes used computers at school more often. With fewer computers in rural homes, more students from homes in villages used computers at school (29%) or a library (18%) compared with children living in cities who used them less often both at school (19%) and at libraries (4%).

Issues of access to information, selectivity, and interactivity all touch on significant developmental concerns and affect the impact on children of recent technological advances as well as those sure to come. Greater access will alter children's knowledge base and perhaps even the tempo of their development. Such increases in information and the interactivity that is possible also affect children's developing sense of mastery and means of coping with their expanding world. Whether they use the media primarily for information or for entertainment and whether they have easy access to computers and other technological devices, technology will have a definite influence on their developing attitudes and knowldge, and on their psychological, social, and emotional development.

SUMMARY

The rapid growth in technology options now available to children and adolescents and the impact of new technologies on children's use and experience of media is an important area of investigation. The increased availability of cell phones, pagers, e-mail, and computers has affected all areas of children's lives, including language use, social interaction, school performance, and family relationships. Technology can have an important influence on children's developing attitudes and behavior and on their psychological, social, intellectual, and emotional development.

Because of the huge impact of technology on child and adolescent development, questions of access and availability become even more important. Children without easy access to this technology are at a distinct disadvantage in an information-rich society. In addition, the interactivity involved allows for more active learning, which developmental theory and research shows is the most effective. Children with less access are once again at a disadvantage.

Research studies have reported differential access for children from rural and urban homes and important gender differences in computer competency. These differences can affect children's developing sense of mastery and ability to cope in the world. Although most children now have greater access to computers, television still occupies the biggest portion of the time they spend with technology. More sophisticated and realistic video games as well as developing virtual reality technology make the fantasy–reality distinction ever more elusive. Difficulty making this separation, coupled with children's significantly increased access to adult information, has important developmental, social, interpersonal, and psychological implications.

DISCUSSION QUESTIONS

1. Discuss the ways in which differential access to new technologies could adversely affect children's and adolescents' development.
2. Discuss some possible reasons why TV still appears to dominate children's use of various media and whether you think this is a positive or negative finding.
3. Discuss the positive and negative impact of the new technologies on children's social development and interaction.

CHAPTER TWELVE

Technologies for Information

Technologies for Information

THE INTERNET

Internet Use

The Internet has expanded rapidly since the late 1980s by 50% every year in the 1990s (Paik, 2001). A 1998 survey by the NEC Research Institute estimated that there were 320 million pages of information and entertainment on the Web, and it had increased to 800 million a year later, an increase of 250% in the number of web pages (Lawrence & Giles, 1998, 1999, as cited in Paik, 2001). Almost 45% of homes with children from ages 12 to 17 have access to the Internet (Horizon Media Research, 1999, as cited in National Institute on Media and the Family, 2002g), and 17 million youth in the age group use the Internet (Lenhart, Rainie, & Lewis, 2001).

Internet communication is highly varied and includes e-mail, news groups, chat rooms, and web pages. There are also electronic magazines, or e-zines, that have a huge distribution advantage over print (Everett-Green, 1997). With systems available that combine multimedia computers with large-screen TV sets, users can surf the Internet, play games, or watch TV all on the same receiver (Brockhouse, 1996).

Most Web users are fairly affluent, with an average household annual income over $80,000 (Vivian, 1997). Children who are growing up with computers and who use them with ease have become very familiar with the offerings on the Internet. Some say that counting the hundreds of thousands of information sources is impossible. "Call it the death of the Renaissance ideal: there is simply too much information to consume for anyone to be truly knowledgeable" (Chiose, 1996, p. C1) . Almost all parents and children agree that it helps with learning and with school work (Lenhart et al., 2001).

Uses and gratifications theory is useful here to look at what motivates users of the Internet, whether they use it for information or entertainment, and whether they use it ritualistically or instrumentally (Morris & Ogan, 1996). Census data from 1997 cited by Paik (2001) reported that children and adolescents used the Internet most frequently to find information on government, health, business, or educational information (76%). Fifty-seven percent used it for e-mail; 32% for chat rooms; 28% for information on news, weather, and sports; 5% for newsgroups; and 3% for taking courses (Paik, 2001). Both genders generally used the Internet for similar reasons except boys used it more than girls for news, weather, and sports information, and girls used it more than boys for e-mail (Paik, 2001). Others such as Lenhart et al. (2001) have reported significant gender differences in how the Internet is used and noted that experienced users use it differently from new users.

In the Lenhart et al. (2001) study, half of the adolescents said their use of the Internet improved their relationships with friends. About a third used it to make new friends, but there was less enthusiasm among older adolescents for its usefulness in making new friends, although making new casual contacts was easier. Nearly two thirds of them thought that use of the Internet reduced the time they spent with their families. Nearly 13 million of them use instant messaging to communicate with friends. Over half have more than one e-mail address, and about a fourth of them have pretended to be someone else when communicating online (Lenhart et al., 2001). Many lie about their age. Others find it easier to be their "true selves" online because there is more focus on intellect and personality than on physical appearance or style (Lenhart et al., 2001).

Adolescents do use the Web not only as a resource for school but for information about music and fashion, and many use it to get information about things they find difficult to talk about with others. A substantial number of adolescents seek health information from the Internet and most adolescents from all groups thought that having such information available via the Internet was valuable; few thought that the information was not reliable (Borzekowski & Rickert, 2001).

Valkenburg and Soeters (2001) studied 194 Dutch children, age 8 to 13, to explore their motives for using the Internet and their positive and negative experiences with it. They found that the most important motive was "affinity with computers"; the children liked to use them and were curious about what they could find. Information was second as a motive and entertainment third. Social interaction, either online or offline, was the least important motive, and children did not discuss their Internet activity with peers the way they do with television. Valkenburg and Soeters found that positive experiences with the Internet included computer games, viewing video clips or music, visiting entertainment sites, and getting information about animals. Negative experiences most often included a virus or computer crash, and violence and pornography.

> Clearly, youngsters are fully engaged in the electronic revolution. They enter online chat rooms that allow for anonymous exchanges of ideas and feelings. They also review and download information important to their schooling and access other websites for pleasure…. In addition to their peers, however, others with less friendly motives have also adapted to the medium…. Children and adolescents, in the process of maturation and naïve to adult experience, are legally protected against enter-

ing into contracts. However, they need to be warned about divulging personal information to strangers and following up anonymous exchanges with face-to-face meetings, and possibly cautioned about accessing material unsuitable for their age. (Kaliebe & Sondheimer, 2002, p. 211)

Valkenburg and Soeters (2001) also found age differences in the use of the Internet. Older children used it more for information than younger ones, perhaps for school work or maybe to get product/service information to guide their spending. Use of it for information versus entertainment was moderated by age. There was no difference for younger children in how often they used it for entertainment or information. This confirms earlier uses and gratifications research indicating that developmental level interacts with motives for using TV, and results cannot be interpreted without taking age into account (Valkenburg & Soeters, 2001).

Internet Advertising

Advertising is big business on the Web too. There has been a huge increase in the amount of advertising and shopping that occurs on the Internet, including Web sites directed at young children, many of which are supported by advertising and incorporate online shopping (Tarpley, 2001).

eShop Weekly (1999, as cited by National Institute on Media and the Family, 2002g) reported that two thirds of online teens between 13 and 18 have researched or bought products online, and over half of those between 5 and 17 surveyed have asked their parents to buy products seen on the Web. Children are attracted to Internet commercial sites because they are colorful and interesting, offer items the children recognize, and provide information in their attempt to build brand familiarity and loyalty (National Institute on Media and the Family, 2002g). By offering interactive games, chat rooms, or free downloads, they attract children and teens, and the line becomes blurred between information or educational content and advertising (National Institute on Media and the Family, 2002g). In a survey of Internet use by nearly 6,000 Canadian youth from age 9 to 17 (Media Awareness Network, 2001), 90% of the parents who responded wanted online advertising that is directed at children to be regulated (Media Awareness Network, 2003e).

Impact of the Internet

A number of difficult questions and issues arise when attempts are made to study what impact use of the Internet might have on users. According to Morris and Ogan (1996), credibility is more of a problem with the Internet, even whether "contributors" are who they say they are. It can be very difficult for users, child or adult, to distinguish between valid information and opinion or questionable information on the Internet. Morris and Ogan predicted that more emphasis will fall to users to judge the credibility of given sources.

The Internet is different from traditional gatekeepers of information who check facts, proofread, and review material to make sure that it is accurate. On the Internet, anyone can develop his or her own Web site and give opinions, and sometimes verification of the information on the Internet is very difficult if not impossible. The Media Awareness Network (2003c) has a program to help users evaluate information they get online and to help them avoid plagiarism.

Although the Internet does raise new social and interpersonal opportunities, there are also risks, and parents today are justifiably concerned. They recognize its huge informational advantage, but they also realize that it is used for entertainment as well, and it can take up many hours, most of which are spent in isolation from other family members. Consideration of possible addictive behavior and the effects of overuse of the Internet on social relationships and on psychological and emotional development is important too. Greater use of the Internet has been associated with less communication among family members, decreased size of social circles, and increased loneliness and depression (Kraut, Patterson, Lundmark, Kiesler, Mukopadhyay, & Scherlis, 1998, as cited in Tarpley, 2001). As with other media, parents need to monitor the extent and nature of their children's Internet use.

Parents are also concerned about the discussion groups their children use, about the pornographic content that is easily available to them, and about relationships they may form with strangers, especially when the online contacts lead to face-to-face meetings. Parks and Floyd (1996) noted that online personal relationships are fairly common (60% in their sample), and that was true across the board, not just in certain newsgroups. The more involved someone was in newsgroups, the more likely they were to develop relationships, and it seemed more a matter of experience than of personal or demographic variables (Parks & Floyd, 1996).

Parks and Floyd (1996) claimed that often, perhaps two thirds of the time, relationships that developed online expanded from computer-mediated communication to other kinds of contact such as by phone, mail, or face-to-face communications, and relationships that began online rarely stayed there. This finding is especially important regarding children and adolescents who lack experience. There is growing parental concern that relationships children form on the Internet can turn dangerous if carried over into real life, such as agreeing to meet someone they met on the Internet. Researchers in one study (Boyd, 2003) noted that certain groups are more vulnerable, including girls, older adolescents, troubled young individuals, and frequent users of the Web and chat rooms. Children and teens may be more vulnerable because they can access the Internet from the safety of their rooms and can misrepresent their age to try things out (Boyd, 2003).

Others have noted the way in which relationships on the Internet can interfere with or replace real-life relationships. The problems they pose are very different in many ways from real-life relationships because individuals who get involved with strangers on the Internet cannot be sure that even age or other physical characteristics of the person with whom they are relating are true. The line between virtual reality and real life can easily be crossed.

In interviews with a sample of 1,501 youths between 10 and 17 who regularly used the Internet, approximately 1 in 5, or 20%, were exposed to unwanted sexual material and solicitations during the previous year, and 1 in 4 came across explicit sexual material inadvertently (National Coalition for the Protection of Children and Families, 2003). Almost a third of children between 10 and 17 in homes with a computer had seen a pornographic Web site (National Public Radio, 1999). According to NetValue, over a fourth of those under 17, or 3 million underage children, had visited an adult Web site, and just over 20% were under 14 ("NetValue Report," 2000). In 1998, a fourth of the roughly 700 new cases of online pedophilia opened for investigation by the FBI dealt with predators attempting to get minor children to meet with them (Nordland & Bartholet, 2001). Moreover, software to filter the Internet failed to block out 20% of sites seen as objectionable (*Consumer Reports* as cited in Jesdanun, 2001). Old ideas about senders of messages and receivers are not adequate to study the Internet, and we need to look at the interactivity and interchangeability involved (Morris & Ogan, 1996).

An added factor is the amount of information people can get about others online. Johnson (2003) reported that Google™ currently can access 4 billion documents on the Web, and individuals have no control over what goes there. Now individuals can even "google" prospective escorts by entering their names into the Google search engine and finding out every last detail about the person before dating him or her. There have also been reports of girls planting damaging information about former partners or publishing other material on the Web (Johnson, 2003).

COMPUTERS IN SCHOOLS

Computers can facilitate learning immeasurably in the classroom. They are interactive, allow students to work at their own pace, provide access to unlimited information, and allow simulation and graphic depictions of many complex concepts or events. They can also improve writing and editing skills by making rewriting and revising much easier.

Lepper and Gurtner (1989) described the uses or purposes that could be made of computers: as tutor, as a medium for experiential learning (e.g., learning skills not usually taught in the regular curriculum and complex simulations), as a multipurpose tool for creative work and expression (e.g., spell check, editing, writing skills), and as a motivator making learning more enjoyable and facilitating cooperative work. Because of advances in word processing, more children now have access to inexpensive quality publishing tools (Kaliebe & Sondheimer, 2002). Subrahmanyam, Greenfield, et al. (2001) found a positive relation between computer use and academic performance. Students used the computer for word processing and the Web to get information for class projects, and parents generally saw it as an educational resource (Subrahmanyam, Greenfield, et al., 2001).

Technology can also be used to enhance learning in the classroom by providing the opportunity to develop new approaches to teaching (Nickerson, 1995). Technology allows exploration of various aspects of the world through simulation and helps identify misconceptions, it can facilitate active learning and discovery, and it can provide visual representations of processes that occur, such as a supernova explosion, at different times and in different levels of detail controlled by the user, providing a wide range of information sources and tools, all within a non-threatening environment (Nickerson, 1995).

Enthusiastic proponents of computers in school praise the impact they can have. In the fall of 2002, every Grade 7 student in Maine received a laptop computer along with the usual school supplies and books (Atkin, 2002). The government provided 15,000 Apple® iBook computers with wireless high-speed Internet access. Supporters said that after only a month or so, the teacher–student experience was being fundamentally altered. Maine Governor Angus King was quoted as saying that his laptop initiative was "way beyond anyone's expectations.... The one-to-one relationship of this incredible tool has exploded the educational process in Maine. Teachers who were opponents are now proponents. Parents are involved. The students are engaged" (Atkin, 2002, p. F7). At one school, the enthusiasm prompted the posting of a sign that read "Students are reminded that they must eat lunch" (Atkin, 2002).

When a similar project was undertaken at Brewer Middle School in Brewer, New Brunswick, Canada, a school with a broad cross-section of students from affluent to lower income families, all of the students in Grades 6, 7, and 8 were given laptop computers (Atkin, 2002). The principal reported that the largest group that was positively affected were the at-risk students, and many who had not "bought into" school before now did. The computers had also improved attendance. Teachers enthused about their ability to correct and edit student writing, monitor student activity on their own screen, and freeze student machines when the class's attention was needed. The biggest advantage, however, was Internet access, and a teacher could refer students to various Web sites related to a current topic under discussion (Atkin, 2002).

Some who are less enthusiastic about computers in the schools worry that they will result in a homogenization of classroom experiences, more regimentation, less social interaction with peers and guidance from teachers, undue influence in shaping the curriculum, and perhaps insufficient transfer of learning to other areas in which basic skills will not be strong enough to deal with complex problems in the future (Santrock & Yussen, 1992). A more recent report (Stanger, 1998), however, indicated that children from homes with computers spend more time with school work and reading newspapers and less time watching videos than children without computers, although computer access did not seem to affect the amount of time they spend playing video games or reading books.

Some teachers have begun to complain that electronic chats going on in the classroom are a downside to the use of computers there. They are concerned that although a computer can be a solid educational tool, it can also distract some students or even result in cheating. Now many schools have begun to crack down on instant messaging, the "new plaything among teens" (Alphonso, 2003, p. A3). Some disable the software for it or limit when it can be used. Others use it like a carrot, allowing students to use it when they have demonstrated that they need it and are responsible. There is even software available that allows teachers to monitor the screens of their students (Alphonso, 2003).

NEW INITIATIVES

One interesting program, The Fifth Dimension, is an activity system that includes electronic and nonelectronic games and activities. The program builds cognitive and social skills by offering tasks that children must master that are set in a mix of games and activities including education, social interaction with peers, play, and use of computer games and educational software (Subrahmanyam, Kraut, Greenfield, & Gross, 2001). It consists of after school programs located in recreation centers, schools, clubs, and YMCA and YWCAs in a number of countries. The software contains academic subject matter, and there is also a nonelectronic component with board games and crafts. The positive results from the program included advances in computer knowledge and gains in academic skills and achievement tests and in following directions, demonstrating that the maximum positive influence of these activities come when they are part of a total constructive, socially mediated environment (Subrahmanyam, Kraut, et al., 2001).

One program designed to close the gender gap in computer interest and competency is a computer science seminar for adolescent young women at the University of Waterloo in Ontario, Canada (Weidner, 2003). With a million dollar donation from Imperial Oil, Grade 9 and 10 girls are provided with a week-long computer science program that combines hands-on work such as taking a computer apart, programming, and wiring digital hardware, with lectures. They also explore university-level content such as theory, information retrieval, and networks, and they learn about the field before they make career decisions. The enthusiastic participants learn quickly about computers and about the career opportunities that open up with those skills, careers they had never heard about. This type of encouragement of adolescent girls became a priority when the number of women at the University of Waterloo who were pursuing degrees in computer science dropped substantially from 33% in the mid-1980s to 15% in 2003 (Weidner, 2003) .

SUMMARY

Children use computers primarily for information or for entertainment, although there clearly is overlap between those two uses. Children and adolescents, for example, may use information seeking on the Internet as a form of entertainment, or they may use entertainment media to get information about the world. The Internet is used frequently to obtain information, and it is heavily used for educational purposes such as research and school projects. There are gender, age, and socioeconomic differences in the use of the Internet and in children's motivations for using it. Children and adolescents have reported both positive and negative experiences with the Internet, and parents are concerned about online chat rooms, relationships that can develop, and exposure to unwanted material such as pornography.

Computers in the schools facilitate learning immeasurably and can provide unique learning experiences. Some critics worry, however, about their possible undue influence and decreases in the amount of time that will be spent on traditional academic activities and pursuits. Used reasonably, however, they are a strong supplement to the school learning environment.

DISCUSSION QUESTIONS

1. What age and gender differences would be especially predictive of Internet use and activity?
2. Discuss the positive and negative effects of having computers available and used extensively in schools. How would these differ from effects of their use at home?
3. What differential effect is Internet advertising likely to have on children and adolescents? What characteristics of the advertising make it attractive to them?

Technologies for Entertainment

Technologies for Entertainment

Although the technologies discussed in this chapter are focused on media that children and adolescents use primarily for entertainment, users also derive significant amounts of information from them that affect their developing attitudes and beliefs. In this chapter, we will take a look at the kinds of content involved in these media options and their impact on the children and adolescents who use them.

VCRs, DVDs, AND CABLE

The rapid increase in the number of VCRs and DVDs as well as cable has significantly increased the options and range of content available to children and adolescents. The new technologies mean access to more channels and more kinds of programs on cable, some considered to be positive (e.g., educational) and some negative (e.g., graphic violence). Children who have access to VCRs, DVDs, and cable are exposed to content that is not available on commercial television, including mature themes, violence, and graphic sexual content.

With so many more channels and program variety, users have unprecedented choice, or so it seems. Some warn, however, that choice in itself does not guarantee quality. As Feldman (1994) put it, "Television choice is sold to us with surprisingly little reference to what is to be chosen. There is far more talk about 500 channel television sets and direct broadcast satellites than there is about the actual choices they will offer. It is assumed that choice itself is a sufficient guarantee of quality" (p. 29).

Feldman (1994) went on to note that many of the channels offer significant amounts of repetition and commercialism. Morgan and Shanahan (1991) noted that society looks at media diversity in terms of number of channels rather than content and that technological changes may bring superficial changes in how people use media but are not likely to decrease the central role of television. "All this suggests that traditional messages can be transmitted in nontraditional ways with decidedly traditional results" (Morgan & Shanahan, 1991, p. 134).

A new 24-hour cable channel offers a new way for teens to learn about and use media, however. Varsity TV (VTV) is a network of American high schools as "affiliates" with students as producers ("Varsity TV," 2003). Billed as a "network exclusively by, for, and about teen life," it is aiming at 36 million adolescents in several media, including cable, video on demand, and a Web site. Each has content from other sources but its main appeal is from the collection of more than 20,000 videos created by do-it-yourselfers with camcorders at 1,900 affiliated schools. Videos include sports, music, news, drama, and animation that reflect the teens' lives. Its developer, Joe Shults, started VTV in response to teen complaints that they felt portrayed poorly by the media and that "nothing on TV speaks to us." VTV focuses on mainstream teens rather than celebrities or trendsetters. The teens also learn about TV in the process and how it can mislead, making it an effective media literacy vehicle as well. Estimates are that the cable channel will be available to about 12 million homes by the end of 2004 ("Varsity TV," 2003).

Some have suggested that VCRs and specialty channels have in fact contributed to decreasing amounts of viewing time by children and adolescents (Beauchesne, 1994), but this seems due more to a concurrent increase in the use of other media. A reported 6% drop in children's overall viewing of TV on Saturday mornings and weekday afternoons could be attributed to the fact that they were watching videos or playing computer games instead (Stead, 1997).

Lindlof and Meyer (1998) compared VCRs to microwaves in that they are valuable even though they are used in a more limited way than had been expected. For example, VCRs are used primarily to simply play tapes rather than time shifting, which is like a microwave used for simply heating food rather than preparing whole meals for a family. Morgan and Shanahan (1991) found that overall, VCR use tends to strengthen television's effects and cultivation because although there is more diversity, it is not necessarily incorporated by all viewers. Heavy viewers concentrated on their favorite programs and did not really use the greater diversity (Dobrow, 1990).

VCRs are quickly being replaced by digital versions that allow users to create their own replays, take breaks without missing anything, and fast forward through advertising (Tarpley, 2001). Furthermore, personal video recorders can "learn" an individual's preferences and then automatically record any programs that correspond to those (Tarpley, 2001). The digital revolution means that viewers can be more selective in their choice of programs and can choose from a much wider selection, they can edit the content more easily, they can download huge amounts of material from the Internet onto compact disks (CDs), and they can store and transport them more easily. The speed with which DVDs have taken over the market is testimony to the fact that they are more compact, provide more information and entertainment, and are highly portable.

In Canada, it took only 5 years to move from 1% of households having at least one DVD player in 1998 to nearly half (48%) having one in 2003, whereas CD players, PCs, and VCRs took about 12 years each to penetrate the market to the same degree (Damsell, 2003). Individuals between 12 and 24, the so-called Generation Y, spend more than 30% of TV time playing DVDs, and in 2002, U.S. consumers spent $12.1 billion on DVDs (Damsell, 2003). There is even a booming market of DVDs and videotapes aimed at infants from 1 to 18 months of age (Rideout et al., 2003).

The use of VCRs and DVDs also allows for changes in who controls a child's viewing, and they enhance viewer selectivity. A steady increase in the use of VCRs and DVDs gives parents less control over their older children's viewing choices and patterns, but it can actually allow parents of younger children greater control. Parents of young children can determine which programs will be viewed, and videotaping helps them control when and for how long a child watches television.

VCRs appear to make little difference in parental mediation, however, and VCR and DVD use in the family is likely to be part of a much broader and more complex context of parental values and competence, characteristics of the children, and activity patterns in the home. The VCR has some impact on viewing times and viewing frequencies, but generally its impact on families' more basic functioning and well-being is modest or small (Lindlof & Shatzer, 1990).

MUSIC VIDEOS

Preadolescents and adolescents listen to music for 3 to 4 hours a day, including CDs, radio, and music videos (Roberts & Christenson, 2001). They consider musicians heroes more frequently than athletes and say they are influenced more by them than by religion or books ("Popular Music's Influence," 1999, as cited in National Institute on Media and the Family, 2002j).

MTV, 20 years old in 2001, has had a significant effect on how TV programs and advertising are produced and has affected programming in all types of media (National Institute on Media and the Family, 2001i). MTV reaches 350 million households globally (PBS On-line, 2001, as cited in National Institute on Media and the Family, 2002i) and is watched by about three fourths of youth of both genders in the 12 to 19 age group (Rich, 1998, as cited in National Institute on Media and the Family, 2002i). It is the most frequently watched cable channel for college students and is becoming the favorite of much younger 9- to 11-year-olds, introducing them to the most undesirable elements of the "grown-up" world, including abuse of women, sexism, racism, and bigotry (Hattemer & Showers, 1995a), as well as violence and casual sex.

Content and Use of Music Videos

Attractive and aggressive role models appear in 80% of the violent videos, and 25% involve tobacco or alcohol use (DuRant, Rich, et al., 1997; DuRant, Rome, et al., 1997; Rich, Woods, Goodman, Emans, & DuRant, 1998). There is also significant exposure to violence and carrying weapons that is glamorized on music videos (DuRant, Rich, et al., 1997). MTV, for example, has at least one violent ocurrence in over half of its videos, a much higher rate than commercial television (Donnerstein et al., 1994).

By 1998, Rich et al. reported that three fourths of the music videos they analyzed portrayed individuals engaged in overt violence, with an average of six violent acts per video with violence. There was an interaction effect for gender and race, with gender differences in how Blacks and Whites were portrayed. Although about three fourths of both White females and Black males were portrayed as victims, males were more than three times as likely to be shown as aggressors, with Black males overrepresented in that group and White males underrepresented compared with their actual numbers in the U.S. population.

There is some disagreement in the literature about the amount of violence in music videos as compared with prime-time television, however. Comstock and Scharrer (1999), for example, said that violence in music videos, at an average rate of 1½ violent acts per video, exceeds or is higher than for prime-time TV. They concluded that MTV is an especially violent channel, but it is largely confined to specific genres and videos.

Smith and Boyson (2002), on the other hand, reported a lower incidence of violence overall in music videos (15%) than in other programs, movies, or children's shows. They also found significant differences in the prevalence and type of violence across channels and genres of music, including rap, heavy metal, contemporary, rhythm and blues, and rock, which would help to explain discrepancies among studies. According to Smith and Boyson, not all channels or types of music videos pose the same level of risk for viewers. Some channels such as Black Entertainment Television (BET) presented violence in ways that increase the likelihood of effect on viewers such as showing repeated violence, unpunished acts, and more violence by Blacks. This increases the risk for African American viewers who would be more likely to identify with and emulate those individuals. BET also showed less gun violence and less gore, however, which would be expected to lower the risk of harmful effects. MTV, on the other hand, more often showed attractive characters engaging in violent behavior, and the violence was more often to be extensive and bloody and most likely to be rewarded or punished. It was also least likely to show violence using natural means, like kicking, that could more easily be imitated by younger viewers (Smith & Boyson, 2002).

The violence and its likely effect on viewers also varied by genre. Rap, for example, was more likely to depict violence by Black adults, which increases the likelihood of African American viewers learning aggression or fear. Rap was also more likely to show violence that would increase the likelihood of aggression such as showing justified violence, repeated violence, and violence that went unpunished. Rock, on the other hand, showed predominantly White characters involved in violence and thus raised the risk for White viewers. Rhythm and blues was in the middle on many of the features (Smith & Boyson, 2002). Thus, different channels and different genres present different risks to different sets of viewers.

On the other hand, Zillmann et al. (1995) found no strong social effects on African American adolescents of radical political rap, but it made White students more tolerant and compassionate and more motivated to support racial harmony initiatives and oppose White supremacy views. One news director has started using the language of music videos to broadcast news in the hope of attracting younger audiences with short attention spans (Gill, 2003). The likelihood that this would further blur the distinction between reality and fiction, especially for young viewers, seems high.

According to Christenson and Roberts (1998), children and adolescents use music for many reasons. These include affective uses that are usually solitary (to escape, to fill time, ease tension or drudgery of some tasks), more social uses (to avoid loneliness, help make conversation, enliven parties), or to intensify or change their moods (Christenson & Roberts, 1998). There were also gender differences in how music is used; boys use it more often to get energized and girls to change or enhance moods (Christenson & Roberts, 1998).

Impact of Music Videos

According to some research, even modest viewing of music videos leads to significant exposure to depictions of alcohol and tobacco use that are glamorized, alcohol use that is linked with sexuality, and violence and weapons (National Institute on Media and the Family, 2002i). The impact of the lyrics is greater when they are acted out in a story, and the videos appear to contribute to adolescents' desensitization to violence. Finally, because it is portrayed by music video stars, it is made to seem more normal and acceptable (National Institute on Media and the Family, 2002i). A longitudinal study (Robinson, Chen, & Killen, 1998) revealed a positive association between music video and TV viewing and consumption of alcohol by teens. Rock videos are likely to be as influential as other TV programs, maybe more so because of their slick and addictive quality, their rhythms, and their appeal for teens and preteens with VCRs (Lefrancois, 1992).

An American Psychological Association study involving 500 college students found that violent lyrics, even humorous ones, increased aggression-related emotions and thoughts and could indirectly create a more hostile social environment ("Violent Music," 2003). Students were more likely to make aggressive interpretations of ambiguous words and increased the rate at which they read aggressive words compared with nonaggressive ones. This contributed to an escalation of antisocial interactions, although the researchers did say that these effects might be short-term.

In one study (Johnson, Jackson, & Gatto, 1995), African American males were exposed to violent rap music videos, nonviolent rap music videos, and music (control) videos. They were then asked to interpret a couple of vignettes: one with violence and one with academic pursuits. Those who had watched violent videos were more accepting of using violence than the other two groups. When controls were compared with participants exposed to the violent material, the latter group indicated greater likelihood that they would engage in violence, expressed more acceptance of violence against women, and were less likely to think that someone pursuing academics would achieve his goals (Johnson et al., 1995). Exposure clearly affected participants' attitudes and perceptions. The nonviolent videos did not affect ideas about the use of violence but did affect perceptions of education. Johnson et al. concluded that it is likely that repeated exposure activates the violence construct and increases the likelihood that it will be used to process information. The association of violence with a positive outcome may lead to more acceptance of violence and the idea that more education is unnecessary.

What effects are associated with listening to a lot of heavy metal music? Studies have shown that a preference for heavy metal music is correlated with greater drug use and casual sex, conflict with parents, problems at school, and other problems (Roberts & Christenson, 2001). In addition, Roberts and Christenson noted that violent and depressive lyrics may increase the risk for violence or suicide in those youths who are already suicidal, alienated, depressed or have drug, alcohol, and family problems. Most heavy metal fans are not at risk or on drugs, depressed, or failing in school. Troubled youths who are alienated from the mainstream school culture, use drugs, or are in trouble with the law, however, are very likely to gravitate toward heavy metal. In other words, there is more of a "troubled youth syndrome" than a "heavy metal syndrome" (Roberts & Christenson, 2001).

Arnett (1991) compared adolescents who liked heavy metal music with those who did not on various outcome measures, especially reckless behavior. Both genders who liked the music were distinct from their peers in a number of ways including being higher in sensation seeking and being more self-assured regarding dating and sexuality. Boys who liked heavy metal music reported more frequent reckless behavior including sexual behavior, drug use, a higher rate of drunk driving, and less satisfaction with family relationships. Girls who liked it reported more reckless behavior in the areas of sexual behavior, shoplifting, drugs, vandalism, and low self-esteem. Arnett reported that the hypothesis that adolescents who liked the music may have been rejected socially and looked to heavy metal music for a different social group was not confirmed here. The participants were not more awkward socially generally or with the opposite sex, and Arnett noted that there is a need to look at the more general socialization of adolescents in contemporary life.

In a study of the cognitive effects of music videos and rock music lyrics, Greenfield, Bruzzone, and Koyamatsu (1987) found that although understanding of lyrics increased with age, they were often poorly understood, especially by younger children who lack experience and knowledge and are at a concrete level of cognitive development. Music videos were enjoyed less than songs alone and had a negative impact on imagination. Songs alone evoked more feelings than those in music videos (Greenfield et al., 1987).

Possible hearing loss is also a concern. Regular sustained exposure to sound that hits 90 to 95 dB can cause permanent hearing damage, and the average for rock concerts is between 110 and 120 dB, although they can peak at 150 dB. The average setting for a Walkman is 94 dB (National Institute on Media and the Family, 2002i).

COMPUTER AND VIDEO GAMES

Although the first games were introduced in the 1970s, studies of their impact on health, school achievement, personality, and other variables, began in the 1980s (Funk & Buckman, 1996). In the early 1990s, with the growth of CD technology, more realistic CD-ROM games and other software appeared on the market (Paik, 2001). Violent games also took hold in the 1990s with games like Mortal Kombat whose chief aim is to hurt, maim, or kill opponents (C. Anderson & Bushman, 2001).

Video games include arcade games, games for systems such as Nintendo® and Sega®, stand-alone games, or interactive toys; computer games include those either downloaded from or played on a computer (Subrahmanyam, Kraut, et al., 2001).

Video game sales were projected to reach $8 billion in sales by 2001, with over 280 million units sold in 2000 alone, and 60% of all Americans are estimated to play video games regularly (Children Now, 2001). Worldwide annual sales of video games reached $20 billion (Cohen, 2000, as cited in National Institute on Media and the Family, 2002d), and electronic games are especially important in boys' lives (Subrahmanyam, Kraut, et al., 2001). Seventy percent of the M rated games (rated for mature audiences, with more intense violence, mature sexual themes, and profanity) were targeted to children under 17, and unaccompanied children between 13 and 16 were able to buy them 85% of the time (Federal Trade Commission, 2000, as cited in National Institute on Media and the Family, 2002e). Individuals in households with income under $35,000 a year spend 50% more time playing these games than those with income over $74,000 ("Video Games," 2003).

According to Funk and Buckman (1996), research on electronic games typically uses similar strategies to those evaluating TV's effects such as modeling effects. Although computer and video games offer opportunities for observational learning as does television, the games add an interactive dimension that may intensify their impact. Many of the concerns about children and adolescents' use of violent video games have centered on the possibility that the users would imitate some of that violent behavior in real life and become more aggressive or violent. Whether or not the content is modeled or imitated, however, depends on many other factors including why users are playing and what needs the game playing satisfies and how the game content fits in with the rest of their thoughts, beliefs, attitudes, and behavior. New research has looked at possible effects of game playing from a uses and gratifications perspective and from a cognitive-neo-associationist perspective.

In a recent series of studies that looked at the effects of game-playing from a uses and gratifications perspective, for example, Sherry and his colleagues

(Sherry, 2001; Sherry, deSouza, Greenberg, & Lachlan, 2003; Sherry, Holmstrom, Binns, Greenberg, & Lachlan, 2003; Sherry, Lucas, Rechsteiner, Brooks, & Wilson, 2001) focused on three main components of the game-playing experience: amount of time spent playing, genre preference in choice of games to play, and motives or reasons for playing. Gender, age cohort, and developmental differences in these three components were studied, and many interesting and provocative findings and questions emerged.

In one study, Sherry et al. (2001) surveyed over 500 young adults on how much they played games, which types of games they preferred, and what uses and gratifications they sought from their game playing. As Sherry et al. (2001) pointed out, this age cohort reflected the first generation to grow up with access to computer games and the first to develop long-term patterns of game use. Sherry et al. (2001) found that uses and gratifications were strong predictors of the players' use of games and their genre preferences. Individuals who spent the most hours playing more often reported playing for diversion and social interaction. They were not isolated, solitary players as is often assumed, and they did not choose games to avoid interaction with others. Rather, their diversion involved others in social interaction. Although this study involved young adults, another one by Sherry, de Souza, et al. (2003) found socially oriented motives to be important in adolescents as well.

Uses and gratifications were associated with preference for various genre clusters, and game types were related to specific reasons for playing. Playing to beat the game, for example, was associated with traditional games like puzzles and trivia and likely to be played alone, whereas the high-action games were preferred by those who enjoyed arousal. Imagination games and role-playing games were preferred by those who played games to engage in fantasy (Sherry et al., 2001).

Sherry et al. (2001) suggested that this pattern of game use is more active and purposeful than the use of television because of the costs involved and the need to purchase individual games, which would make it less likely that players would use game content that was not sure to give them the gratification they were looking for.

Gender Differences

Researchers have reported gender differences in the use of video entertainment, including music videos, video games, and videocassettes (Kubey & Larson, 1990) and in the way in which males and females are represented. For boys in Kubey and Larson's study, use of these media was related to higher reported arousal and more positive affect than there was with reading, watching television, or listening to popular music. Girls showed lower arousal and affect relative to boys, especially for music videos and video games. Kubey and Larson used the ESM that elicits not only time spent but more information regarding viewers' subjective experience of various activities that can help to evaluate the assumptions of uses and gratifications theory and assess whether viewers are active or passive.

Funk and Buckman (1996) also found significant gender differences in game habits and in self-perceptions. Boys spent more time playing and preferred more violent games; for girls, spending more time with games was associated with lower self-esteem. Funk and Buckman suggested that lack of attention to gender may have obscured differences in some past studies. They found no evidence that playing games leads to major adjustment problems for most players and no significant relationship between preference for violent games and self-concept.

According to Haddon (1993), games in arcades became a collective leisure activity for young males but not for girls. Girls tended to play them at home or with friends, but their use of them was not the same as that of boys who also talked about them and exchanged them. Girls tended to play whatever was available, which was often determined by boys.

A Children Now (2001) study reported that although video games are sometimes described as "designed 'by boys for boys,'" 45% of computer and video game players are girls. Girls like to play but they appreciate different features such as creative possibilities, less violence, and a reality-based environment. Based on this research, Children Now (2001) developed a 13-point "girl-friendly" scale to see how many of the games had features that appealed to girls. Very few did. Such scarcity of girl-friendly material is important because it may lead girls to think that computers and games are not acceptable for them, it ignores their potential to be an important segment of that market, and it causes them to miss out on the improved computer literacy that results from their use (Children Now, 2001). If playing helps improve relatively weak spatial skills as Subrahmanyam and Greenfield (1994) reported, girls presumably could perhaps improve their skills, but they tend to play less because they are less attracted to most of the games available to them.

Pronounced gender differences in patterns of preference for games and in the hours of use have also emerged (Sherry, Holmstrom, et al., 2003). Sherry, Holmstrom, et al. reported that males played about twice as much as females within and across age groups. Females preferred quieter games with an emphasis on intellectual challenge such as the classic board games like Monopoly®, trivia games, quiz games like Jeopardy!®, and puzzle games like FreeCell® or Tetris®. Males preferred games that require fast reactions, flashy graphics, and more violence such as fighters, action and adventure, and sports games. They preferred fantasy games and games that require strategy. These types of games usually take longer to play. They often have multiple levels and can take weeks, unlike card games like Solitaire or puzzle games like FreeCell that take much less time, a fact that accounts for gender differences in time spent playing them (Sherry, Holmstrom, et al., 2003). Sherry, Holmstrom, et al. suggested that these preferences are consistent with early socialization pressures, and both girls and boys were very sensitive to which were "boy games" and which were "girl games." Sherry, Holmstrom, et al. also suggested, however, that there was more to these differences than socialization, important as that is.

Recent data (Rideout et al., 2003) revealed that gender differences in game playing appear as early as 4 to 6 years of age when boys are more likely to play games and they play for longer periods of time. Rideout et al. found that three times as many boys as girls in that age group play video games in a typical day, and nearly five times as many boys as girls play them every day.

Sherry, Holmstrom, et al. (2003) noted that although there are many games that involve strategy, fantasy role playing, and action and adventure that are not violent, they still do not seem to appeal to girls. Conversely, boys enjoy some nonviolent games such as sports and racing games, but they do not seem to like other nonviolent games such as card games or trivia games, so perhaps it is the form of the game rather than the content that provides the attraction (Sherry, Holmstrom, et al., 2003).

The main motivation for playing games for all age and gender groups, except for eighth-grade boys, was for the challenge, and respondents liked challenge and feelings of mastery. Sherry, Holmstrom, et al. (2003) said they would expect cognitive ability to be a predictor of game preferences and the differences in preferences may be related to which genres boys and girls can master more easily. They noted, for example, that there are gender differences in problem-solving skills. Males do better with three-dimensional object rotation and motor skills directed at targets such as guiding projectiles. These are the skills needed to excel at the games males prefer (like scoring in soccer or hockey in sports games or moving through 3-dimensional space in shooter games). Females, on the other hand, are better at verbal fluency and memory, matching, and remembering displaced objects, skills that serve them well in card games such as Solitaire, trivia games, or puzzle games such as FreeCell (Sherry, Holmstrom, et al., 2003).

According to Sherry, Holmstrom, et al. (2003), these differences in game play are important because they are related to later high-paying, high-tech job opportunities that are greater for boys because they spend more time with games and computers. They urged development of games that will give girls the same feelings of mastery, but the games need to be more substantial to do so. Examples would be games that tap into their verbal and memory skills, that engage them for longer, that require more knowledge of technology, and that are appealing to girls. Currently, according to Sherry, Holmstrom, et al., trivial games lead to trivial amounts of involvement with technology. Perhaps girls would like action and adventure games and enjoy more feelings of mastery if the games tapped into their cognitive strengths.

Games with appeal for girls are not easy to find. Girls are not generally interested in the violent games boys like, but many of those targeted to girls promote stereotypic interests like fashion and makeup (Media Awareness Network, 2003f). The Media Awareness Network noted the need for more creative games that require interaction, cooperation, and strategic and problem-solving skills.

Developmental Differences

Children at different developmental stages also differ in their motives for playing video games, in the types of games they prefer, and in the amount of time they spend playing them (Sherry, de Souza, et al., 2003). Sherry, de Souza, et al. found that uses and gratifications predictors for heavy use of games differed among the three age groups they studied: fifth graders, eighth graders, and college students. These three groups represent preadolescent, adolescent, and young adult stages of cognitive and social development. There was a gradual increase in the amount of time spent playing games between fifth and eighth grade, after which there was a dramatic decrease. Young adults played games for about half the amount of time they spent with them in eighth grade, a trend that mirrors reports of television viewing peaking at around eighth grade. Sherry, de Souza, et al. (2003) suggested that one reason for these findings might be that fifth graders' cognitive skills are less highly developed than those of eighth graders, making complex games harder for them to play.

There was a small effect size with a decrease in preference for physical enactment and imagination and an increase in interest in traditional games. Children in fifth grade preferred physical enactment and imagination games. This preference corresponds with their two top motives for using video games—challenge and fantasy—which are provided by the games they prefer, and there is less fantasy in more traditional games. Strategy games rated lowest, perhaps because of the cognitive skills and demands involved, or they may pose challenges that do not appeal to fifth graders (Sherry, de Souza, et al., 2003).

The most popular games with eighth graders were action and adventure and speed games that allow them to do things they cannot do in real life. Strategy games were also popular with them, supporting the suggestion that children's levels of cognitive development are an important factor in their media choices. College students preferred traditional games and liked imagination ones the least, perhaps because traditional games take less time, the rules are already known, and they are available on PCs (Sherry, de Souza, et al., 2003).

Sherry, de Souza, et al. (2003) also discovered differences in motives among the three age groups. Fifth graders played for challenge and fantasy, but as they got into adolescence, they started to play games for competition and social interaction, more socially oriented motives consistent with theories of social development. Sherry, de Souza, et al. suggested that game playing may be a nonthreatening way for them to interact with peers. In college, users once again played for challenge and fantasy, which are more personal motives.

Motivation among heavy users, however, was different. Both adolescent and college age heavy users used games more for diversion, suggesting that perhaps heavy users shift from purposeful use of games toward more ritualistic use (Sherry, de Souza, et al., 2003). According to Sherry, de Souza, et al., adolescents may use games as a means of escaping adult responsibility. Although appropriate for young adolescents, such withdrawal into a fantasy world in late adolescence may signal bigger socialization problems (Sherry, de Souza, et al., 2003).

Realism did not predict heavy game play in any of the age groups, nor was it a popular reason for playing. According to Sherry, de Souza, et al. (2003), this has important theoretical implications for the debate over video game violence. Because games were used primarily for challenge, these results do not support a modeling explanation or a use of games to learn about the real world. Sherry, de Souza, et al. concluded that adolescents have a different cognitive relation with games than they do with TV. This does not mean that games do not have effects but that the effects do not likely come through learning and imitation. According to Sherry, de Souza, et al., games could have effects through activation of aggression-related schemas (C. Anderson & Bushman, 2001), priming of aggression-related networks (Berkowitz & Rogers, 1986), or general arousal (Tannenbaum & Zillmann, 1975, as cited in Sherry, de Souza, et al., 2003), or there may be a cathartic component to game playing that needs further study. In any case, effects may be likely even though users do not think the games reflect the real world and do not use them to learn behavior (Sherry, de Souza, et al., 2003).

Effects of Game Playing

Positive Effects.   According to The National Institute on Media and the Family (2002e), video game playing has both positive and negative effects. Positive effects include introducing children to information and computer technology, providing practice in following instructions, some practice in logic, problem solving, and fine motor coordination, providing occasions for adults and children to play together, and providing entertainment. Several studies now also confirm the improvement in some spatial and attentional skills as a result of playing computer games (Subrahmanyam, Kraut, Greenfield, & Gross, 2000; Subrahmanyam, Kraut, et al., 2001). Playing electronic games provides the "'training wheels' for computer literacy" (Subrahmanyam, Kraut, et al., 2001, p. 96). Researchers have found that playing games helps to improve spatial visualization skills and performance and visual attention (Okagaki & Frensch, 1994; Subrahmanyam & Greenfield, 1994; Subrahmanyam, Kraut, et al., 2001), manual dexterity, and ease with electronic equipment (Kaliebe & Sondheimer, 2002), although there are gender differences. Subrahmanyam and Greenfield (1994), for example, found boys' spatial skills to be better than those of girls in Grade 5. After practice on action video games or computer word games, the action games were more effective than the word games in improving spatial skills on posttest. The greatest effect was on children whose starting spatial skills were relatively poor, and practice did improve relatively weak skills.

A study by researchers at the University of Rochester found that individuals who played action-packed games such as Grand Theft Auto III® or Counter-Strike® regularly showed better visual skills ("Some Video Games," 2003). They were better able to keep track of objects that appeared simultaneously and to process rapidly changing visual information. The researchers also found that individuals who did not ordinarily play the games but were trained to do so developed enhanced visual/perceptual skills, ruling out the possibility that their previous findings were simply due to people with better visual skills being drawn to video games.

The most popular games, then, may lead to increases in specific information-processing skills including visual/spatial skills and the development of strategies for divided attention in keeping track of multiple events on a screen; they have in fact changed the emphasis from verbal to visual skills (Subrahmanyam, Kraut, et al., 2001). If such a shift has occurred, girls would be at a disadvantage because of their typically stronger verbal skills.

Negative Effects.   Although there may be some benefits to video games such as improved visual attention, spatial skills, computer skills, and academic performance with educational games, a common view is that there is much more evidence to suggest an association between game playing and unhealthy results including loneliness and isolation, obesity, increased aggression, and maintenance of gender stereotypes (Children Now, 2001a). Negative effects also include possible social isolation with overdependence on games, practicing violence that may lead to more aggressive behavior than simply watching TV, and displacing time that could be spent on other activities such as reading and playing with friends (National Institute on Media and the Family, 2002e). Other negative effects include the development of an environment of violence and making violence necessary to win; antisocial themes such as irresponsible sex, gender bias, or stereotypes; and blurring of fantasy and reality (National Institute on Media and the Family, 2002e). A great diversity of sources sends similar messages that reinforce the original message, and popular video games show violence as a problem-solving technique (Dietz, 1998).

Many feel that because of their interactivity, games may have a stronger influence on children's beliefs, attitudes, and behaviors than other forms of media (Children Now, 2001a). Specific features of some of the newer games may increase the risk of negative effects on players because they feature increasing levels of difficulty and violence, and they can be customized by inserting images of real people and places to make them more realistic (Kaiser Family Foundation, 2002a). There is also concern about the growing trend toward the marketing of violence in the form of action figures and advertising for violent games (Oldberg, 1998, as cited in Subrahmanyam, Kraut, et. al., 2001).

Games and Aggression

There have been fairly consistent findings of a relation between playing violent video games and behaving aggressively. C. Anderson and Bushman's (2001) general aggression model (GAM) includes three routes to aggressive behavior: cognitive, aggressive affect, and arousal. C. Anderson and Bushman noted that the cognitive route is the only one specifically related to the violent content of video games. Aggressive affect can also be increased by nonviolent games because frustration and arousal can also be increased in nonviolent games, but C. Anderson and Bushman argued that only violent games directly prime aggressive thoughts. According to the GAM perspective,

> Long-term effects of exposure to violent media result primarily from the development, rehearsal, and eventual automatization of aggressive knowledge structures such as perceptual schemata (Was this bump accidental or intentional?), social expectations (Are other people expected to be cooperative or vengeful?), and behavioral scripts (insult → retaliation). (C. Anderson & Bushman, 2001, p. 356)

Once a child's arousal level is increased, toys and other materials in the environment become especially important. In one study (Josephson, 1987), boys noted as characteristically high-aggressive boys showed more aggressive behavior after they had viewed violent television and after they had also been shown a related cue subsequently than did those boys who viewed violent television but did not receive a subsequent cue. However, both the violent content and the cue may have suppressed aggressive behavior in boys rated as characteristically low in aggression (Josephson, 1987).

Indirect support for the arousal hypothesis also came from an earlier study by Silvern and Williamson (1987) of the effects of violent video games on aggression. Silvern and Williamson hypothesized that exposing 4- and 6-year-olds to violent video games would lead to increased aggression; they found no difference in results between the video game and television conditions. The children were more aggressive after exposure to violent video games whether the child was playing or observing, which is similar to findings about behavior that follows viewing of violent cartoons on TV.

Level of arousal may vary with the context of playing, such as whether one is playing against another person instead of a machine, or games may be used to balance arousal levels, suggesting a drive reduction or catharsis hypothesis that needs to be tested further to see if the use of video games leads to decreased anger (Sherry, 2001).

In their meta-analysis of 35 research reports from 2000 that included a total of 4,262 participants, about half of whom were under 18, C. Anderson and Bushman (2001) compared movies/TV with video games because they have similar underlying processes. C. Anderson and Bushman's meta-analysis offered clear support for the hypothesis that exposure to violent video games is hazardous to children and adolescents, including university-age individuals. Adolescents who were not "naturally aggressive" on a standard psychological profile but who played violent video games for a lot of time, were nearly 10 times more likely to get involved in fights than other adolescents who also were nonaggressive but did not play as many violent games (C. Anderson & Bushman, 2001). Exposure was positively correlated with higher levels of aggression in both experimental and nonexperimental studies and in both genders and was negatively correlated with prosocial behavior. Exposure was positively associated to aggressive cognition, which is the main factor underlying long-term effects, and exposure was positively related to aggressive affect and physiological arousal. According to C. Anderson and Bushman, there is now a need for longitudinal research as well as study of whether exciting games could be developed to teach nonviolent solutions to problems and conflicts.

Anderson and Dill (2000) found playing violent video games to be positively related to aggressive behavior and delinquency, especially for characteristically aggressive individuals and for men. Time spent playing was negatively related to academic achievement. Anderson and Dill also suggested that the interactive nature of the games makes them potentially more dangerous than violent movies and television, especially with more graphic violence and greater realism.

Anderson and Dill (2000) claimed that the general affective aggressive model predicts more aggression in both the short term (laboratory) and in the long term (delinquency) after playing violent video games. According to Anderson and Dill, these games provide a venue for learning and rehearsing violent solutions to conflicts. The effect is cognitive: In the short term, it affects aggression by priming aggressive thoughts, and in the long-term, it becomes incorporated into scripts that are increasingly accessible in real-life conflicts. Chory-Assad and Mastro (2000) also used a cognitive-neoassociationistic view to study the impact of aggressive media and the relation between use of violent video games and other media and hostility. Chory-Assad and Mastro noted that continued exposure to violent media content over time leads to aggressive mental constructs becoming accessible over a long period and hence a long-term effect of increased hostility.

Griffiths (1991) reported short-term aggressive effects, especially in young children, after either playing or observing someone playing violent video games, but he raised some questions about the measures used and the effects of long-term exposure. Although many studies have demonstrated a positive correlation between time spent playing violent video games or watching violent television and engaging in aggressive behavior, correlation cannot be used as evidence of causation, and such behaviors could also be due to other factors such as school problems or poor parental supervision. Moreover, perhaps children who prefer violent video games tend to be more aggressive to begin with rather than the other way around. In fact, preference for such games may be critical, as those who liked aggressive games were rated by their peers as more aggressive (Wiegman & van Schie, 1998). Frequent exposure to violent games may, however, have subtle long-term negative effects and may lead to disinhibition of aggressive responses (Comstock & Strasburger, 1993a).

Findings from other research programs, however, have not found the same strong evidence of a relation between playing violent games and aggressive behavior. Gender, cognitive skill level, and reasons for playing, as well as amount of time spent with games, appear to mediate the impact of game playing on children's and adolescents' development.

van Schie and Wiegman (1997), for example, found no significant relation between the time spent with games and aggressive behavior. In another study (Fleming & Rickwood, 2001), significantly increased arousal (both in heart rate and self-reported arousal) followed playing of a violent video game compared with a nonviolent video game and a pencil-and-paper game. However, there was no significant increase in scores for aggressive mood for either boys or girls after the violent game. Heart rate and aggressive mood were not positively correlated after the violent game, and aggression did not increase after the violent or nonviolent game, perhaps because the violence seemed justified (rescue mission) or maybe because it was not seen as especially violent. Fleming and Rickwood also noted that these were short games, and longer ones may have stronger effects; repetition could lead to development of aggressive scripts and more aggressive behavior later, given specific cues.

In a meta-analysis of the effects of violent video games on aggression, Sherry (2001) reported results that suggested a smaller effect for violent games than for TV violence on aggression. Moreover, the effect was positively associated with the type of game violence and, surprisingly, negatively related to the amount of time spent playing the games. The effect size for games that involved fantasy and human characters engaged in violence was greater than for games that involved sport-related violence, perhaps because of the greater amount of action in the fantasy- and human-violence games or perhaps because they may have been more graphic and hence a more powerful prime for associated networks.

Sherry (2001) noted, however, that the type of game was confounded with the year of the study. The games with human violence were not tested until recently because of availability and hence were also tested on a generational cohort with different video game experience because of the increase in faster and more graphic game violence in the 1990s. The effect size was negatively related to the time spent playing when age of the players and year of the study were controlled. Sherry (2001) said that his results suggest that playing even very violent games for extended periods of time may not lead to increased aggression. Sherry (2001) suggested further that the studies may have measured an initial arousal that fell off sharply after extended play, perhaps replaced by boredom or fatigue. With decreased arousal, one would predict reduced aggressiveness as well. This needs to be explored further in studies with different types of games and playing times (Sherry, 2001).

According to Sherry (2001), the implications of these findings are significant socially. Children and adolescents who play games for long stretches may carry less aggression from the game playing to the real world than those who play for a shorter time. If so, limiting playing time would be counterproductive and would have parents ending their children's play when the most aggressive effects were likely, or the decreased effect could reflect boredom, catharsis, or desensitization to the violence (Sherry, 2001). Interestingly, in the Fleming and Rickwood (2001) study, girls reported higher arousal than boys, perhaps because of the greater experience and desensitization of the boys. This finding appears to support Sherry's (2001) findings of less effect over time and/or with experience.

In Sherry's (2001) meta-analysis, the average size of the effect with paper-and-pencil measures, which reflect attitudes or affect, was somewhat higher than with behavioral measures. Sherry (2001) said this result would be expected because cultural constraints may keep someone who feels hostile from acting on that hostility, and there is evidence to indicate that playing violent games is not a strong enough prime to overcome such social sanctions against aggression. Further study needs to focus on individuals who do override such sanctions after playing games and who behave aggressively (Sherry, 2001).

Sherry (2001) reported that surveys, which measure attitudes or memory of past aggressive behavior, had a bigger effect size than experimental studies that used both paper-and-pencil and behavioral measures, and differences in methodology may have led to differences in outcome measures. There was also some indication of an increased effect size with age rather than a decrease, as one might expect; therefore, further study of this with longitudinal designs as well as cohort studies are necessary to settle whether the priming effects (short-term) or social learning (long-term) are most significant and which predict real-world behavior (Sherry, 2001).

In general, then, Sherry's (2001) correlational findings suggest that the types of violence in games predicted aggression, with human and fantasy violence having stronger effects than sports violence. There was a trend toward longer playing times to be associated with less aggression. Study is needed of the characteristics of games that best predict aggressive behavior and of what social and experiential differences exist between video game playing and TV viewing in, for example, modeled rewards, involvement, concentration, time spent, social setting, and the social purpose of playing games (Sherry, 2001). As the active or interactive dimension may intensify a game's impact, the implications of pervasive preferences for violent media and whether there are high-risk players or high-risk habits need to be examined (Funk & Buckman, 1996).

Games and Prosocial Behavior

Researchers have also reported negative game-playing effects on prosocial behavior (Chambers & Ascione, 1987; van Schie & Wiegman, 1997; Wiegman & van Schie, 1998). Chambers and Ascione (1987) exposed children in grades 3 to 4 and 7 to 8 to four conditions: playing alone or cooperatively with another child and playing aggressive or prosocial video games. Levels of donating and helping behavior were then measured. Chambers and Ascione found that the older children donated more than the younger ones, and children who played aggressive games donated significantly less than children who played prosocial games alone. There were no significant differences in helping behavior. Although playing prosocial games did not lead to more prosocial behavior, playing the aggressive game led to less prosocial behavior. Chambers and Ascione speculated that the failure to improve prosocial behavior after prosocial games may have been due to the brief responses or the particular game used, and longer exposure may have greater effects.

In another study to explore the positive and negative effects of playing video games, van Schie and Wiegman (1997) studied 346 seventh- and eighth-grade children. van Schie and Wiegman found that playing such games did not seem to displace other leisure activities, social integration, or school performance. A negative relation between time with video games and prosocial behavior did not hold when boys and girls were analyzed separately, so that relation was not clear. van Schie and Wiegman did not distinguish among types of games, however, which may have been a factor in their findings, and boys spent more time with video games than girls. van Schie and Wiegman recommended longitudinal research to get better insight into the effects of video game playing on cognitive, social, and psychic development and more research into the relationship between the content of games and aggressive and prosocial behavior, school performance, and social integration.

Subrahmanyam, Greenfield, et al. (2001) noted that games and the Internet blur the line between real life and simulation, and they commented on virtual pets that also blur the line. They said that virtual pets contribute to cognitive socialization to a world of computers because the pets have specific requirements presented to children in iconic codes that must be mastered, and children are stimulated to consider the pets to be real.

VIRTUAL REALITY

The key to a definition of virtual reality is the strong sense of actually being present in an environment or destination (Biocca, 1994; Steuer, 1992). Entering virtual reality means going into a computer-generated world where objects exist in a three-dimensional space (Pryor & Scott, 1993). Pryor and Scott explained that there is not only input and output with a computer but also information into and out of the individual who is in the virtual reality setting, such as what the person is seeing, hearing, and feeling. The user moves through it with hand and head movements, not actually with legs, and the person is represented by an arrow cursor.

Biocca (1994) described virtual reality as a medium designed to extend our senses. According to Biocca, in virtual reality, a person's perception is so immersed in the simulation that he or she feels a sense of actually being there. It uses the way we ordinarily interact with the physical world except that intuitive actions and unconscious or conscious movements become commands or potential input. Even the sound is interactive and changes as the user's head moves. Virtual reality includes tactile images as well (Biocca, 1994; Steuer, 1992), which enhance the idea of presence and can communicate subtle information.

Some research adds weight to the basis for concern about the impact of these experiences. In one study (Calvert & Tan, 1994), participants in an aggressive virtual reality game showed higher physiological arousal, such as heart rate, and more aggressive thoughts than did observers, but this was not true of hostile feelings. Calvert and Tan interpreted this as support for arousal theory because although both control and virtual reality groups moved, the latter showed more arousal.

Of more concern in the Calvert and Tan (1994) study was their finding that violent virtual reality interactions overrode personal characteristics like pregame hostility or gender, resulting in similar aggressive levels or effects for all players. Calvert and Tan explained that shifts in technologies from observational to interactional allow linking of emotions, thought, and behavior, and societal and personal aggression may increase when participants become actively involved in such violence-filled entertainment.

Shapiro and McDonald (1992) also have considered some of the ramifications of virtual reality on users. First, Shapiro and McDonald noted that people are likely to be influenced most when they do not have other experiences to help them evaluate the information. Although users may know fiction from reality, virtual reality has additional sensory experiences and feelings of being immersed in an environment that might have greater emotional and physiological effects. The detail in virtual reality makes memories more vivid and thus more likely to affect reconstruction over time. Unreal items can seem as real or more real than actual ones, and although it may be easier for healthy individuals to make judgments about virtual reality than it is for those with mental illness or those under stress, with more and more realistic media technology, such judgments become more difficult (Shapiro & McDonald, 1992).

Tamborini, Eastin, et al. (2000) suggested that because virtual reality's (VR) technology increases identification with aggressive characters by increasing the sense of presence or telepresence, the short-term impact of those games should be greater than for regular violent games. Participants were randomly assigned to four media conditions: playing a VR violent game, a standard violent game, observing a violent game, and observing a nonviolent game. They then responded to a questionnaire about their experience of telepresence and a task to assess the frequency of their hostile thoughts. Tamborini, Eastin, et al. (2000) found that greater presence was experienced by those in the game conditions than by those in the observation conditions. More hostile thoughts were found in the three violent media conditions than in the one nonviolent observation control condition. Surprisingly, however, hostile thoughts tended to be higher in the violence observation condition than in the virtual reality game condition. Trait differences in telepresence tendency and hostility in combination with the media environment and experience of presence predicted hostile thoughts (Tamborini, Eastin, et al., 2000).

In a related study, Tamborini et al. (2001) again assigned participants to the four conditions described for the other study. After exposure to these conditions, they not only completed the questionnaire about presence but also a self-report questionnaire about their physiological distress and a task that was coded for indications of boredom as well as hostile thoughts. Tamborini et al. (2001) found that neither boredom nor physiological distress accounted for the influence of the violent games on hostile thoughts, and they found only minimal support for the expected relation between exposure to game violence and hostility, but physiological distress was a strong predictor of hostility.

Although Tamborini et al. (2001) found an association between human video game violence and acceptance of hostility and physical aggression, they concluded that relative to demographic variables and other media sources, video game use was relatively inconsequential in the prediction of aggression beliefs or dispositions. Television was a stronger predictor of aggression in the high school sample. In the college sample, however, the relation between video game use and aggressive traits was much stronger. Tamborini et al. (2001) suggested that perhaps characteristics of certain games make them less able to act as aggressive primes. They suggested further that exposure to more intense and realistic aggression versus animated or cartoon forms may affect the intensity and types of mental constructs that are activated and that might be manifested in different ways. The context for playing the games may also promote arousal, which facilitates learning (Tamborini et al., 2001). If certain game characteristics are less likely to prime aggressive scripts or constructs, then gender differences in genre preference would be an important factor in the effects on later behavior.

Shapiro and McDonald (1992) warned that spending too much time in a virtual reality environment could be harmful to those who need to confront reality rather than escape from it and could be especially damaging to children and adolescents. People might even have to make internal or external checks to see if something is real or virtual reality (e.g., "Did I turn on the machine?"). Shapiro and McDonald also foresaw its potential use in advertising, as, for example, in having a virtual reality ad that allowed children to "play" with a product toy.

SUMMARY

Children and adolescents spend a considerable amount of time using technology for entertainment. They view TV, videos, DVDs, and cable; they enjoy a wide range of music videos; and they engage in significant amounts of time playing video games and computer games. There are important gender and developmental differences in their media use and in the impact that the media have on children's aggressive behavior, attitudes toward others, prosocial behavior, and general psychological well-being. Music videos often depict glamorized alcohol and tobacco use, sexual behavior, and violence, and they tend to perpetuate gender and racial stereotypes.

New research has raised important questions about differences between TV and video games in terms of their effect on behavior. It has pointed to important gender differences in game preferences and reasons for playing that include challenge, fantasy, imagination, social interaction, diversion, and escape. Modeling, uses and gratification, and cognitive-neoassociationist theories have been used to explain the impact of game playing and other media experiences as well as children's television experience. Many variables interact to produce the relations that are observed between use of the media for entertainment and behavior in the real world.

DISCUSSION QUESTIONS

1. Discuss the ethical issues involved in research on the effects of children's exposure to violent video games.
2. What research designs or methodology could best discern the complex interactions among gender, genre preference, developmental level, and game content? Discuss the interactions of gender, genre preferences, cognitive skill level, and game content as they affect the impact of game playing on users.
3. How might a uses and gratification paradigm be used to explain the effects of music videos?

PART V

Interventions and Conclusions

CHAPTER FOURTEEN

Intervention Strategies

Intervention Strategies

The act of watching television need not require much of viewers. Without ever leaving their easy chairs, viewers can be stimulated, entertained, educated, horrified, or intrigued by a never-ending smorgasbord of material. They need not respond to or interact with the material, they do not have to analyze it or criticize it, they do not have to remember it, they do not even have to attend to it continuously, and they frequently engage in other activities simultaneously. The television set simply provides continuous stimuli until someone turns it off. On the other hand, viewers can interact with, attend to, remember, analyze, and criticize what they see, and they certainly interact with many of the new technologies like video games. Several authors have underscored the need to help children develop critical viewing skills to help them derive greater benefits from their media experience.

Possible solutions to counter potential negative effects of the media include having public debate and "common ground" talks among producers, teachers, and politicians; the development of professional conduct and self-discipline codes for producers; and innovative forms of education about media to create more critical users of media (Groebel, 2001).

MEDIA LITERACY EDUCATION

Kubey and Csikszentmihalyi (1990) considered it essential to teach children formally about television, as most will spend 1,000 hours of each of their childhood and adult years watching television. They pointed out that no one doubts the benefits of teaching children how to read essays or novels or poems, but they will spend far less time reading those than viewing television.

Hobbs (1997) defined media literacy as "the ability to access, analyze, evaluate and communicate messages in a variety of forms" (p. 7). One of the problems in media literacy is a paradox according to Hobbs (1998): The diversity of views among scholars and educators reflects the widespread appeal and relevance of the idea that critical evaluation of the media is an essential skill. At the same time, it is just that diversity that precludes consensus and leads to fragmentation and polarization. Hobbs (1998) noted two important phases in the emerging area of inquiry: a need to bring information about media analysis and production to a wider variety of settings and individuals and the need for the development of theory and research that can predict and evaluate complex learning and teaching processes about the media with educators, children, and youth.

Types of Media Literacy

Most media literacy programs aim to increase children's understanding of types of programs and how they are created and about the technical aspects of television such as special effects. They also aim to help students analyze advertising and the persuasive appeals used and how they affect buying behavior; to help them compare information they are exposed to in various media with information from the real world; to inform them about potential effects of media violence on real-life aggression and on other behavior, feelings, academic achievement, and self-concept; to help them see the good that they can derive from media; to help them understand how the media cover and affect world events; and to help them devise positive media strategies and schedules.

Meyrowitz (1998) argued for the need for different types of literacy. These include content literacy (messages sent by the media), grammar literacy (the distinct languages and production variables used within each medium), and medium literacy (studying the relatively fixed characteristics of each medium). *Content literacy* is the most common and seeks to analyze messages sent by the various media including violent, racist, or sexist content; news programming; advertising; and behavior models that are portrayed. *Grammar literacy* involves studying the unique grammar of each medium and how it and the production variables used in each interact with the content. For example, some of the production variables for print would include size of the page, spacing, and paragraph breaks. Photography would use depth of focus, framing, cropping, and shutter speed. Radio/audio would use volume and tone, echo, and fade-outs, and TV/film would include cuts, zooms, close-ups, and length of shots to communicate, and all of these interact with content. Close-ups, for example, might encourage more connection to the person or suggest other meanings of distance between individuals.

The third type of literacy, *medium literacy,* is the least commonly studied. It involves study of a medium as a setting or environment that influences communication in a fixed and particular way regardless of content or production variables. Particular interactions differ, for example, depending on the form such as e-mail versus phone versus face-to-face contact (Meyrowitz, 1998).

Media Literacy Programs

Most media literacy programs have been designed for use in the classroom and have been integrated into the educational curriculum. Kubey and Csikszentmihalyi

(1990) pointed out that children can be taught to view television more critically both through formal educational channels and in less formal ones. In school, for example, students can be taught about many aspects of television such as techniques of persuasion, character development, advertising, and economics and can be taught to think about how television reflects society and why it does so in certain ways. They suggested that parents can also help their children view television more critically, but it should be done in a relaxed way—not to develop "right" answers but to help them learn various ways to perceive and evaluate television (Kubey & Csikszentmihalyi, 1990).

There are many examples of specific interesting and creative programs that have been developed to work with children on these issues, some of which are described in the following paragraphs.

The *NEWSWEEK* Extra! program provides classroom activities to help students start to explore media literacy skills (Hobbs, 2003). The program aims to strengthen reading skills with topics and activities of high interest, increase teamwork and collaborative problem solving through work in small groups, improve data analysis and interpretive skills and reflect their use of media outside the classroom. For example, one activity for students was to read the Kaiser Family Foundation report on *Kids & Media @ the New Millennium* (Rideout et al., 1999) and discuss specific questions about it. Another had them review some of the statistics from the report and interpret the data.

Austin and Johnson (1997) studied alcohol-specific media literacy training with third-grade children. They examined children's perceptions of advertising for alcohol, norms for alcohol, and expectancies for and behaviors toward alcohol. This was an experimental study with two levels of the treatment factor to assess how effective the in-school media training was. Training affected both immediate and delayed effects. Immediate effects included better understanding of advertising's persuasive intent, seeing the characters as less real and less desirable with less desire to be like them, decreased expectation of positive results from drinking, and less likelihood to choose an alcohol product. Training was more effective for girls than for boys, and it was more effective when it was specific to alcohol.

Gadow, Sprafkin, and Watkins (1987) used the critical viewing skills curriculum that they developed for exceptional children, Curriculum for Enhancing Social Skills Through Media Awareness (CESSMA), with typical elementary school classes of kindergartners and second graders. Increased knowledge about television did not lead to changes in kindergartners' attitudes or beliefs in the reality of the characters or the aggression. They seemed to think the television aggression was real, that victims were really hurt, and that the aggression they saw happens frequently in real life. Second graders recognized and understood the fantasy portrayals, and even without instruction, they could interpret aggressive scenes more accurately. Interestingly, both groups had difficulty understanding animation and attributed real-life characteristics, such as having a home and money, to cartoon characters. Testing of sixth graders revealed that they had acquired most of the CESSMA information on their own.

Another project, the Television Literacy Project, was designed to look at skills involved in "reading" television to see if those skills were equally applicable to different kinds of programming such as news and drama. Kelley, Gunter, and Buckle (1987) found that a classroom course on television programming and production techniques led to significant improvements in critical viewing.

According to Brown (2001), however, the focus has shifted from developing viewing plans and curricula with audiovisual and print materials to staff development and teacher training as a better way to go in introducing media literacy programs into the schools. Moreover, the teacher training should not only teach teachers how to use prepared materials in their classes, but it should stimulate them to create their own materials and connections with activities involving media production and analysis.

Increased attention is also being paid to the need to introduce media curricula and training into pediatric training programs and physicians' practices to encourage them to include viewing habits and media use in their work with children and adolescents (Gruber & Grube, 2000; Rich & Bar-on, 2001; Strasburger, 1993; Strasburger & Donnerstein, 1999, and many others). Beresin (1999) also urged psychiatrists to discuss the problem with parents, medical students and residents, and other school and health professionals.

Even television shows can be used to increase children's media awareness. *Street Cents,* for example, is a program of the Canadian Broadcasting Corporation on which viewers can examine advertising and criticize ads and other television messages (Saunders, 1996). It also has an e-zine for teens that features online articles for adolescent consumers.

Other new and innovative programs, including joint ventures, have been launched recently. An Internet education initiative, for example, was launched in Canada by the Girl Guides and the Media Awareness Network (2002). "You go girl in technology" was designed to help Canadian girls from ages 5 to 17 and over become effective, responsible, and safe users of the Internet.

The Media Awareness Network (2003a) also developed checklists for parents for children 9 to 12 and for adolescents 13 to 17 to assess their awareness of how to use the Internet effectively and safely. The checklists include questions to test awareness about accessing the Internet, how to monitor it, which chat rooms to use, what personal information not to reveal, how to verify information received on the Web, restrictions on arranging meetings, how to handle disturbing material or messages, and copyright practices. Another of their programs takes students on a "cybertour" in an interactive module online. It visits 12 mock sites to allow users to test their surfing skills and savvy (Media Awareness Network, 2003d). The *Media Literacy Review* (Ferrington, 2003) is an online publication of the Media Literacy Online Project and is an information resource linking media education sites around the world.

Critical viewing skills should also include metacognitive skills and awareness of the effort involved so that children learn not only about television content but also about television's role as a displacer of activities that offer other advantages (Williams, 1986). The differences and benefits of perusing information from a wide range of sources, including print, should also be a part of such critical viewing skills, according to Williams (1986), so that the importance of such mental activities as elaboration and reflection can be underscored.

The Committee on Public Education of the American Academy of Pediatrics (2001b) urged more media literacy, more responsible portrayal of violence by producers, more thoughtful use of the media by parents and children, and better ratings as possible solutions to the harm that can come from exposure to violence in the media.

Providing additional and alternate information to television content can work against any undue influence of the television information. Research has demonstrated that if children are taught about media messages and how they are produced and about the hidden values and assumptions they convey, they become less susceptible to negative effects of using media (Brown et al., 2002). Brown et al. (2002) noted that Canada and Australia, among other countries in the world, have extensive media literacy curricula in the schools, and some states now include it in their educational goals. Yet, the United States is one of only a few Western countries without a comprehensive school-based media education program (Strasburger & Donnerstein, 1999).

Although critical viewing skills programs can help children to learn about television, there have not been studies of the long-term impact of such programs either on children's viewing patterns or on the way they process the television content (Anderson & Collins, 1988).

RATINGS SYSTEMS

Violence ratings for TV can help parents judge how violent specific television programs are without having to watch them. Not only are parents encouraged to use the rating system often, but cable operators and videocassette distributors should prominently post ratings for films they are broadcasting or renting (Donnerstein et al., 1994; Kunkel et al., 2002).

The ratings include the following (Kunkel et al., 2002; *New York Times* Service and Staff, 1997):

1. TV–Y, All Children (appropriate for all children, but designed specifically for preschool age children 2 to 6 and not expected to frighten them).

2. TV–Y7, Directed to Older Children (for children 7 and older, better for children who can distinguish fantasy from reality; may include mild comedic or physical violence and might frighten younger children).

3. TV–G, General Audience (appropriate for all ages; not designed specifically for younger children but alright for them as there is little or no violence, strong language, or sexual situations or dialogue).

4. TV–PG, Parental Guidance (may contain material unsuitable for young children, and parents may want to be present if younger children are viewing it; may contain some strong language, suggestive situations, and limited violence).

5. TV–14, Parents Strongly Cautioned (may contain material unsuitable for children younger than 14, and parents should monitor it carefully and not let younger children watch; may contain mature themes, sexual and more violent content, and strong language).

6. TV–M, Mature Audience Only (designed specifically for adults and maybe unsuitable for those younger than 17; may contain graphic violence, explicit sex, mature themes, and profanity) (*New York Times*, 1997).

Although the general audience ratings reasonably reflect program content, television industry content descriptors that were added to supplement the age-based ratings such as V for violence, S for sex, D for dialogue, L for adult language, and FV for fantasy violence, are often not used for many programs containing them (Kunkel et al., 2002). Almost 80% of violent shows did not have a V rating despite averaging five moderately intense violent scenes per program (Kunkel, 1999). This makes it difficult for parents to monitor and control their children's exposure to violence.

The whole issue of classification is controversial, however. Some have argued, for example, that classification ignores the context of content, that providing an objective rating or assessment of content is impossible, and that some valuable and acceptable programming would be banned as a result of an "objective" rating of the content (King, 1995).

According to Donnerstein et al. (1994), the problem with the current rating system is that content is rated according to what has been seen to be offensive traditionally rather than what is likely to be harmful to children. For example, Donnerstein et al. suggested that violence should be rated separately from factors such as mature themes, profanity, or sexual content. Donnerstein et al. also pointed out that the system rates explicit sex more restrictively than violence. Short sex scenes can lead to an R rating, whereas many gory scenes can still appear in PG movies. Moreover, the system stresses amount and explicitness in content and pays little attention to context (Donnerstein et al., 1994).

Video games played on PCs and games on the Internet are rated by the Entertainment Software Rating Board (ESRB). The ratings are based on age and include descriptors for violence and gore; nudity; sexual or suggestive themes; drug, alcohol, and tobacco use; language; lyrics; hate speech; and gambling (Kaiser Family Foundation, 2002a; National Institute on Media and the Family, 2002e). They include the following:

1. EC (Early Childhood): For 3 and older with no inappropriate content.

2. E (Everyone): For 6 and older; may have minimal violence, slapstick comedy, crude language.
3. T (Teens): For age 13 and older; may contain some language, violence, mild sexual themes.
4. M (Mature): For age 17 and older; may have more intense violence, language, mature sexual themes.
5. A (Adult only): May contain graphic violence and sexual themes; not for sale or rented to those under 18.

Arcade games are labeled with a color-coded "traffic light" system to warn parents of sex, violence, or language. Green means a game is appropriate for all ages, yellow means mild violence—either lifelike or animated—and red means strong violence with blood and serious injury or death (Kaiser Family Foundation, 2002a).

Children Now (2001) provided a game-by-game comparison of the top selling games such as Nintendo®, Game Boy®, PlayStation®, and Dreamcast®, and PC games. The games were compared on the amount and type of violence they contained, racial and gender diversity, "girl friendliness," revealing clothing, and average body type. PC games ranked the highest overall with "better than average" scores in 7 out of 10 categories.

Parents often disagree with game ratings, however, and some games do not include appropriate descriptors. Ratings by the industry do not match those of game-playing children or other adults (C. Anderson & Bushman, 2001). The *KidScore* content-based system for evaluating computer and video games, TV programs, and movies "from a family-friendly perspective" (National Institute on Media and the Family, 1997–2000, p. 1) may help. It applies one system to all of the media and includes two sets of ratings: those made by visitors to the site—allowing anyone to rate games, movies, or TV shows—and ratings done by a panel of qualified "SuperRaters."

TECHNOLOGICAL AIDS

One rather controversial weapon in the war against children's viewing of violence or explicit sexual content is the V-chip. Designed to deal with TV violence without restricting creative freedom, the V-chip is an electronic device that flags programs that exceed a chosen level of violence or language or sexually explicit content and screens them out, thus allowing parents to block children's reception of sensitive content.

Gruber and Grube (2000) and many others have emphasized the importance of parental supervision and direction in what and how much their adolescents use media. Gruber and Grube recommended coviewing, but if that is not possible, V-chip and screening software to decrease the access to inappropriate content and to help their teens develop critical viewing skills.

The following descriptions for violence are contained in the V-chip guidelines that have been put out by the industry (Kunkel, Maynard-Farinola, Farrar, Donnerstein, & Zwarun, 2002). They differ slightly from the ratings described earlier, although they are generally approximate: TV–G, no violence; TV–PG, moderate violence; TV–14, intense violence; and TV–MA.

The second area included in the V-chip system for sensitive material includes sexual behavior. The following descriptions are contained in the guidelines that have been put out by the industry: TV–G, little or no sexual situations; TV–PC, some sexual situations; TV–14, intense sexual situations; and TV–MA, explicit sexual activity. There is also a section for sexual dialogue and adult language as well (Kunkel et al., 2002).

In an extensive study by Kunkel et al. (2002), a large program sample was taken from most frequently viewed channels including broadcast network, cable, and independent channels. Programs were examined for their depictions of violence, sexual behavior and language, and adult language. These findings were then compared to the ratings that were applied to them to see how accurate the ratings were. Kunkel et al. (2002) found that age-based ratings were reasonably accurate in reflecting the program content but descriptors such as violent or sexual content and language were not used on the majority of programs containing them. They also found that children's programs had a significant amount of violence that was not identified by the relevant descriptor such as fantasy violence. Kunkel et al. (2002) concluded that there are significant limits to the ability of V-chip technology to limit effectively the exposure of children to sensitive content.

Some concern has arisen that the use of the V-chip would mean that broadcasters might then increase levels of violence and explicit sexual content, and children would be exposed to even higher levels. Parental monitoring and responsibility for their children's viewing clearly is still essential, and V-chip technology also requires parental involvement.

Despite the obvious need for parental involvement, however, a Kaiser Family Foundation report (2001) revealed that fewer than 10% of parents actually use a V-chip to block programs from their children, whereas over half use TV ratings to decide what their children can or cannot watch, even though there is some confusion about key elements of the ratings. Over half of parents who had a TV with a V-chip as standard equipment did not know it was there, and two thirds of those who knew it was there did not use it (Kaiser Family Foundation, 2001). Those parents who use it are likely the ones who already are monitoring or limiting their children's access to violent programming.

Such technology or others such as an electronic lock on the television set to preset available times and channels can help parents, but such technology would exclude poor families unless it was made widely available as was done for 24 million hearing impaired individuals (Centerwall, 1995).

PARENT STRATEGIES AND EDUCATION

Many researchers, pediatricians, and other professionals have urged parents to monitor their children's computer use, TV viewing, and video game playing; to use ratings and other information; to look for games that require strategies and problem solving, not just violent activity; to limit the amount of time they spend with each; and to encourage participation in other activities. Parents need to be aware of which television shows their children are viewing and what messages are being conveyed to make sure the material is understandable and appropriate for their age. They should discuss media content with their children in the context of their own views, preferences, and values. They should also be aware of the video games their children are playing and the level of violence involved. Young children need to be protected from graphic sex and violence that might frighten or confuse them. Similar advice holds for viewing music videos.

Parents also need to monitor their children's online activity. They need to caution their children about the people they meet on the Internet and the fact that they are strangers and may not be whom they appear to be. They need to teach their children not to give out personal information or agree to meet strangers in person (National Institute on Media and the Family, 2002l).

Whether TV, video games, music, or the Internet, parents are generally well advised to limit the amount of time children spend on them and to encourage other activities. Most experts discourage having TVs, computers, and video games in children's rooms, which makes monitoring and supervision more difficult and can increase isolation and loneliness. Finally, parents need to model healthy media practices themselves including selective viewing, limited or reasonable amounts of time, and engagement in many other activities including reading.

Warren and Bluma (2002) compared parents' mediation of children's Internet use and of their TV viewing. They found that parents apply their TV mediation practices to the Internet and Web surfing by their children. What they do with TV they tend to use with the new media as well, and there were similar concerns about sexual and violent content for both (Warren & Bluma, 2002). On a brighter note, there is more quality programming available for preschoolers now, with more child development theory working its way into the shows (McGinn, 2002). McGinn suggested that some parents use TV and quality programs the way previous generations used Dr. Spock—as an essential part of their children's healthy development.

The Alliance for Children and Television's (ACT) media literacy kit, *Prime Time Parent* (Media Awareness Network, 1995), is full of information and activities to help parents to better understand TV and its effects on their children. It aims to make parents more media literate. It informs them about various stages of child development, what content is appropriate viewing content for their children, and what fears are common at each developmental stage. It alerts them to values that are being portrayed on TV and helps them cope with new technologies (Media Awareness Network, 1995).

OTHER INITIATIVES

In addition to media literacy programs aimed at children and guidance including ratings and technological aids provided to parents, other initiatives have demonstrated creative ways to use TV, cable, and new technologies to guard against possible negative effects of media use and to increase the positive contributions the media can make to children's, and adolescents' development.

Educational Resources

A comprehensive and helpful compendium of 33 advocacy organizations in the United States can be found in Trotta's (2001) chapter. Trotta organized them by the approach and methodology they use and the audiences they serve, and she included a brief synopsis of each one, including their philosophies, major initiatives, goals, and strategies. All of the material was taken from the organizations' own materials, either published or on their Web sites. The National Institute on Media and the Family also has an extensive list of resources available at its Web site.

Dirr (2001) also provided a helpful summary of educational resources on television for children in early childhood, primary grades, middle grades, and junior high, as well as adolescents, high school students, and adults. Dirr noted that the major barriers to greater use of cable programs and the Internet by teachers is a lack of time, insufficient information, and budget constraints.

In response to school shootings in the United States, the American Psychological Association (Barrett, 1999a, personal communication) prepared materials for youth to recognize warning signs of violence in themselves and others. The American Psychological Association cited MTV research findings that revealed violence to be the top concern among its viewers. Other poll results indicated that 40% of youth said they had been concerned about a classmate who was potentially violent, and 71% said they wanted to learn the warning signs of violence (Barrett, 1999a).

The American Psychological Association and MTV joined to give information to youth about identifying warning signs of violence and how to get help if they saw the signs in themselves or others. This joint initiative was part of MTV's "Fight for your rights: Take a stand against violence" supported by U.S. Departments of Education and Justice, other federal agencies, and other organizations (Barrett, 1999a). The MTV president, Judy McGrath, was quoted as saying that the goal of the "Fight for your rights" initiative was to give MTV viewers a voice in the national debate and to provide specific ways for them to fight violence in their communities (Barrett, 1999a). There was a "Warning Signs" documentary with a toll-free number to call for a "Warning Signs" guide with information about normal anger and signs of potential violence. Demand for the guide was so great that an additional 100,000 guides had to be printed within 2 weeks of the launch of the project. Moreover, special kits were available to American Psychological Association members to help them organize activities in their own communities, including information about how to work with local MTV cable affiliates (Barrett, 1999b, personal communication).

As television has been found to be "an effective and pervasive teacher of children and youth" (Slaby, Barham, Eron, & Wilcox, 1994, p. 451), television should be used to contribute to solving the violence issue, according to Slaby et al. Slaby et al. suggested that to accomplish that the Federal Communications Commission should require limits on dramatized violence during prime time when children are likely to be watching, television programs should be used in educational programs and activities to prevent violence, and the film rating system should be revised to flag violent content more adequately.

Broadcaster and Government Responsibility

In Canada, 200,000 Canadians petitioned the Canadian Radio-Television and Telecommunications Commission (CRTC) after the Montréal massacre in 1989 in which 14 young women were gunned down at their university, 1.3 million signed a petition demanding legislative action against violence that was circulated by a young woman whose sister had been raped and murdered, and 350,000 teachers also had urged action (Spicer, 1995). The Canadian approach by the CRTC to violence was to try to reduce it on a number of fronts: 80% by way of public education through various groups and associations, 10% through technological devices such as the V-chip, and 10% through voluntary codes. In addition to trying to reduce violent content, the CRTC also aimed to encourage more creative and intelligent children's programming. The hope was to balance creative expression and children's health through consensus and cooperation rather than through regulations and new laws (Spicer, 1995).

When voluntary guidelines on violence were announced by the networks in 1992, however, reporters could not find any producers who thought those guidelines would require any changes in their programming (Centerwall, 1995). The 3-hour rule that requires commercial broadcasters to offer educational programs for a minimum of 3 hours per week requires that those programs have education as a primary focus and must air between 7 a.m. and 10 p.m. If broadcasters air less, they must have their licenses reviewed and demonstrate that they are serving child viewers in other ways (Jordan, 2001).

Other steps have been taken to protect children and adolescents who use the Internet. In 2002, for example, Canada amended its criminal code to make Internet luring an offense, making it a crime for adults to try to entice children via the Web for sexual purposes (Boyd, 2003).

Strasburger and Donnerstein's (1999) suggested solutions included parental control over their children's media use, more physician and public health counseling, effective government regulation of the media, and entertainment industry efforts to improve the viewing product. All play a role and need to take responsibility. Strasburger and Donnerstein also called for a year 2002 National Institute of Mental Health Report on Children, Adolescents, and the Media, as the last one appeared in 1982 (National Institute of Mental Health, 1982).

SUMMARY

Many media literacy programs have been developed and introduced into school curricula in an effort to encourage and develop children's critical viewing skills and more general media literacy. Such programs appear to be effective in increasing children's awareness of many aspects of the media and hopefully in making them less susceptible to negative messages, but their long-term influence on behavior has not been definitively demonstrated. It is hoped that such programs will enable children to enjoy television and other media and to benefit from the many positive aspects while at the same time minimizing their potential negative influence or manipulation.

Other interventions have also been developed and studied to assess their usefulness in helping parents monitor their children's and adolescents' media experience and in reducing negative media impact. There are ratings systems for TV content, movies, and video games that parents can use to assess programs their children watch and games they play. There are problems with use of the ratings, however, because they frequently to not adequately or accurately reflect actual levels of sexual content and violence in the TV programs or games. Technological aids such as the V-chip are also available, but similar problems exist, and many parents do not know about them or do not use them.

There is increasing emphasis in the literature on the need for physicians and pediatricians to incorporate media content into their training programs and practices and to be aware of some of the problems as they deal with their patients. There are also many strategies and practices that parents can incorporate into their families' media experiences to enhance the positive aspects and reduce the negative ones.

DISCUSSION QUESTIONS

1. Discuss the discrepancies between TV and video game ratings systems and the actual content that sometimes includes more sexual behavior, language, and violence than the assigned ratings indicate.
2. What other developmental and experiential factors should be taken into account in the development of ratings systems?
3. Discuss what you consider to be the most important recommendations to make to parents about their children's media use.

CHAPTER FIFTEEN

Summary, Conclusions, and Future Directions

CHAPTER FIFTEEN

Summary, Conclusions, and Future Directions

SUMMARY AND CONCLUSIONS

Children's use of technology has expanded rapidly with the proliferation of cell phones, pagers, music videos, video games, DVDs, and other digital devices, but television still retains its prominent spot in the media world. The pace of the current research and the number of studies on the impact of all of these media on the social, emotional, physical, and intellectual development of children and adolescents is breathtaking. Interesting findings regarding the frequency and patterns of use of each of the media have emerged. New variables have been identified as significant factors, and more diverse relations among old ones have been revealed.

The complexity of the issues and the interactions among dozens of variables, however, provide ongoing challenges to researchers. There are differences among viewers such as age, gender, socioeconomic level, past experience, motivations, and needs. There are differences in viewer choices, patterns of use, and viewing contexts. There are major differences in media content, technological options, and access to technology. The choice of research design and methodology is a critical component in studies of the interactions and impact of all of these variables, in the clarity of results, and in the interpretation of findings. Posing questions effectively and planning data collection and analysis to answer those questions is a vital part of getting useful and applicable information.

Current research has built on the strong foundation provided by earlier studies. The role of major theoretical perspectives in explaining and refining the complex interactions among many variables has become increasingly clear. Social cognitive theory, cultivation theory, and a uses and gratification approach have all made significant contributions to a better understanding of the impact of media on children and adolescents.

The emphasis on children's social learning and cognitive processes such as attention, retention, and motivation, as well as on their information-processing ability and cognitive skills, is clearly important to understand how they use and react to media content and when they are likely to emulate what they see. There is growing emphasis on the role of cognitive skills and cognitive activity, not just in children's level of comprehension of media content but in game preferences, associative networks of aggressive or violent responses, and development of scripts about behavior.

Cultivation theory's emphasis on the effects of heavy viewing of common messages is helpful in understanding how children come to develop attitudes and beliefs. Heavy viewing in the absence of competing information, for example, may result in users' attitudes and beliefs falling more in line with the media content to which they are being exposed. A uses and gratifications perspective reminds us that children and adolescents have different needs and use the media for different purposes and in different contexts, all of which affect their perceptions and reactions and the media's impact on them.

An integration of cultivation and uses and gratifications theories from the communication field and social and cognitive learning and other developmental theories from psychology can be useful in explaining many of the attitudinal and behavioral differences among child and adolescent media users that abound in the literature.

A considerable body of research suggests that when viewers use the media seriously to obtain information they need, especially when the content is perceived to be realistic and when there are few alternate sources of information, the media's potential impact is great. Influence is less significant when media use is primarily for diversion, is less frequent, is taken less seriously, and when users have other sources of information and knowledge. However, these patterns are mitigated by developmental, gender, contextual, and family variables; by the amount of media use engaged in by children and adolescents; and by the choices they make:

> The message is clear. Media messages do not affect all of the people all of the time, but some of the messages affect some of the people some of the time. As we move into an age of ever-expanding technological options in the mass media, we need to recognize that the process is as complex on the human side as it is on the technological side. (Heath & Gilbert, 1996, p. 385)

One of the most promising directions in current studies lies in the refinement of research questions by splitting some of the most relevant variables into subgroups or subtypes. Current research programs, for example, have focused on types of violence; different genres of video games and music videos; varied reasons for playing games or viewing TV; and the interaction of these subgroups with developmental, cognitive, and gender differences. The study of different types of violence, for example, has shed new light on previous findings of gender differences in levels of aggressive behavior.

Developmental and Gender Differences

Children's information processing abilities determine what they attend to, what they understand, and what they remember. There are important developmental changes in what messages and features children attend to, how well they understand what they are viewing, whether they can distinguish reality from fantasy, and in what they remember and what they fear. Young children's greater attention to perceptually salient information means they may attend to material that attracts their attention but at the same time confuses or frightens them. They may also recall vivid visual images for a long time but not be able to put them in contexts the way older children and adults can. Moreover, young children's limited verbal expressive skills may prevent them from accurately articulating what they actually do understand.

As children get older, cognitive processes and challenges become more important and affect their attention to TV, their choice of games and other media, and the skills they need to use them. Girls, for example, tend to be stronger in verbal areas and focus more on those; boys tend to have stronger visual/spatial skills. If television relies more heavily on language and video games rely more on visual input, gender differences in these skill areas will affect the impact of various media.

Developmental differences in cognitive skills are significant in the context of children's increased access to all kinds of information, and they have important social, interpersonal, and psychological implications. Children now have fairly easy access to adult information, violence, sexual content, and even pornography on the Internet, but they lack the cognitive skills and emotional development and maturity to deal with them satisfactorily.

Media Violence

Several current research programs have suggested new ways to pursue the relation between media violence and real-life aggressive behavior and other responses. Rather than measuring largely physical violence, for example, which is more typical of boys, researchers have found some answers by defining different types of violence and distinguishing between direct and indirect aggression or between physical and relational aggression.

Research has generally shown differences between boys and girls in their response to violence and in their use of violent or aggressive behavior. When greater attention is paid to different types of violence, however, the interaction between gender and types of aggression as well as different skills becomes apparent. Girls tend to be involved more in relational aggression, perhaps because of their verbal strengths and their socialization.

The fantasy–reality distinction can be difficult to make with more sophisticated and realistic video games. Difficulties in making that distinction, coupled with the interactivity of games, makes them a potentially more potent influence. However, some research suggests that they may have less impact, especially if played over a prolonged period. A renewed interest in the possibility of a cathartic or drive-reduction effect has arisen from a convergence of several research programs that suggest decreased arousal with continued play. The meaning and significance of varying arousal levels, such as whether decreased arousal indicates boredom and fatigue or desensitization to violence needs to be studied further.

Research findings on the importance of identification with characters has been quite consistent, however. Viewers who identify with characters who are engaged in violence are more strongly affected by what they view. Perceptions of the violence as justified, provoked, realistic, or rewarding also affect its impact. Daydreaming about violent content, playing violent games, and viewing violence on TV or in movies all provide rehearsal of aggressive responses in fantasy that would be expected to increase the likelihood of aggressive behavior.

Developmental factors also play a large role in the impact of media violence on children. Younger children differ from older children and adolescents in what they perceive to be violent, how they reason about it, how they think it affects them, and what they fear. They also differ in how much they can weigh motivation and justification as factors and in how fully they can comprehend the consequences of violence or even the finality of death. As realism is an important factor in media impact, young children's inability to separate fact from fantasy makes them more vulnerable to media influence.

Video Games

Although children and adolescents spend a considerable amount of time using technology for information, they also use it a good deal for entertainment. Children play games for various reasons or purposes including challenge, fantasy, imagination, social interaction, diversion, or escape. Evidence is surfacing that the television experience is not as similar to the game-playing experience as has frequently been assumed. TV viewing, for example, is a more passive experience; game playing is interactive and requires different cognitive skills. Social cognitive theory, uses and gratification, and cognitive-neoassociationistic views have all been used to explain the impact of game playing as well as other media experiences.

The types of games that are available, the choices children and adolescents make, the length of time they play, and the gratifications they seek, as well as gender differences in cognitive skills, interests, and socialization experiences, all affect the impact of game playing on development. The findings in game-playing choices and behavior mirror closely children's and adolescents' social, cognitive, and emotional development in interesting and significant ways. Boys prefer more action-oriented and violent media, whereas girls tend to prefer more intellectually challenging and language-based games such as card games, trivia games, or puzzles.

More attention is now being paid to their game choices because they reflect important gender differences in the reasons for playing, the amount of time spent playing, and in the cognitive skills required. What has sometimes been viewed as less interest of girls in games or computers may instead reflect the fact that many of the games available do not connect well with girls' skills and interests. Therefore, they play less frequently and develop less experience with computers. Specific efforts can be made to change that situation with content that has more appeal for girls and requires more of their stronger skills.

Game preferences also affect what scripts or cues are activated and what thoughts and responses are rehearsed. When media use becomes associated with children's beliefs and cognitions and becomes part of their script, it is more likely to have long-term effects. Cues in the environment can play an important role in the activation and perpetuation of aggressive scripts and the increased likelihood of aggressive behavior. Parental monitoring, then, not only of TV viewing and game playing but also of toys and environmental conditions, becomes an even more important aspect of children's media experience.

Variation in motivations for playing games appears to be a significant factor in the effect of game playing on children. If a user's motive is diversion rather than seeking information or learning about behavior, there should be less impact. Conversely, if users are using game playing as a model for social interaction, or are playing to avoid other responsibilities or problems, the effects would likely be quite different.

Cultural Diversity

Research on cultural diversity in the media has demonstrated that minority groups, women, and the elderly continue to be underrepresented. Much of the entertainment media such as music videos and video games tend to perpetuate gender and racial stereotypes. Given the developmental theory that children identify with individuals who are most like themselves and model their behavior after them, the chances of a negative impact are increased if there are few individuals like them and/or if the few who are like them engage in less appropriate or less successful behavior. From a modeling and social cognitive view, users in those groups have fewer positive and strong media models to emulate. They also pay less attention to certain aspects of the media that have less relevance for them. A cultivation theory perspective might also lead to concern about the impact of the information on children's developing attitudes and beliefs about themselves and others. Blacks and Hispanics who see relatively few individuals like themselves may come to feel that they are inconsequential or less important than Whites. A uses and gratifications' perspective would also suggest that for those children who are viewing TV or using media to learn more about others and who have little competing information, views and attitudes may become skewed.

Advertising

Children are still exposed to a considerable amount of advertising on television and more recently on the Internet. They are also increasingly exposed to significant amounts of advertising in other contexts such as product placement in movies, corporate sponsorship of sporting events, and advertising within schools. The impact of all of this advertising, however, is mediated by important developmental, gender, and racial differences that affect children's comprehension of the advertising and their reactions to it. Younger children, for example, are particularly vulnerable to advertising because of their attention to perceptually salient material, their inability to distinguish between real and unreal, and their lack of comprehension of the persuasive purpose of advertising and its techniques. Black girls may attend to different aspects of messages than White girls and may be less affected by some media content because the depictions may be less relevant to them.

Children and adolescents can be taught to view advertising more critically, but despite greater knowledge about it, they are still likely to be influenced by it.

Advertising techniques are sometimes used in campaigns to try to change behavior such as getting people to stop smoking or drinking excessively. Research is increasingly being directed at the effects of embedding such messages in popular programs to see if they have more of an effect on children and adolescents there than they would in more straightforward, direct messages such as PSAs. In any case, the research still indicates that it is easier to change knowledge and attitudes than to change actual behavior in most areas.

Parent Mediation and the Family

Research has consistently demonstrated that parental involvement and mediation is an important component of children's media experience. Coviewing of television and monitoring of game playing and computer use have been considered essential ways to facilitate comprehension and prevent misunderstanding or negative effects. It also helps to reduce any inordinate influence of the media by providing competing information and alternative views and values. However, most children have multiple media options in their own rooms, and there is relatively little parental monitoring or supervision. The number of parents who actually are involved is surprisingly low given the frequent exhortation to do so, and much of children's media use occurs in isolation in their own rooms.

Media use, especially television viewing, has been blamed for interfering with family life, and it has also been credited with bringing families together in a common activity. The media are also sometimes blamed for interfering with children's social development by increasing the number of hours they spend in isolation with TV, games, or other media, but the media have also been used in a social context, especially by adolescent boys. Motivation for using the media and the context in which they are used as well as family makeup, activities, and values influence the types of interactions that will occur in a family and the effects on the children and adolescents in those families. Simply coviewing is not enough, however, and may serve as a model for more ritualistic viewing. Parental comments, mediation, and restrictions or rules about viewing and other media use are also important.

Health-Related Effects of Media Use

A good deal of new research has focused on the effects on children and adolescents of frequent exposure to negative or unhealthy behaviors that are shown in the media. Music videos, for example, also often depict alcohol and tobacco use, sexual innuendo and behavior, and violence. Sexual behavior is a common feature of many movies and TV programs that air at times when children and adolescents are likely to be watching. Most of the portrayals do not include much reference to risks, potential negative consequences, or responsibility, although this appears to be changing somewhat.

Frequent portrayals of attractive characters on television or in movies, music videos, or magazines using alcohol, tobacco, or drugs can play an important role in users' attitudes and decisions to use those substances. The media, including TV and print material, continue to present a thin ideal for female users such that many of them become dissatisfied with their own bodies and become more vulnerable to eating disorders.

Social/Emotional Effects

In addition to media effects on aggressive behavior, stereotypes, self-concept, and susceptibility to advertising, media use also has the potential to affect children's social and emotional development in other ways. A large proportion of children have reported experiences of fear and anxiety, stress, nightmares, reduced concentration, and poor school performance after watching frightening content. Although viewing violence has not been directly related causally to psychopathology in children, some researchers have reported higher levels of depression, posttraumatic stress disorder, and other emotional problems following media use. It is also clear that children who have various kinds of learning, emotional, and behavioral disorders tend to view larger amounts of television, see it as more realistic, and have fewer skills to deal with the information in a constructive way and are therefore more vulnerable. They may also use the media to avoid academic or social problems and to get information that they cannot get from print.

Differential Access

Given the ubiquity of technology in the lives of children and adolescents and its potential impact on their development, the issue of unequal access to the new technologies is an important one. Computers can increase children's learning immeasurably and children without easy access will be at a distinct disadvantage in an information-rich society. As the interactivity of the new technologies allows for more active learning, which developmental theory and research has demonstrated is the most effective type of learning, differential access leads to different learning experiences. Socioeconomic level also affects children's access to the media, the availability of other educational resources, and their patterns of media use. Limited access to technology for some children may reduce their apparent computer competency but does not necessarily indicate a lack of interest or an inability to learn the necessary skills. Although children and adolescents with less access are exposed to fewer unhealthy messages, they also miss more positive messages and all of the benefits that computer use can confer, both for information and academic work and for entertainment. Weaker computer competency may also jeopardize future employment opportunities.

Use of the Internet

The Internet and online activities have become an increasingly significant part of children and adolescents' experience with technology. Children use the Internet frequently for educational purposes such as research or school projects, and they also enjoy e-mail and online chat rooms. Many report significant exposure to unwanted material such as pornography, however, and parents worry about the relationships that can develop on the Internet. The Internet can be used to communicate with friends and meet new ones, and many teens appear to use it as a testing ground for various personas. They also use it to get information that is difficult for them to discuss.

Interventions

Various media literacy programs have been developed to help children learn critical viewing skills and more general media literacy so they can make the best use of the media. Rating systems have been developed for television content, movies, and video games to help parents screen their children's media use and to reduce their exposure to undesirable content such as violence. However, ratings frequently do not match the content sufficiently to allow effective control or screening by parents. There is growing encouragement for parents, family physicians, pediatricians, and other professionals to intervene to ensure that children's media experiences are positive and healthy.

FUTURE RESEARCH QUESTIONS AND DIRECTIONS

Despite the wealth of data now available on all aspects of the media experiences of children and adolescents, many questions remain to fascinate and challenge researchers. One area that will undoubtedly command a good deal more attention is the study of the differences in the use that is made of television and game playing and whether children and adolescents use the media ritualistically or instrumentally. The purpose for which they engage in media use appears to be a major factor in their choices, in the nature of their information processing, and in the media's impact on them.

If children and adolescents are playing games or watching TV primarily for relaxation and diversion, they likely invest less effort, and there should be less effect than if they are seriously seeking information. Some researchers have suggested that new technologies are used more instrumentally, which should increase their impact. On the other hand, those using the media more purposefully and instrumentally likely spend less time with them, which also affects media impact. More research also needs to be done to further explore important gender differences in cognitive skills and preferences in games and TV viewing and how they interact with motivation and use of the media to affect media impact or influence.

There are suggestions in recent research findings that despite games' greater realism and graphic violence, game playing may be less predictive of aggression than is commonly assumed. Some inconsistencies in research findings in this area have been reported, however, and more study of the possible reasons for the inconsistencies, such as interactions among types of games, types of aggression, reasons for playing, and gender and developmental differences needs to be done.

Others have suggested that game playing can provide an important social context. More research is needed on the differences between television viewing and game playing and their relative impact on children's and adolescents' social behavior and development. Questions also remain about why some children seem relatively unaffected by either.

More attention to the importance of different types of auditory and visual stimuli and the different kinds of processing that are required for holistic and linguistic stimuli is needed. Study of the interactions of these stimuli types with gender, cognitive skills, and media content might lead to further clarification of some of the differential gender effects of game playing and television viewing that have been reported in the research literature, perhaps due in part to their respective emphases on visual and verbal skills.

Another intriguing area of study is in the role of arousal in media impact and whether lower levels of arousal mean fatigue and boredom, and consequently less effect, or desensitization to violence and therefore, perhaps, greater likelihood of aggressive behavior. More research is needed to explore whether the arousal and cueing effect is short-term and subsides over longer periods of extended play or whether the lower arousal over longer periods means that the individual is becoming more desensitized to and accepting of violence as normal. In other words, is the lower arousal level a positive or negative effect?

Greater attention needs to be paid to the difference between impact on attitudes, emotions, and beliefs and effects on actual behavior. Although behavior controls exist in most media users, researchers need to learn whether continued exposure and possible desensitization lead to weaker controls, and if so, which aspects of the exposure (e.g., social interaction, competition, type of violence, context, and many others) make a critical difference. More research on the subtypes of violence and the interactions of types of violence with gender and developmental levels would likely reveal different patterns of aggression for both genders than have been apparent previously. Further study of the differences between short-term and long-term effects of media use and of media literacy programs and other interventions is also needed.

The most important and difficult research challenge remains to be that of unraveling the interactions among gender, racial, socioeconomic, developmental, and cognitive variables on one hand and the purposes for media use, time spent, alternate information and entertainment sources, and patterns of use on the other. Finally, expansion of theoretical and methodological means to study and explain these interactions will result in a clearer understanding of media influence on the social, psychological, intellectual, and physical development of children and adolescents and will provide ways to study the many future technological changes and media options that are sure to come.

References

Abelman, R. (1987). Television literacy for gifted children. *Roeper Review, 9*(3), 166–168.

Abelman, R. (1990). Determinants of parental mediation of children's television viewing. In J. Bryant (Ed.), *Television and the American family* (pp. 311–326). Hillsdale, NJ: Lawrence Erlbaum Associates, Inc.

Adler, T. (1991, October). By age 4, most kids see what's real. *APA Monitor.*

Adventures in learning. (1992). Toronto, Ontario, Canada: Discis Knowledge Research.

Alphonso, C. (2003, February 15). An instant way to get teachers' dirty looks. *The Globe and Mail,* p. A3.

Alvarez, M. M., Huston, A. C., Wright, J. C., & Kerkman, D. D. (1988). Gender differences in visual attention to television form and content. *Journal of Applied Developmental Psychology, 9,* 459–475.

Ambrose, M. (1991, June 20). Cross current. *The Globe and Mail,* p. C1.

American Academy of Child and Adolescent Psychiatry. (2002). Children and the news. *Facts for Families, 67.*

American Academy of Pediatrics. (2001a, July). Alcohol use and abuse: A pediatric concern. *Pediatrics, 108,* 185–189.

American Academy of Pediatrics. (2001b, November). Media violence. *Pediatrics, 108*(5), 1222–1226. Abstract retrieved January 13, 2003, from http://www.pediatrics.org/cgi/content/abstract/108/5/1222

American Psychological Association. (1995, December). Violence is sowing the seeds for educational, emotional setbacks. *APA Monitor,* pp. 6–7.

Anderson, C., & Bushman, B. (2001). Effects of violent video games on aggressive behavior, aggressive cognition, aggressive affect, physiological arousal, and prosocial behavior: A Meta-analytic review of the scientific literature. *Psychological Science, 12,* 353–359.

Anderson, C. A., & Dill, K. E. (2000). Video games and aggressive thoughts, feelings, and behavior in the laboratory and in life. *Journal of Personality and Social Psychology, 78,* 772–790.

Anderson, D. R., & Collins, P. A. (1988). *The impact on children's education: Television's influence on cognitive development* (Working Paper No. 2). U.S. Department of Education, Office of Educational Research and Improvement.

Anderson, D. R., Field, D. E., Collins, P. A., Lorch, E. P., & Nathan, J. G. (1985). Estimates of young children's time with television: A methodological comparison of parent reports with time-lapse video home observation. *Child Development, 56,* 1345–1357.

Anderson, D. R., Huston, A. C., Schmitt, K. L., Linebarger, D. L., & Wright, J. C. (2001). Early childhood television viewing and adolescent behavior: The recontact study. *Monographs of the Society for Research in Child Development, 66*(Serial No. 264).

Anderson, D. R., & Levin, S. R. (1976). Young children's attention to *"Sesame Street." Child Development, 47,* 806–811.

Anderson, D. R., & Smith, R. (1984). Young children's tv viewing: The problem of cognitive continuity. In F. J. Morrison, C. Lord, & D. P. Keating (Eds.), *Applied developmental psychology* (Vol. 1, pp. 116–163). Orlando, FL: Academic.

Anderssen, E. (2003, February 15). R u sure u no wht yr kds r doin? *The Globe and Mail,* p. F9.

Andsager, J. L., Austin, E. W., & Pinkleton, B. E. (2002). Gender as a variable in interpretation of alcohol-related messages. *Communication Research, 29,* 246–269.

Annas, G. J. (1996). Cowboys, camels, and the First Amendment—The FDA's restrictions on tobacco advertising. *The New England Journal of Medicine, 335,* 1779–1783. Retrieved January 13, 2003, from http://content.nejm.org/cgi/content/full/335/23/1779?ijkey=OGNN q5a787kfk

Annenberg Public Policy Center. (1999). *Media in the home 1999: The fourth annual survey of parents and children.* Retrieved July 2, 2002, from http://www.apj3cpenn.org/mediainhome/survey

Argenta, D. M., Stoneman, Z., & Brody, G. H. (1986). The effects of three different television programs on young children's peer interactions and toy play. *Journal of Applied Developmental Psychology, 7,* 355–371.

Arnett, J. (1991). Heavy metal music and reckless behavior among adolescents. *Journal of Youth and Adolescence, 20,* 573–592.

Associated Press. (2003a, July 14). Camera phones lead to mischief. *The Record,* p. B4.

Associated Press. (2003b, February 28). Sons copied Sopranos killing, police say. *The Globe and Mail,* p. A13.

Atkin, D. (2002, November 2). It computes: Laptops equal better learning. *The Globe and Mail,* p. F7.

Augoustinos, M., & Rosewarne, D. L. (2002). Stereotype knowledge and prejudice in children. *British Journal of Developmental Psychology, 19,* 143–156.

Austin, E. W., & Johnson, K. K. (1997). Effects of general and alcohol-specific media literacy training on children's decision making about alcohol. *Journal of Health Communication, 2*(1), 17–42.

Austin, E. W., & Meili, H. K. (1994). Effects of interpretations of televised alcohol portrayals on children's alcohol beliefs. *Journal of Broadcasting & Electronic Media, 38,* 417–435.

Austin, E. W., Pinkleton, B. E., & Fujioka, Y. (1999). The role of interpretation processes and parental discussion in the media's effects on adolescents' use of alcohol. *Pediatrics, 105,* 343–349. Abstract retrieved January 14, 2003, from http://www.pediatrics.org/cgi/content/abstract/105/2/343

Austin, E. W., Roberts, D. F., & Nass, C. I. (1990). Influences of family communication on children's television-interpretation processes. *Communication Research, 17,* 545–564.

Babrow, A. S., O'Keefe, B. J., Swanson, D. L., Meyers, R. A., & Murphy, M. A. (1988). Person perception and children's impressions of television and real peers. *Communication Research, 15,* 680–698.

Bandura, A. (1967). The role of modelling processes in personality development. In W. W. Hartup & N. L. Smothergill (Eds.), *The young child: Reviews of research* (pp. 42–58). Washington, DC: National Association for the Education of Young Children.

Bandura, A. (1977). *Social learning theory.* Englewood Cliffs, NJ: Prentice Hall.

Bandura, A. (1986). *Social foundations of thought and action: A social-cognitive theory.* Englewood Cliffs, NJ: Prentice Hall.

Bandura, A. (1990). Selective activation and disengagement of moral control. *Journal of Social Issues, 46,* 27–46.

Bandura, A. (1994). Social cognitive theory of mass communication. In J. Bryant & D. Zillmann (Eds.), *Media effects: Advances in theory and research* (pp. 61–90). Hillsdale, NJ: Lawrence Erlbaum Associates, Inc.

Bar-on, M. E. (2000). The effects of television on child health: Implications and recommendations. *Archives of Disease in Childhood, 83,* 289–292. Retrieved January 13, 2003, from http://adc.bmjjournals.com/cgi/content/full/archdischild;83/4/289

Barr, R., & Hayne, H. (1999). Developmental changes in imitation from television during infancy. *Child Development, 70,* 1067–1081.

Beasley, B., & Standley, T. C. (2002). Shirts vs. skins: Clothing as an indicator of gender role stereotyping in video games. *Mass Communication and Society, 5,* 279–293.

Beatty, S. (2003, March 18). In a time of anxiety, a 'safe zone' for kids. *The Globe and Mail.*

Beauchesne, E. (1994, November 5). Canadians spend less time in front of TV, study shows. *The Kitchener-Waterloo Record.*

Beentjes, J. W., & Van der Voort, T. H. (1988). Television's impact on children's reading skills: A review of research. *Reading Research Quarterly, 23,* 389–413.

Beentjes, J. W. J., & Van der Voort, T. H. A. (1993). Television viewing vs. reading: Mental effort, retention, and inferential learning. *Communication Education, 42,* 191–205.

Beresin, E. V. (1999). Media violence and youth Abstract. *Academic Psychiatry, 23,* 111–114.

Berkowitz, L. (1986). Situational influences on reactions to observed violence. *Journal of Social Issues, 42*(3), 93–106.

Berkowitz, L. (1988). Frustrations, appraisals, and aversively stimulated aggression. *Aggressive Behavior, 14,* 3–11.

Berkowitz, L. (1994). Is something missing? Some observations prompted by the cognitive-neoassociationist view of anger and emotional aggression. In L. R. Huesmann (Ed.), *Aggressive behavior: Current perspectives* (pp. 35–57). New York: Plenum.

Berkowitz, L., & Rogers, K. H. (1986). A priming effect analysis of media influences. In J. Bryant & D. Zillmann (Eds.), *Perspectives on media effects* (pp. 57–81). Hillsdale, NJ: Lawrence Erlbaum Associates, Inc.

Berry, G. L. (1998). Black family life on television and the socialization of the African American child: Images of marginality. *Journal of Comparative Family Studies, 29,* 233–242.

Bianculli, D. (1994). *Teleliteracy: Taking television seriously.* New York: Touchstone.

Billings, A. C., Halone, K. K., & Denham, B. E. (2002). "Man, that was a pretty shot": An analysis of gendered broadcast commentary surrounding the 2000 men's and women's NCAA final four basketball championships. *Mass Communication and Society, 5,* 295–315.

Biocca, F. (1994). Virtual reality technology: A tutorial. *Journal of Communication, 42*(4), 23–72.

Boehm, H. (2003). Should youngsters watch the news? *Advice on raising kids from FamilyFun.* Retrieved March 18, 2003, from http://www.family.msn.com/tool/article.aspx?dept=raising&sdept=rks&name=ff_021703

Borzekowski, D. L. (1996). Embedded anti-alcohol messages on commercial television: What teenagers perceive. *Journal of Adolescent Health. 19,* 345–352.

Borzekowski, D. L. G., & Rickert, V. I. (2001). Adolescents, the Internet, and health: Issues of access and content. *Applied Developmental Psychology, 22,* 49–59.

Botta, R. A. (2000). The mirror of television: A comparison of black and white adolescents' body image. *Journal of Communication, 50*(3), 144–159.

Boyd, C. (2003, July 17). Girl's abduction exposes extent of Internet luring. *The Globe and Mail,* p. A11.

Brockhouse, G. (1996, December). A computer for couch potatoes. *Home Computing,* pp. 38–39.

Brown, D., & Bryant, J. (1990). Effects of television on family values and selected attitudes and behaviors. In J. Bryant (Ed.), *Television and the American family* (pp. 253–274). Hillsdale, NJ: Lawrence Erlbaum Associates, Inc.

Brown, J. A. (2001). Media literacy and critical television viewing in education. In D. G. Singer & J. L. Singer (Eds.), *Handbook of children and the media* (pp. 681–697). Thousand Oaks, CA: Sage.

Brown, J. D., & Keller, S. N. (2000). Can the mass media be healthy sex educators? *Family Planning Perspectives, 32*(5). Retrieved December 20, 2002, from http://www.agi-usa.org/pubs/journals/3225500.html

Brown, J. D., Steele, J. R., & Walsh-Childers, K. (2002). Introduction and overview. In J. D. Brown, J. R. Steele, & K. Walsh-Childers (Eds.), *Sexual teens, sexual media: Investigating media's influence on adolescent sexuality* (pp. 1–24). Mahwah, NJ: Lawrence Erlbaum Associates, Inc.

Brown, J. D., & Walsh-Childers, K. (1994). Effects of media on personal and public health. In J. Bryant & D. Zillmann (Eds.), *Media effects: Advances in theory and research* (pp. 389–415). Hillsdale, NJ: Lawrence Erlbaum Associates, Inc.

Brown, P. L. (2003, July 27). Hey there, couch potatoes: Hot enough for you? *The New York Times*, pp. 1, 7.

Brucks, M., Armstrong, G. M., & Goldberg, M. E. (1988). Children's use of cognitive defenses against television advertising: A cognitive response approach. *Journal of Consumer Research, 14*, 471–482.

Buchanan, A. M., Gentile, D. A., Nelson, D. A., Walsh, D. A., & Hensel, J. (2002). *What goes in must come out: Children's media violence consumption at home and aggressive behaviors at school.* Retrieved December 29, 2002, from the National Institute on Media and the Family Web site: http://www.mediafamily.org/research/report_issbd_2002.shtml

Bushman, B. J. & Huesmann, L. R. (2001). Effects of televised violence on aggression. In D. G. Singer & J. L. Singer (Eds.), *Handbook of children and the media* (pp. 223–254). Thousand Oaks, CA: Sage.

California Assessment Program. (1980). *Television and student achievement.* Sacramento, CA: State Department of Education.

California Assessment Program. (1988). *Annual report, 1985–1986.* Sacramento, CA: California State Department of Education.

Calvert, S. L. (1988). Television production feature effects on children's comprehension of time. *Journal of Applied Developmental Psychology, 9*, 263–273.

Calvert, S. L., & Gersh, T. L. (1987). The selective use of sound effects and visual inserts for children's television story comprehension. *Journal of Applied Developmental Psychology, 8*, 363–374.

Calvert, S. L., & Tan, S. L. (1994). Impact of virtual reality on young adults' physiological arousal and aggressive thoughts: Interaction vs. observation. *Journal of Applied Developmental Psychology, 15*, 125–139.

Campbell, T. A., Wright, J. C., & Huston, A. C. (1987). Form cues and content difficulty as determinants of children's cognitive processing of televised educational messages. *Journal of Experimental Child Psychology, 43*, 311–327.

Canadian Advertising Foundation. (1987). *Sex-role stereotyping guidelines.* Ottawa, Ontario, Canada: Author.

Cannon, C. M. (1995). Media violence increases violence in society. In C. Wekesser (Ed.), *Violence in the media* (pp. 17–24). San Diego, CA: Greenhaven.

Cantor, J. (1994). Fright reactions to mass media. In J. Bryant & D. Zillmann (Eds.), *Media effects: Advances in theory and research* (pp. 213–245). Hillsdale, NJ: Lawrence Erlbaum Associates, Inc.

Cantor, J. (2001). The media and children's fears, anxieties, and perceptions of danger. In D. G. Singer & J. L. Singer (Eds.), *Handbook of children and the media* (pp. 207–221). Thousand Oaks, CA: Sage.

Cantor, J., & Nathanson, A. (1996). Children's fright reactions to television news. *Journal of Communication, 46*(4), 139–152.

Cantor, J., & Sparks, G. G. (1984). Children's fear responses to mass media: Testing some Piagetian predictions. *Journal of Communication, 34*, 90–103.

Carpenter, E. (1986). The new languages. In G. Gumpert & R. Cathcart (Eds.), *Inter/media: Interpersonal communication in a media world* (3rd ed., pp. 353–367). New York: Oxford University Press.

Caughey, J. L. (1986). Social relations with media figures. In G. Gumpert & R. Cathcart (Eds.), *Inter/media: Interpersonal communication in a media world* (3rd ed., pp. 219–252). New York: Oxford University Press.

Celebrating television. (1989, Summer). *People. Extra,* p. 6.

Centerwall, B. S. (1995). Television and violent crime. In R. L. DelCampo & D. S. DelCampo (Eds.), *Taking sides: Clashing views on controversial issues in childhood and society* (pp. 180–187). Guilford, CT: Dushkin.

Chambers, J. H., & Ascione, F. R. (1987). The effects of prosocial and aggressive videogames on children's donating and helping. *Journal of Genetic Psychology, 148,* 499–505.

Chapin, J. (2002). Third-person perception and school violence. *Communication Research Reports, 19,* 216–225.

Cheney, G. A. (1983). *Television in American society.* New York: F. Watts.

Children Now. (1995). *Sending signals: Kids speak out about values in the media.* Retrieved November 7, 2003, from http://www.childrennow.org/media/mc95/poll.html

Children Now. (1997). *Reflections of girls in the media: A two-part study on gender and media. Summary of key findings.* Retrieved July 14, 2003, from http://www.childrennow.org/media/mc97/ReflectSummary.html.

Children Now. (1999). *Study shows that media reinforces gender strait jacket.* Retrieved December 29, 2002, from http://www.childrennow.org/media/boystomen/index.html

Children Now. (2000). *Top-selling video games 'unhealthy' for girls* (Children and the Media Program). Retrieved December 12, 2002, from http://www.childrennow.org/newsroom/news-00/pr-12-12-00.htm

Children Now. (2001a). *Fair play? Violence, gender and race in video games.* Retrieved December 29, 2002, from http://www.childrennow.org/media /video-games/2001/

Children Now. (2001b). *TV networks' "Family Hour" has least diverse prime time programming.* Retrieved December 27, 2002, from http://www.childrennow.org/newsroom/news-01/pr-5-1-01.cfm

Children Now. (2002a). Anti-smoking ads may influence teen habits: Study. *Preventive Medicine, 35,* 511–518. Retrieved December 29, 2002, from http://www.childrennow.org/newsroom/news-02/cam-ra-12-10-02a.htm

Children Now. (2002b). *Children and advertising.* Retrieved December 29, 2002, from http://www.mediafamily.org/facts/facts_childadv.shtml

Children Now. (2002c). *Newscasts too often employ scare tactics.* Retrieved December 29, 2002, from http://www.childrennow.org/newsroom/news-02/cam-ra-10-16-02.htm

Children Now. (2002d). *Why it matters ... Diversity on television.* Retrieved December 29, 2002, from http://www.childrennow.org/media/medianow/mnsummer2002.htm

Chiose, S. (1996, December 14). Bombarded by culture. *The Globe and Mail* p. C1.

Chory-Assad, R. M., & Mastro, D. E. (2000, November). *Violent videogame use and hostility among high school students and college students.* Paper presented as part of the panel "Violent Video Games and Hostility" to the Mass Communication Division of the National Communication Association, Seattle, WA. Retrieved July 4, 2003, from http://web.ics.purdue.edu/~sherryj/videogames/VGU&H.pdf

Christenson, P. G., & Roberts, D. F. (1998). *It's not only rock & roll: Popular music in the lives of adolescents.* Cresskill, NJ: Hampton.

Clifford, B. R., Gunter, B., & McAleer, J. (1995). *Television and children: Program evaluation, comprehension, and impact.* Hillsdale, NJ: Lawrence Erlbaum Associates, Inc.

Cohen, A. A., & Salomon, G. (1979). Children's literate television viewing: Surprises and possible explanations. *Journal of Communication, 29*(3), 156–163.

Committee on Public Education. (2001, January). Sexuality, contraception and the media. *Pediatrics, 107,* 191–194.

Comstock, G. (1998). Television research: Past problems and present issues. In J. K. Asamen & G. L. Berry (Eds.), *Research paradigms, television, and social behavior* (pp. 11–65). Thousand Oaks, CA: Sage.

Comstock, G., & Paik, H. (1991). *Television and the American child.* San Diego, CA: Academic.

Comstock, G., & Scharrer, E. (1999). *Television: What's on, who's watching, and what it means.* San Diego, CA: Academic.

Comstock, G., & Strasburger, V. C. (1993a). Deceptive appearances: Television violence and aggressive behavior. *Journal of Adolescent Health Care, 11,* 31–44.

Comstock, G., & Strasburger, V. C. (1993b). Media violence: Q & A. In V. C. Strasburger & G. A. Comstock (Eds.), *Adolescents and the media, adolescent medicine: State of the art reviews, 4*(3), 495–509. American Academy of Pediatrics. Philadelphia: Hanley and Belfus.

Considine, J. D. (2003, July 17). Manga mania comes to the West. *The Globe and Mail,* p. R3.

Cope-Farrar, K. M., & Kunkel, D. (2002). Sexual messages in teens' favorite prime-time television programs. In J. D. Brown, J. R. Steele, & K. Walsh-Childers (Eds.), *Sexual teens, sexual media: Investigating media's influence on adolescent sexuality* (pp. 59–78). Mahwah, NJ: Lawrence Erlbaum Associates, Inc.

Corteen, R. S., & Williams, T. M. (1986). Television and reading skills. In T. M. Williams (Ed.), *The impact of television* (pp. 39–86). Orlando, FL: Academic.

Cotrane, S., & Messineo, M. (2000). The perpetuation of subtle prejudice: Race and gender imagery in 1990's television advertising. *Sex Roles, 42,* 363–389.

Crain, W. (1992). *Theories of development: Concepts and applications.* Englewood Cliffs, NJ: Prentice Hall.

Crawley, A. M., Anderson, D. R., Santomero, A., Wilder, A., Williams, M., Evans, M. K., & Bryant, J. (2002). Do children learn how to watch television? The impact of extensive experience with *Blues Clues* on preschool children's television viewing behavior. *Journal of Communication, 52*(2), 264–280.

Crespo, C. J., Smit, E., Troiano, R. P., Bartlett, S. J., Macera, C. A., & Andersen, R. E. (2001). Television watching, energy intake, and obesity in U.S. children. *Archives of Pediatric and Adolescent Medicine, 155,* 360–365. Cited in National Institute on Media and the Family. Television and obesity among children. Retrieved December 29, 2002, from http://www.mediafamily.org/facts/facts_tvandobchild.shtml

Crick, N. R. (1996). The role of overt aggression, relational aggression, and prosocial behavior in children's future social adjustment. *Child Development, 67,* 2317–2327.

Crick, N., & Grotpeter, J. (1995). Relational aggression, gender, and social-psychological adjustment. *Child Development, 66,* 710–722.

Csikszentmihalyi, M., & Larson, R. (1987). Validity and reliability of the Experience-Sampling Method. *Journal of Nervous and Mental Disease, 175,* 526–536.

Cuff, J. H. (2005, January). Television: The real victims of constant viewing. *The Globe and Mail,* p. D1.

Cullingsford, C. (1984). *Children and television.* Aldershot, England: Gower.

Damsell, K. (2003, April 9). DVDs a hit in Canada, especially among Generation Y. *The Globe and Mail,* p. B4.

de Groot, G. (1994, June). Psychologists explain 'Barney's' power. *APA Monitor,* p. 4.

Dennison, M. D., Barbara, A., Erb M. S., Tara A. E., & Jenkins, P. L. (2002). Television viewing and television in bedroom associated with overweight risk among low-income preschool children. *Pediatrics, 109,* 1028–1035.

Desmond, R. J., Singer, J. L., & Singer, D. G. (1990). Family mediation: Parental communication patterns and the influences of television on children. In J. Bryant (Ed.), *Television and the American family* (pp. 293–309). Hillsdale, NJ: Lawrence Erlbaum Associates, Inc.

Dietz, T. L. (1998). An examination of violence and gender role portrayals in video games: Implications for gender socialization and aggressive behavior. *Sex Roles, 38,* 425–442.

Dirr, P. J. (2001). Cable television: Gateway to educational resources for development at all ages. In D. G. Singer & J. L. Singer (Eds.), *Handbook of children and the media* (pp. 533–545). Thousand Oaks, CA: Sage.

Disney, A. (1995). Media violence should be treated as a public health problem. In C. Wekesser (Ed.), *Violence in the media* (pp. 130–131). San Diego, CA: Greenhaven.

Dixon, T. L., & Linz, D. (2002). Race and the misrepresentation of victimization on local television news. *Communication Research, 27,* 547–573.

Dobrow, J. R. (1990). Patterns of viewing and VCR use: Implications for cultivation analysis. In N. Signorielli & M. Morgan (Eds.), *Cultivation analysis: New directions in media effects research* (pp. 71–83). Newbury Park, CA: Sage.

Doerken, M. (1983). *Classroom combat: Teaching and television.* Englewood Cliffs, NJ: Educational Technology Publications.

Dominick, J. R. (1987). *The dynamics of mass communication.* New York: Random House.

Donnerstein, E., Slaby, R. G., & Eron, L. D. (1994). The mass media and youth aggression. In L. D. Eron, J. H. Gentry, & P. Schlegel (Eds.), *Reason to hope: A psychosocial perspective on violence and youth* (pp. 219–250). Washington, DC: American Psychological Association.

Dorr, A., Kovaric, P., & Doubleday, C. (1989). Parent–child coviewing of television. *Journal of Broadcasting and Electronic Media, 33,* 35–51.

Dorr, A., Kovaric, P., & Doubleday, C. (1990). Age and content influences on children's perceptions of the realism of television families. *Journal of Broadcasting and Electronic Media, 34,* 377–397.

Douglas, W. (1996). The fall from grace? The modern family on television. *Communication Research, 23,* 675–702.

Douglas, W., & Olson, B. M. (1996). Subversion of the American family? An examination of children and parents in television families. *Communication Research, 23,* 73–99.

Doyle, J. (2003, March 12). Setting up for the really cool Iraq war show. *The Globe and Mail,* p. R2.

Duke, L. (2000). Black in a blonde world: Race and girls' interpretation of the feminine ideal in teen magazines. *Journalism and Mass Communication Quarterly, 77,* 367–392.

Dunn, J., & Hughes, C. (2001). "I got some swords and you're dead!": Violent fantasy, antisocial behavior, friendship, and moral sensibility in young children. *Child Development. 72,* 491–505.

Dunn, L. M. (1965). *Peabody picture vocabulary test.* Circle Pines, MN: American Guidance Service.

Dunn, L. M., & Dunn, L. M. (1981). *Peabody picture vocabulary test—revised: Manual for forms L and M.* Circle Pines, MN: American Guidance Service.

DuRant, R. H., Rich, M., Emans, S. J., Rome, E. S., Allred, E., & Woods, E. R. (1997). Violence and weapon carrying in music videos: A content analysis. *Pediatric Adolescent Medicine, 151,* 443–448.

DuRant, R. H., Rome, E. S., Rich, M., Allred, E., Emans, S. J., & Woods, E. R. (1997). Tobacco and alcohol use behaviors portrayed in music videos: Content analysis. *American Journal of Public Health, 87,* 1131–1135.

Durham, M. G. (1999). Girls, media, and the negotiation of sexuality: A study of race, class and gender in adolescent peer groups. *Journalism and Mass Communication Quarterly, 76,* 193–216.

Durkin, K. (1985). *Television, sex roles and children: A developmental social psychological account.* Philadelphia: Open University Press.

Durkin, K., & Judge, J. (2002). Effects of language and social behaviour on children's reactions to foreign people in television. *British Journal of Developmental Psychology, 19,* 597–612.

Edell, J. A. (1988). Nonverbal effects in advertisements: A review and synthesis. In S. Hecker & D. W. Stewart (Eds.), *Nonverbal communication in advertising* (pp. 11–28). Lexington, MA: D. C. Heath.

Elber, L. (2002, December 21). Group helps TV practise safe sex. *The Globe and Mail,* p. R20.

Elkind, D. (1993). Adolescents, parenting, and the media in the twenty-first century. In V. C. Strasburger & G. A. Comstock (Eds.), *Adolescents and the media. Adolescent medicine: State of the art reviews,* pp. 599–606. American Academy of Pediatrics. Philadelphia: Hanley and Belfus.

Engelhardt, T. (1987) The shortcake strategy. In T. Gitlin (Ed.), *Watching television: A pantheon guide to popular culture* (pp. 68–110). New York: Pantheon.

Eron, L. D. (1980). Prescription for reduction of aggression. *American Psychologist, 35,* 244–252.

Eron, L. D. (1982). Parent–child interaction, television violence, and aggression of children. *American Psychologist, 37,* 197–211.

Eron, L. D. (1986). Interventions to mitigate the psychological effects of media violence on aggressive behavior. *Journal of Social Issues, 42*(3), 155–169.

Eron, L. D. (1994). Theories of aggression: From drives to cognitions. In L. R. Huesmann (Ed.), *Aggressive behavior: Current perspectives* (pp. 3–33). New York: Plenum.

Everett-Green, R. (1997, January 28). E-zines explore uncharted Internet territory. *The Globe and Mail*, p. C1.

Farrington, D. P. (1991). Childhood aggression and adult violence: Early precursors and later life outcomes. In D. J. Pepler & K. H. Rubin (Eds.), *The development and treatment of childhood aggression* (pp. 5–29). Hillsdale, NJ: Lawrence Erlbaum Associates, Inc.

Feldman, S. (1994, November 15). Chameleon in a box: Where TV is taking us. *The Globe and Mail*, p. 29

Ferrington, G. (2003). Youth and multimedia. *Media Literacy Review, 3*(2), 1.

Fetler, M. (1984). Television viewing and school achievement. *Journal of Communication,34*(2), 104–118.

Fischer, P. M., Schwartz, M. P., Richards, J. W., Jr., & Goldstein, A. O. (1991). Brand logo recognition by children aged 3 to 6 years: Mickey Mouse and Old Joe the Camel. *Journal of the American Medical Association, 266*, 3145– 3148.

Fleming, M. J., & Rickwood, D. J. (2001). Effects of violent versus nonviolent video games on children's arousal, aggressive mood, and positive mood. *Journal of Applied Social Psychology, 31*, 2047–2071.

Flynn, B. S., Worden, J. K., Secker-Walker, R. H., Badger, G. J., Geller, B. M., & Costanza, M. C. (1992). Prevention of cigarette smoking through masss media intervention and school programs. [Abstract]. *American Journal of Public Health, 82*, 827–834. Retrieved January 13, 2003 from http://www.ajph.org/cgi/content/abstract/82/6/827?ijkey=ovrebH5xYPLIg

Forge, K. L. S., & Phemister, S. (1987). The effect of prosocial cartoons on preschool children. *Child Study Journal, 17*(2), 83–88.

Foss, K. A., & Alexander, A. F. (1996). Exploring the margins of television viewing. *Communication Reports, 9*, 61–68.

Fouts, G., & Burggraf, K. (1999). Television situation comedies: Female body images and verbal reinforcements. *Sex Roles, 40*, 473–481.

Fowles, J. (1992). *Why viewers watch: A reappraisal of television's effects.* Newbury Park, CA: Sage.

Friedrich-Cofer, L., & Huston, A. C. (1986). Television violence and aggression: The debate continues. *Psychological Bulletin, 100*, 364–371.

Fullerton, J. A., & Kendrick, A. (2000). Portrayal of men and women in U.S. Spanish-language television commercials. *Journalism and Mass Communication Quarterly, 77*, 128–142.

Funk, J. B., & Buckman, D. D. (1996). Playing violent video and computer games and adolescent self-concept. *Journal of Communication, 46*(2), 19–32.

Gadow, K. D., Sprafkin, J., & Ficarrotto, T. J. (1987). Effects of viewing aggression-laden cartoons on preschool-aged emotionally disturbed children. *Child Psychiatry and Human Development, 17*, 257–274.

Gadow, K. D., Sprafkin, J., Kelly, E., & Ficarrotto, T. (1988). Reality perceptions of television: A comparison of school-labeled learning-disabled and nonhandicapped children. *Journal of Clinical Child Psychology, 17*, 25–33.

Gadow, K. D., Sprafkin, J., & Watkins, T. L. (1987). Effects of a critical viewing skills curriculum on elementary school children's knowledge and attitudes about television. *The Journal of Educational Research, 81*, 165–170.

Gardner, H., & Krasny Brown, L. (1984). Symbolic capabilities and children's television. In J. P. Murray & G. Salomon (Eds.), *The future of children's television* (pp. 45–51). Boys Town, NE: Father Flanagan's Boys' Home.

Geen, R. (1994, October). Psychologists explore the origins of violence. *APA Monitor.*

Gender gap persists in computer studies. (2003, June 24). *The Record*, p. A4.

Gentile, D. A., & Walsh, D. A. (2002, January 28). A normative study of family media habits. *Journal of Applied Developmental Psychology, 23*, 157–178.

Gentile, D., Walsh, D., Bloomgren, B., Jr., Atti, J., & Norman, J. (2001, April). *Frogs sell beer: The effects of beer advertisements on adolescent drinking knowledge, attitudes and behavior.* National Institute on Media and the Family paper presented at the Biennial Conference of the Society for Research in Child Development. Cited in National Institute on Media and the Family (2002), Alcohol Advertising and Youth. Retrieved Dec. 29, 2002, from http://www.media family.org/facts/facts_alcohol.shtml

Gerbner, G. (1998). *Casting the American scene: A look at the characters on prime time and daytime television from 1994–1997. The 1998 Screen Actors Guild report: Casting the scene.* Retrieved December 27, 2002, from the Media Awareness Network Web site: http:// www.media-aware-ness.ca/eng/issues/minrep/resource/reports/gerbner.htm

Gerbner, G., Gross, L., Morgan, M., & Signorielli, N. (1980). The 'mainstreaming' of America: Violence profile no. 11. *Journal of Communication, 30*(3), 10–29.

Gerbner, G., Gross, L., Morgan, M., & Signorielli, N. (1982). Charting the mainstream: Television's contributions to political orientation. *Journal of Communication, 32*(2), 100–127.

Gerbner, G., Gross, L., Morgan, M., & Signorielli, N. (1986). Living with television: The dynamics of the cultivation process. In J. Bryant & D. Zillmann (Eds.), *Perspectives on media effects* (pp. 17–40). Hillsdale, NJ: Lawrence Erlbaum Associates, Inc.

Gerbner, G., Gross, L., Morgan, M., & Signorielli, N. (1994). Growing up with television: The cultivation hypothesis. In J. Bryant & D. Zillmann (Eds.), *Media effects: Advances in theory and research* (pp. 17–41). Hillsdale, NJ: Lawrence Erlbaum Associates, Inc.

Gibbons, J., Anderson, D. R., Smith, R., Field, D. E., & Fischer, C. (1986). Young children's recall and reconstruction of audio and audiovisual narratives. *Child Development, 57,* 1014–1023.

Gidwani, P. P., Sobol, A., DeJong, W., Perrin, J. M., & Gortmaker, S. L. (2002). Television viewing and initiation of smoking among youth. *Pediatrics, 110,* 505–508.

Gill, A. (2003, January 27). Below zero. *The Globe and Mail,* pp. R1, R7.

Goldstein, A. O., Sobel, R. A., & Newman, G. R. (1999). Tobacco and alcohol use in G-rated children's animated films. *Journal of the American Medical Association, 281,* 1131–1136 [Abstract]. Retrieved January 14, 2003, from http://www.ncbi.nlm.nih.gov/entrez/query.fcgi?cmd=retrieve&db=pubmed&list_uids=101

Gow, J. (1996). Reconsidering gender roles on MTV: Depictions in the most popular music videos of the 1990's. *Communication Reports, 9,* 151–161.

Greenberg, B. S. (1986). Minorities and the mass media. In J. Bryant & D. Zillmann (Eds.), *Perspectives on media effects* (pp. 165–188). Hillsdale, NJ: Lawrence Erlbaum Associates, Inc.

Greenfield, P. M., Bruzzone, L., & Koyamatsu, K. (1987). What is rock music doing to the minds of our youth? A first experimental look at the effects of rock music lyrics and music videos. *Journal of Early Adolescence, 7,* 315–329.

Griffiths, M. D. (1991). Amusement machine playing in childhood and adolescence: A comparative analysis of video games and fruit machines. *Journal of Adolescence, 14,* 53–73.

Grimes, T., & Bergen, L. (2001). The notion of convergence as an epistemological base for evaluating the effect of violent programming on psychologically normal children. *Mass Communication and Society, 4,* 183–198 [Abstract]. Retrieved January 6, 2003, from http://operatix.ingentaselect.com/v1=37615266/c1=35/nw=1/rpsv/wwwtemp/c135tmp57.htm

Groebel, J. (2001). Media violence in cross-cultural perspective: A global study on children's media behavior and some educational implications. In D. G. Singer & J. L. Singer (Eds.), *Handbook of children and the media* (pp. 255–268). Thousand Oaks, CA: Sage.

Grube, J., & Wallack, L. (1994, February). Television beer advertising and drinking knowledge, beliefs, and intentions among schoolchildren. *The American Journal of Public Health, 24,* 254–259 [Abstract]. Retrieved January 13, 2003, from http://www.ajph.org/cgi/content/abstract/84/2/254?ijkey=f8ZGjPW1BUglA

Gruber, E., & Grube, J. W. (2000). Adolescent sexuality and the media. *Western Journal of Medicine, 172,* 210–214.

Guerra, N. G., Nucci, L., & Huesmann, L. R. (1994). Moral cognition and childhood aggression. In L. R. Huesmann (Ed.), Aggressive behavior: Current perspectives (pp. 13–33). New York: Plenum.

Gunter, B. (1985). Dimensions of television violence. Aldershot, England: Gower.

Gunter, B., McAleer, J., & Clifford, B. (1991). Children's views about television. Aldershot, England: Avebury.

Haddon, L. (1993). Interactive games. In P. Hayward & T. Wollen (Eds.), Future visions: New technologies of the screen (pp. 123–147). London: British Film Institute.

Hardin, M., Lynn, S., Walsdorf, K., & Hardin, B. (2002) The framing of sexual difference in SI for kids editorial photos. Mass Communication and Society, 5(3), 341–359.

Harrison, K. (2000). The body electric: Thin-ideal media and eating disorders in adolescents. Journal of Communication, 50(3), 119–143.

Harrison, L., & Williams, T. (1986). Television and cognitive development. In T. M. Williams (Ed.), The impact of television: A natural experiment in three communities (pp. 87–142). New York: Academic.

Hattemer, B., & Showers, R. (1995a). Heavy metal rock and gangsta rap music promote violence. In C. Wekesser (Ed.), Violence in the media (pp. 150–158). San Diego, CA: Greenhaven.

Hattemer, B., & Showers, R. (1995b). Prosocial programming by the media can be effective. In C. Wekesser (Ed.), Violence in the media (pp. 86–93). San Diego, CA: Greenhaven.

Hawkins, R. P., & Daly, J. (1988). Cognition and communication. In R. P. Hawkins, J. M. Wiemann, & S. Pingree (Eds.), Advancing communication science: Merging mass and interpersonal processes (pp. 191–223). Newbury Park, CA: Sage.

Hawkins, R. P., Kim, Y., & Pingree, S. (1991). The ups and downs of attention to television. Communication Research, 18, 53–76.

Hawkins, R. P., & Pingree, S. (1986). Activity in the effects of television on children. In J. Bryant & D. Zillmann (Eds.), Perspectives on media effects (pp. 233–250). Hillsdale, NJ: Lawrence Erlbaum Associates, Inc.

Hayes, D. S., & Birnbaum, D. W. (1980). Preschoolers' retention of televised events: Is a picture worth a thousand words? Developmental Psychology, 16, 410–416.

Hayes, D. S., & Kelly, S. B. (1984). Young children's processing of television: Modality differences in the retention of temporal relations. Journal of Experimental Child Psychology, 38, 505–514.

Hearold, S. (1986). A synthesis of 1043 effects of television on social behavior. In G. Comstock (Ed.), Public communication and behavior (Vol. 1, pp. 65–133). Orlando, FL: Academic.

Heath, L., & Gilbert, K. (1996). Mass media and fear of crime. American Behavioral Scientist, 39, 379–386.

Henning, B., & Vorderer, P. (2001). Psychological escapism: Predicting the amount of television viewing by need for cognition. Journal of Communication, 51(1), 100–120.

Hepola, S. (2003, June 22). Her favorite class: 'Sex' education. The New York Times, p. 1.

Higgins, M. (2003, March 11). In this unsettled world, Mr. Rogers exemplified safety. The Record, p. A9.

Hirsch, B. Z., & Kulberg, J. M. (1987). Television and temporal development. Journal of Early Adolescence, 7, 331–334.

Hobbs, R. (1997). Literacy for the information age. In J. Flood, S. B. Heath, & D. Papp (Eds.), Handbook of research on teaching literacy through the communicative and visual arts (pp. 7–14). New York: Macmillan.

Hobbs, R. (1998). The seven great debates in the media literacy movement. Journal of Communication, 48(1), 16–32.

Hobbs, R. (2003). Media literacy in the classroom. Newsweek Education Program. Retrieved April 20, 2003, from http://school.newsweek.com/online_activities/media.php

Hodge, R., & Tripp, D. (1986). Children and television. Cambridge, England: Polity.

Hodges, C. (1996). Beyond the computer. Random House/Broderbund.

Hoffner, C. (1995). Adolescents' coping with frightening mass media. *Communication Research, 22*, 325–346.

Hoffner, C., Cantor, J., & Thorson, E. (1988). Children's understanding of a televised narrative. *Communication Research, 15*, 227–245.

Hoffner, C., & Haefner, M. J. (1997). Children's comforting of frightened coviewers. *Communication Research, 24*, 136–152.

Hoffner, C., Plotkin, R. S., Buchanan, M., Anderson, D., Kamigaki, L. A., Hubbs, L. A., et al. (2001). The third-person effect in perceptions of the influence of television violence. *Journal of Communication, 51*(2), 283–299.

Hofschire, L. J., & Greenberg, B. S. (2002). Media's impact on adolescents' body dissatisfaction. In J. D. Brown, J. R. Steele, & K. Walsh-Childers (Eds.), *Sexual teens, sexual media: Investigating media's influence on adolescent sexuality* (pp. 125–149). Mahwah, NJ: Lawrence Erlbaum Associates, Inc.

Huesmann, L. R. (1986). Psychological processes promoting the relation between exposure to media violence and aggressive behavior by the viewer. *Journal of Social Issues, 42*(3), 125–139.

Huesmann, L. R. (1988) An information processing model for the development of aggression. *Aggressive Behavior, 14*, 13–24.

Huesmann, L. R., & Eron, L. D. (1986). The development of aggression in American children as a consequence of television violence viewing. In L. R. Huesmann & L. D. Eron (Eds.), *Television and the aggressive child: A cross-national comparison* (pp. 45–80). Hillsdale, NJ: Lawrence Erlbaum Associates, Inc.

Huesmann, L. R., Eron, L. D., Lefkowitz, M. M., & Walder, L. O. (1984). Stability of aggression over time and generation. *Developmental Psychology, 20*, 1120–1134.

Huesmann, L. R., Eron, L. D., & Yarmel, P. W. (1987). Intellectual functioning and aggression. *Journal of Personal and Social Psychology, 52*, 232–240.

Huesmann, L. R., Lagerspetz, K., & Eron, L. D. (1984). Intervening variables in the TV violence-aggression relation: Evidence from two countries. *Developmental Psychology, 20*, 746–775.

Huesmann, L. R., & Miller, L. S. (1994). Long-term effects of repeated exposure to media violence in childhood. In L. R. Huesmann (Ed.), *Aggressive behavior: Current perspectives* (pp. 153–186). New York: Plenum.

Huntemann, N., & Morgan, M. (2001). Mass media and identity development. In D. G. Singer & J. L. Singer (Eds.), *Handbook of children and the media* (pp. 309–322). Thousand Oaks, CA: Sage.

Huston, A. C., Donnerstein, E., Fairchild, H., Feshbach, N. D., Katz, P. A., Murray, J. P., Rubinstein, E. A., Wilcox, B. L., & Zuckerman, D. (1992). *Big world, small screen: The role of television in American society.* Lincoln: University of Nebraska Press.

Huston, A. C., Greer, D., Wright, J. C., Welch, R., & Ross, R. (1984). Children's comprehension of televised formal features with masculine and feminine connotations. *Developmental Psychology, 20*, 707–716.

Huston, A. C., Wartella, E., & Donnerstein, E. (1998). *Measuring the effects of sexual content in the media: A report to the Kaiser Family.* Retrieved December 20, 2002, from http://www.kff.org/content/archive/1389/content.html

Huston, A. C., & Wright, J. C. (1983). Children's processing of television: The informative functions of formal features. In J. Bryant & D. R. Anderson (Eds.), *Children's understanding of television* (pp. 35–68). New York: Academic.

Irvin, L. K., Walker, H. M., Noell, J., Singer, G. H. S., Irvine, A. B., Marquez, K., & Britz, B. (1992). Measuring children's social skills using microcomputer-based videodisc assessment. *Behavior Modification, 16*(4), 475–503.

Janz, K. F., Burns, T. L., Torner, J. C., Levy, S. M., Paulos, R., Willing, M. C., & Warren, J. J. (2001). Physical activity and bone measures in young children: The Iowa bone development study. *Pediatrics, 107*, 1387–1393.

Jesdanun, A. (2001, February 15). Filtering out bad software? abcnews.com. Retrieved November 8, 2003, from http://abcnews.go.com/sections/scitech/DailyNews/netfilters 010215.html

Johnson, J. (2003, February 15). Boy meets girl, boy gets Googled. *The Globe and Mail*, p. L1.

Johnson, J. D., Jackson, L. A., & Gatto, L. (1995). Violent attitudes and deferred academic aspirations: Deleterious effects of exposure to rap music. *Basic and Applied Social Psychology, 16,* 27–41.

Johnston, D. D. (1995). Adolescents' motivations for viewing graphic horror. *Human Communication Research, 21,* 522–552.

Johnston, J., & Ettema, J. S. (1986). Using television to best advantage: Research for prosocial television. In J. Bryant & D. Zillmann (Eds.), *Perspectives on media effects* (pp. 143–164). Hillsdale, NJ: Lawrence Erlbaum Associates, Inc.

Jordan, A. B. (2001). Public policy and private practice: Government regulations and parental control of children's television use in the home. In D. G. Singer & J. L. Singer (Eds.), *Handbook of children and the media* (pp. 651–662). Thousand Oaks, CA: Sage.

Josephson, W. L. (1987). Television violence and children's aggression: Testing the priming, social script and disinhibition predictions. *Journal of Personality and Social Psychology, 53,* 882–892.

Joy, L. A., Kimball, M. M., & Zabrack, M. L. (1986). Television and children's aggressive behavior. In T. M. Williams (Eds.), *The impact of television* (pp. 303–360). Orlando, FL: Academic.

Junk-food marketing goes elementary. (2000, January). *Education Digest, 65*(5), 32.

Kaiser Family Foundation. (2001). *Few parents use V-chip to block TV sex and violence, but more than half use TV ratings to pick what kids can watch.* Retrieved December 20, 2002, from http://www.kff.org/content/2001/3158/V-chip%20release.htm

Kaiser Family Foundation. (2002a, Fall). *Children and video games.* Retrieved November 6, 2003, from http://www.kff.org/content/2002/3271/ideo_game_Key_Facts.pdf

Kaiser Family Foundation. (2002b, May). *Teens, sex and TV. Survey snapshot.* Retrieved November 6, 2003, from http://www.kff.org/content/2002/3229/TeenSnapshot.pdf

Kaliebe, K., & Sondheimer, A. (2002). The media: Relationships to psychiatry and children: A seminar. *Academic Psychiatry, 26,* 205–215.

Kaufman, R. (2000). *The impact of television and video entertainment on student achievement in reading and writing.* Retrieved April 20, 2003, from http://www.turnoffyourtv.com/readingwriting.html

Kellermann, K. (1985). Memory processes in media effects. *Communication Research, 12,* 83–131.

Kelley, P., Gunter, B., & Buckle, L. (1987). 'Reading' television in the classroom: More results from the Television Literacy Project. *Journal of Educational Television, 13,* 7–20.

Kelly, A. E., & Spear, P. S. (1991). Intraprogram synopses for children's comprehension of television content. *Journal of Experimental Child Psychology, 52,* 87–98.

Kestenbaum, G. I., & Weinstein, L. (1985). Personality, psychopathology, and developmental issues in male adolescents' video game use. *Journal of the American Academy of Child Psychiatry, 24,* 329–333.

King, A. (1995, October 13). Beware the temptation to classify violent TV shows. *The Globe and Mail*, p. A19.

Klesges, R. C., Shelton, M. L., & Klesges, L. M. (1993). Effects of television on metabolic rate: Potential implications for childhood obesity. *Pediatrics, 91,* 281–286.

Koolstra, C. M., & Van der Voort, T. H. A. (1996). Longitudinal effects of television on children's leisure-time reading. A test of three explanatory models. *Human Communication Research, 23,* 4–35.

Kraut, R., Patterson, M., Lundmark, V., Kiesler, S., Mukopadhyay, T., & Scherlis, W. (1998). Internet paradox: A social technology that reduces social involvement and psychological well-being? *American Psychology. 53*(9), 1017–1031.

Krcmar, M., & Cooke, M. C. (2001). Children's moral reasoning and their perceptions of television violence. *Journal of Communication, 51*(2), 300–316.

Krcmar, M., & Valkenburg, P. M. (1999). A scale to assess children's moral interpretations of justified and unjustified violence and its relationship to television viewing. *Communication Research, 26,* 608–634.

Kubey, R. W. (1986). Television use in everyday life: Coping with unstructured time. *Journal of Communication, 36*(3), 108–123.

Kubey, R. (1990). Television and family harmony among children, adolescents, and adults: Results from the Experience Sampling Method. In J. Bryant (Ed.), *Television and the American family* (pp. 73–88). Hillsdale, NJ: Lawrence Erlbaum Associates, Inc.

Kubey, R., & Csikszentmihalyi, M. (1990). *Television and the quality of life: How viewing shapes everyday experience.* Hillsdale, NJ: Lawrence Erlbaum Associates, Inc.

Kubey, R., & Larson, R. (1990). The use and experience of the new video media among children and young adolescents. *Communication Research, 17,* 107–130.

Kubey, R., Larson, R., & Csikszentmihalyi, M. (1996). Experience sampling method applications to community research questions. *Journal of Communication, 46,* 99–120.

Kunkel, D. (1988). From a raised eyebrow to a turned back: The FCC and children's product-related programming. *Journal of Communication, 38*(4), 61–90.

Kunkel, D. (1992). Children's television advertising in the multichannel environment. *Journal of Communication, 42*(3), 134–152.

Kunkel, D. (1999). *APA Congressional testimony in the Hearing on Television Violence before the U.S. Senate Committee on Commerce, Science, and Transportation.* Retrieved April 20, 2003, from http://www.apa.org/ppo/issues/pkunkel.html

Kunkel, D., Biely, E., Eyal, K., Cope-Farrar, K., Donnerstein, E., & Fandrich, R. (2003). *SEX ON TV3:* A biennial report to the Kaiser Family Foundation. Retrieved November 11, 2003, from http://www.kff.org/content/2003/20030204a/Sex_on_TV_3_Full.pdf

Kunkel, D., Cope, K. M., & Colvin, C. (1996). *Sexual messages in "family hour" television.* Oakland, CA: Children Now, Kaiser Foundation. ED409080. Retrieved December 20, 2002, from http://npin.org/pnews/1999/pnew199/int199c.html

Kunkel, D., Cope-Farrar, K., Biely, E., Maynard-Farinola, W. J., & Donnerstein, E. (2001). *SEX ON TV2.* Menlo Park, CA: Kaiser Family Foundation. Retrieved November 10, 2003, from http://www.kff.org/content/2001/3087/

Kunkel, D., Maynard-Farinola, W. J., Farrar, K., Donnerstein, E. B, & Zwarun, L. (2002). Deciphering the V-chip: An examination of the television industry's program rating judgments. *Journal of Communication, 52*(1), 112–138.

Lacey, L. (1993, February 4). What is going on? *The Globe and Mail,* p. C1.

Lagerspetz, K. M. J., & Bjorkqvist, K. (1994). Indirect aggression in boys and girls. In L. R. Huesmann (Ed.), *Aggressive behavior: Current perspectives* (pp. 131–150). New York: Plenum.

Lauzen, M. M., Dozier, D. M., & Hicks, M. V. (2001). Prime-time players and powerful prose: The role of women in the 1997–1998 television season. *Mass Communication and Society, 4,* 39–59.

Lawrence, F., & Wozniak, P. H. (1989). Children's television viewing with family members. *Psychological Reports, 65,* 395–400.

Lawrence, S., & Giles, L. (1998). Searching the World Wide Web. *Science, 280,* 98–100.

Lawrence, S., & Giles, L. (1999). Accessibility and distribution of information on the Web. *Nature, 400,* 107–109.

Lefrancois, G. R. (1992). *Of children* (7th ed.). Belmont, CA: Wadsworth.

Lemish, D., & Rice, M. L. (1986). Television as a talking picture book: A prop for language acquisition. *Journal of Child Language, 13,* 251–274.

Lenhart, A., Rainie, L., & Lewis, O. (2001). *Teenage life online: The rise of the instant-message generation and the Internet's impact on friendships and family relationships.* Washington, DC: The Pew Internet & American Life Project. Retrieved July 20, 2003, from http://www.pewinternet.org/

Leonard, J. (1995). The negative impact of media violence on society is exaggerated. In C. Wekesser (Ed.), *Violence in the media* (pp. 31–37). San Diego, CA: Greenhaven.

Lepper, M. R., & Gurtner, J. (1989). Children and computers: Approaching the twenty-first century. *American Psychologist, 44,* 170–178.

Levin, S. R., Petros, T. V., & Petrella, F. W. (1982). Preschoolers' awareness of television advertising. *Child Development, 53,* 933–937.

Levine, L. E., & Waite, B. M. (2000). Televiewing and attentional abilities in fourth and fifth grade children. *Journal of Applied Developmental Psychology, 21,* 667–679.

Levine, S. B. (1995). A variety of measures could combat media violence. In C. Wekesser (Ed.), *Violence in the media* (pp. 142–147). San Diego, CA: Greenhaven.

Liebert, R. M., & Sprafkin, J. (1988*). The early window* (3rd ed.). New York: Pergamon.

Lindlof, T. R., & Meyer, T. P. (1998). Taking the interpretive turn: Qualitative research of television and other electronic media. In J. K. Asamen & G. L. Berry (Eds.), *Research paradigms, television, and social behavior* (pp. 237–268). Thousand Oaks, CA: Sage.

Lindlof, T. R., & Shatzer, M. J. (1990). VCR usage in the American family. In J. Bryant (Ed.), *Television and the American family* (pp. 89–109). Hillsdale, NJ: Lawrence Erlbaum Associates, Inc.

Li-Vollmer, M. (2000). Race representation in child-targeted television commercials. *Mass Communication and Society, 5,* 207–228.

Lorch, E. P., Anderson, D. R., & Levin, S. R. (1979). The relationship of visual attention to children's comprehension of television. *Child Development, 50,* 722–727.

Lowry, B. (2002, October 16). Newscasts too often employ scare tactics. *Children Now,* Retrieved December 29, 2002, from http://www.childrennow.org/newsroom/news-02/camra-10-16-02.htm

Lull, J. (1988a). Constructing rituals of extension through family television viewing. In J. Lull (Ed.), *World families watch television* (pp. 237–259). Newbury Park, CA: Sage.

Lull, J. (1988b). The family and television in world cultures. In J. Lull (Ed.), *World families watch television* (pp. 9–21). Newbury Park, CA: Sage.

Lynn, R., Hampson, S., & Agahi, E. (1989). Television violence and aggression: A genotype-environment, correlation and interaction theory. *Social Behavior and Personality, 17*(2), 143–164.

MacBeth, T. M. (1998). Quasi-experimental research on television and behavior: Natural and field experiments. In J. K. Asamen & G. L. Berry (Eds.), *Research paradigms, television, and social behavior* (pp. 109–151). Thousand Oaks, CA: Sage.

MacGregor, R. (2002, October 17). This news just din: When TV is too much. *The Globe and Mail,* p. A2.

MacGregor, R. (2003, January 8). What Canadian economists should learn from the first Product Placement Awards. *The Globe and Mail,* p. A2.

Macklin, M. C. (1988). The relationship between music in advertising and children's responses: An experimental investigation. In S. Hecker & D. W. Stewart (Eds.), *Nonverbal communication in advertising* (pp. 225–244). Lexington, MA: Heath.

Malamuth, N. M., & Impett, E. A. (2001). Research on sex in the media: What do we know about effects on children and adolescents? In D. G. Singer & J. L. Singer (Eds.), *Handbook of children and the media* (pp. 269–287). Thousand Oaks, CA: Sage.

Mathios, A., Avery, R., Bisogni, C., & Shanahan, J. (1998). Alcohol portrayal on prime-time television: Manifest and latent messages. *Journal of Studies on Alcohol, 59,* 305–310 [Abstract]. Retrieved January 14, 2003, from http://www.ncbi.nlm.nih.gov/entrez/query. Fcgi?cmd=retrieve&db=pubmed&list_uids=959

Mayer, W. G. (1994). Trends: The rise of the new media. *Public Opinion Quarterly, 58,* 124–146.

McClure, R. F., & Mears, F. G. (1986). Videogame playing and psychopathology. *Psychological Reports, 59,* 59–62.

McCool, G. (2003, April 8). *Long TV sitting raises obesity risk, study finds.* Retrieved June 19, 2003, from ABC News Web site: http://abcnewsgo.com/wire/US/reuters20030408_504.html

McGinn, D. (2002, November 11). Guilt free TV. *Children Now.* Retrieved December 29, 2002, from http://www.childrennow.org/newsroom/news-02/cam-ra-11-11-02.htm

Meadowcroft, J. M., & Reeves, B. (1989). Influence of story schema development on children's attention to television. *Communication Research, 16,* 352–374.

Media Awareness Network. (1995). *Prime Time Parent workshop kit.* Retrieved August 16, 2002, from http://www.media-awareness.ca/eng/med/home/resource/ptpkit.htm

Media Awareness Network. (2001). *Young Canadians in a wired world: The students' view. Final report.* Retrieved July 15, 2003, from http://www.media-awareness.ca/english/resources/special_initiatives/survey_resources/stu

Media Awareness Network. (2002). *Internet education initiative for Canadian girls launched by Girl Guides and Media Awareness Network* [News release]. Retrieved July 15, 2003, from http://www.media-awareness.ca/english/resources/media_kit/news_releases/2002/go_girl_

Media Awareness Network. (2003a). *Are you Web aware?* Retrieved July 15, 2003, from www.media-awareness.ca/english/parents/internet/fact_or_folly_parents/index.cfm

Media Awareness Network. (2003b). *Cereal and junk food advertising.* Retrieved July 15, 2003, from http://www.media-awareness.ca/english/resources/educational/handouts/advertising_marke

Media Awareness Network. (2003c). *Fact or folly: Authenticating online information.* Retrieved July 15, 2003 from http://www.media-awareness.ca/english/parents/internet/fact_or_folly_parents/index.cfm

Media Awareness Network. (2003d). *Jo cool or Jo fool.* Retrieved July 15, 2003, from http://www.media-wareness.ca/english/special_initiatives/games/joecool_joefool/index.cfm

Media Awareness Network. (2003e). *Kids for sale: Online marketing to kids and privacy issues.* Retrieved July 15, 2003, from http://www.media-awareness.ca/english/parents/internet/kids_for_sale_parents/index.cfm

Media Awareness Network. (2003f). *Special issues for girls.* Retrieved July 15, 2003, from http://www.media-awareness.ca/english/parents/video_games/issues_girls_video games.cfm

Media Awareness Network. (2003g). *Watching for "weasel words."* Retrieved July 15, 2003, from http://www.media-wareness.ca/english/resources/parents_resources/handouts/handouts_w

Messaris, P. (1986). Parents, children, and television. In G. Gumpert & R. Cathcart (Eds.), *Inter/media: Interpersonal communication in a media world* (3rd ed., pp. 519–536). New York: Oxford University Press.

Metzger, M. J., & Flanagin, A. J. (2002). Audience orientations toward new media. *Communication Research Reports,19,* 338–351.

Meyrowitz, J. (1998). Multiple media literacies. *Journal of Communication, 48*(1), 96–108.

Miller, M. C. (1987). Deride and conquer. In T. Gitlin (Ed.), *Watching television: A pantheon guide to popular culture* (pp. 183–228). New York: Pantheon.

Miron, D., Bryant, J., & Zillmann, D. (2001). Creating vigilance for better learning from television. In D. G. Singer & J. L. Singer (Eds.), *Handbook of children and the media* (pp. 153–181). Thousand Oaks, CA: Sage.

Morgan, M. (1993). Television and school performance. In Adolescents and the Media, *Adolescent Medicine: State of the Art Reviews, 4*(3), 607–622. American Academy of Pediatrics. Philadelphia: Hanley and Belfus.

Morgan, M., Alexander, A., Shanahan, J., & Harris, C. (1990). Adolescents, VCRs, and the family environment. *Communication Research, 17,* 83–106.

Morgan, M., & Shanahan, J. (1991). Do VCRs change the TV picture? VCRs and the cultivation process. *American Behavioral Scientist, 35*(2), 122–135.

Morgenstern, J. (1989, January 1). TV's big turnoff: Can "USA Today" be saved? *The New York Times Magazine*, pp. 13–15, 26–28.

Morris, M., & Ogan, C. (1996). The Internet as mass medium. *Journal of Communication, 46*(1), 39–50.

Murray, J. P. (1998). Studying television violence: A research agenda for the 21st century. In J. K. Asamen & G. L. Berry (Eds.), *Research paradigms, television, and social behavior* (pp. 369–410). Thousand Oaks, CA: Sage.

Mutz, D. C., Roberts, D. F., & van Vuuren, D. P. (1993). Reconsidering the displacement hypothesis: Television's influence on children's time use. *Communication Research, 20,* 51–75.

Naigles, L. R., & Mayeux, L. (2001). Television as incidental language teacher. In D. G. Singer & J. L. Singer (Eds.), *Handbook of children and the media* (pp. 135–152). Thousand Oaks, CA: Sage.

Nathanson, A. I. (1999). Identifying and explaining the relationship between parental mediation and children's aggression. *Communication Research, 26*(2), 124–143.

Nathanson, A. I. (2001). Parents versus peers: Exploring the significance of peer mediation of antisocial television. *Communication Research, 28*(3), 251–274.

National Coalition for the Protection of Children and Families. (2003). Retrieved April 20, 2003 from http://www.nationalcoalition.org/stat.phtml?ID=53.

National Institute on Media and the Family. (1997–2000). *KidScore®*. Retrieved from http://www. Mediafamily.org

National Institute on Media and the Family. (2002a). *Alcohol advertising and youth*. Retrieved December 29, 2002, from http://www. mediafamily.org/facts/facts_ alcohol.shtml

National Institute on Media and the Family. (2002b). *Children and advertising*. Retrieved December 29, 2002, from http://www.mediafamil.org/facts/facts_childadv.shtml

National Institute on Media and the Family. (2002c). *Commercial advertising in schools*. Retrieved December 29, 2002, from http://www.mediafamily.org/facts/facts_adsinschool.shtml

National Institute on Media and the Family. (2002d). *Effect of advertising on children's use of tobacco*. Retrieved December 29, 2002, from http://www.mediafamily.org/facts/facts_tobacco.shtml

National Institute on Media and the Family. (2002e). *Effects of video game playing on children*. Retrieved December 29, 2002, from http://www.mediafamily.org/facts/facts_effect.shtml

National Institute on Media and the Family (2002f). *Helping children cope with war and terrorism*. Retrieved December 29, 2002, from http://www.mediafamily.org/facts/tipshelpingkidscope.shtml

National Institute on Media and the Family. (2002g). *Internet advertising and children*. Retrieved December 29, 2002, from http://www.mediafamily.org/facts/facts_internetads.shtml

National Institute on Media and the Family. (2002h). *Media use*. Retrieved December 29, 2002, from http://www.mediafamily.org/facts/facts_mediause.shtml

National Institute on Media and the Family. (2002i). *MTV*. Retrieved December 29, 2002, from http://www.mediafamily.org/facts/facts_mtv.shtml

National Institute on Media and the Family. (2002j). *Music and children*. Retrieved December 29, 2002, from http://www.mediafamily.org/facts/facts_music.shtml

National Institute on Media and the Family. (2002k). Pro-wrestling: Lewd, crude, and on your tube. *Media Wise, 11,* 1–5. Retrieved December 29, 2002, from http://www.mediafamily. org/newsletter/v.11.shtml

National Institute on Media and the Family. (2002l). *Safety tips for surfing the net*. Retrieved December 29, 2002, from http://www.mediafamily.org/facts/tips_ surfsafe.shtml

National Institute on Media and the Family. (2002m). *Television's effect on reading and academic achievement*. Retrieved December 29, 2002, from http://www.mediafamily.org/facts/facts_tveffect.shtml

National Institute on Media and the Family. (2002n). *Television and obesity among children*. Retrieved December 29, 2002, from http://www.mediafamily.org/facts/facts_ tvandobchild.shtml

National Institute on Media and the Family. (2002o). TV in the bedroom. *MediaWise, 10*. Retrieved December 29, 2002, from http://www.mediafamily.org/newsletter/v10.shtml

National Institute of Mental Health. (1982). *Television and behavior: Ten years of scientific progress and implications for the eighties, I*. DHHS #A82-1195. Washington, DC: U.S. Government Printing Office.

National Public Radio. (1999). *Survey shows widespread enthusiasm for high technology*. Retrieved November 5, 2003, from http://www.npr.org/programs/specials/poll/technology

Nelson, J. (1987). *The perfect machine: Television in the nuclear age*. Toronto, Ontario, Canada: Between the Lines.

"The NetValue report on minors online ..." (2000, December 19). (Taken from study by NetValue, Internet activity service.) *Businesswire*.

Neuman, S. B. (1988). The displacement effect: Assessing the relation between television viewing and reading performance. *Reading Research Quarterly, 23*(4), 414–440.

New York Times Service and Staff. (1997, January 2). U.S. TV networks launch ratings system. *The Globe and Mail*, p. C3.

Nickerson, R. S. (1995). Can technology help teach for understanding? In D. N. Perkins, J. L. Schwartz, M. M. West, & M. S. Wiske (Eds.), *Software goes to school: Teaching for understanding with new technologies* (pp. 7–22). New York: Oxford University Press.

Nolen, S. (2000, April 6). Web babies. *The Globe and Mail*, pp. R1, R3.

Nordland, R., & Bartholet, J. (2001, March 19). The Web's dark secret. *Newsweek, 137*(12), p. 44.

Okagaki, L., & Frensch, P. A. (1994). Effects of video game playing on measures of spatial performance: Gender effects in late adolescence. *Journal of Applied Developmental Psychology, 15*, 33–58.

O'Keefe, G. J., & Reid-Nash, K. (1987). Crime news and real-world blues: The effects of the media on social reality. *Communication Research, 14*, 147–163.

Paik, H. (2001). The history of children's use of the electronic media. In D. G. Singer & J. L. Singer (Eds.), *Handbook of children and the media* (pp. 7–27). Thousand Oaks, CA: Sage.

Paik, H., & Comstock, G. (1994). The effects of television violence on antisocial behavior: A meta-analysis. *Communication Research, 21*, 516–546.

Palmer, E. L. (1998). Quantitative research paradigms in the study of television: Field of dreams, world of realities. In J. K. Asamen & G. L. Berry (Eds.), *Research paradigms, television, and social behavior* (pp. 39–65). Thousand Oaks, CA: Sage.

Palmer, E. L., Taylor Smith, K., & Strawser, K. S. (1993). Rubik's tube: Developing a child's television worldview. In G. L. Berry & J. K. Asamen (Eds.), *Children and television: Images in a changing sociocultural world* (pp. 143–154). Newbury Park, CA: Sage.

Parks, M. R., & Floyd, K. (1996). Making friends in cyberspace. *Journal of Communication, 46*(1), 80–97.

Pepler, D. J., & Slaby, R. G. (1994). Theoretical and developmental perspectives on youth and violence. In L. D. Eron, J. H. Gentry, & P. Schlegel (Eds.), *Reason to hope. A psychosocial perspective on violence and youth*. Washington, DC: American Psychological Association.

Perse, E. M., Ferguson, D. A., & McLeod, D. M. (1994), Cultivation in the newer media environment. *Communication Research, 21*, 79–104.

Peterson, L., & Lewis, K. E. (1988). Preventive intervention to improve children's discrimination of the persuasive tactics in televised advertising. *Journal of Pediatric Psychology, 13*, 163–170.

Pezdek, K., & Hartman, E. F. (1983). Children's television viewing: Attention and comprehension of auditory versus visual information. *Child Development, 54*, 1015–1023.

Pingree, S. (1986). Children's activity and television comprehensibility. *Communication Research, 13*, 239–256.

Pingree, S., Hawkins, R. P., Rouner, D., Burns, J., Gikonyo, W., & Neuwirth, C. (1984). Another look at children's comprehension of television. *Communication Research, 11*, 477–496.

Pinon, M. F., Huston, A. C., & Wright, J. C. (1989). Family ecology and child characteristics that predict young children's educational television viewing. *Child Development, 60,* 846–856.

Pool, M. M., Van der Voort, T. H. A., Beentjes, J. W. J., & Koolstra, C. M. (2000). Background television as an inhibitor of performance on easy and difficult homework assignments. *Communication Research, 27,* 293–326.

Postman, N. (1985). *Amusing ourselves to death.* New York: Penguin.

Potter, W. J. (1986). Perceived reality and the cultivation hypothesis. *Journal of Broadcasting and Electronic Media, 30,* 159–174.

Potter, W. J. (1988). Perceived reality in television effects research. *Journal of Broadcasting and Electronic Media, 32,* 23–41.

Potts, R., Huston, A. C., & Wright, J. C. (1986). The effects of television form and violent content on boys' attention and social behavior. *Journal of Experimental Child Psychology, 41,* 1–17.

Pryor, S., & Scott, J. (1993). Virtual reality: Beyond Cartesian space. In P. Hayward & T. Wollen (Eds.), *Future visions: New technologies of the screen* (pp. 166–179). London: British Film Institute.

Rajecki, D. W., McTavish, D. G., Rasmussen, J. L., Schreuders, M., Byers, D. C., & Jessup, K. S. (1994). Violence, conflict, trickery, and other story themes in TV ads for food for children. *Journal of Applied Social Psychology, 24,* 1685–1700.

Reading, writing and buying? (1998, September). *Consumer Reports,* p. 45.

Reeves, B., & Thorson, E. (1986). Watching television: Experiments on the viewing process. *Communication Research, 13,* 343–361.

Reinking, D., & Wu, J. (1990). Reexamining the research on television and reading. *Reading Research and Instruction, 29*(2), 30–43.

Reuters. (2003, January 21). *Yes, your baby really is watching that TV.* Retrieved January 21, 2003, from http://abcnews.go.com/wire/US/reuters20030121_472.html

Rice, M. (1983). The role of television in language acquisition. *Developmental Review, 3,* 211–224.

Rice, M. L. (1984). Television language and child language. In J. P. Murray & G. Salomon (Eds.), *The future of children's television* (pp. 53–58). Boys Town, NE: Father Flanagan's Boys Home.

Rice, M. L., Huston, A. C., Truglio, R., & Wright, J. C. (1990). Words from "Sesame Street": Learning vocabulary while viewing. *Developmental Psychology, 26,* 421–428.

Rice, M. L., Huston, A. C., & Wright, J. C. (1986). Replays as repetitions: Young children's interpretation of television forms. *Journal of Applied Developmental Psychology, 7,* 61–76.

Rice, M. L., & Woodsmall, L. (1988) Lessons from television: Children's word learning when viewing. *Child Development, 59,* 420–429.

Rich, M., & Bar-on, M. (2001). Child health in the information age: Media education of pediatricians. *Pediatrics, 107,* 156–162 [Abstract]. Retrieved January 13, 2003, from http://www.pediatrics.org/cgi/content/abstract/107/1/156

Rich, M., Woods, E., Goodman, E., Emans, J., & DuRant, R. (1998). Aggressors or victims: Gender and race in music video violence. *Pediatrics, 101,* 669–674.

Rideout, V. J., Foehr, U. G., Roberts, D. F., & Brodie, M. (1999). *Kids & media @ the new millennium.* Menlo Park, CA: The Henry J. Kaiser Family Foundation. Retrieved December 20, 2002, from http://www.kff.org/content/1999/1535

Rideout, V. J., Vandewater, E. A., & Wartella, E. A. (2003). *Zero to six: Electronic media in the lives of infants, toddlers, and preschoolers.* Menlo Park, CA: The Henry J. Kaiser Family Foundation. Retrieved November 11, 2003, from http://www.kff.org/content/2003/3878/0to6Report.pff

Ridley-Johnson, R., Surdy, T., & O'Laughlin, E. (1991). Parent survey on television violence viewing: Fear, aggression, and sex differences. *Journal of Applied Developmental Psychology, 12,* 63–71.

Ritchie, D., Price, V., & Roberts, D. F. (1987). Television, reading, and reading achievement. *Communication Research, 14,* 292–315.

Roberts, D. F., Bachen, C. M., Hornby, M. C., & Hernandez-Ramos, P. (1984). Reading and television: Predictors of reading achievement at different age levels. *Communication Research, 11,* 9–49.

Roberts, D. F., & Christenson, P. G. (2001). Popular music in childhood and adolescence. In D. G. Singer & J. L. Singer (Eds.), *Handbook of children and the media* (pp. 395–414). Thousand Oaks, CA: Sage.

Robinson, J. P. (1990). Television's effects on families' use of time. In J. Bryant (Ed.), *Television and the American family* (pp.195–209). Hillsdale, NJ: Lawrence Erlbaum Associates, Inc.

Robinson, T. N. (1999). Reducing children's television viewing to prevent obesity. *Journal of the American Medical Association, 282,* 1561–1567.

Robinson, T. N., Chen, H. L., & Killen, J. D. (1998). Television and music video exposure and risk of adolescent alcohol use. *Pediatrics, 102,* e54.

Rolandelli, D. R., Wright, J. C., Huston, A. C., & Eakins, D. (1991). Children's auditory and visual processing of narrated and nonnarrated television programming. *Journal of Experimental Child Psychology, 51,* 90–122.

Rosenkoetter, L. I. (1999). The television situation comedy and children's prosocial behavior. *Journal of Applied Social Psychology, 29*(5), 979–993.

Rosenkoetter, L.I., Huston, A.C., & Wright, J. C. (1990). Television and the moral judgment of the young child. *Journal of Applied Developmental Psychology, 11,* 123–137.

Roser, C. (1990). Involvement, attention, and perceptions of message relevance in the response to persuasive appeal. *Communication Research, 17,* 571–600.

Ross, R. P., Campbell, T., Wright, J. C., Huston, A. C., Rice, M. L., & Turk, P. (1984). When celebrities talk, children listen: An experimental analysis of children's responses to TV ads with celebrity endorsement. *Journal of Applied Developmental Psychology, 5,* 185–202.

Roxy Girl books draw fire. (2003, April 17). *The Record,* p. E3.

Rubin, A. M. (1984). Ritualized and instrumental television viewing. *Journal of Communication, 34*(3), 67–77.

Rubin, A. M. (1985). Media gratifications through the life cycle. In K. E. Rosengren, L. A. Wenner, & P. Palmgreen (Eds.), *Media gratifications research: Current perspectives* (pp. 195–208). Beverly Hills, CA: Sage.

Rubin, A. M. (1986). Uses, gratifications, and media effects research. In J. Bryant & D. Zillmann (Eds.), *Perspectives on media effects* (pp. 281–301). Hillsdale, NJ: Lawrence Erlbaum Associates, Inc.

Rubin, A. M. (1994). Media uses and effects: A uses and gratifications perspective. In J. Bryant & D. Zillmann (Eds.), *Media effects: Advances in theory and research* (pp. 417–436). Hillsdale, NJ: Lawrence Erlbaum Associates, Inc.

Rubin, A. M., & Perse, E. M. (1987). Audience activity and television news gratifications. *Communication Research, 14,* 58–84.

Rubin, A. M., Perse, E. M., & Taylor, D. S. (1988). A methodological examination of cultivation. *Communication Research, 15,* 107–134.

Ruggiero, T. E. (2000). Uses and gratifications theory in the 21st century. *Mass Communication and Society, 3,* 3–37.

Rule, B. G., & Ferguson, T. J. (1986). The effects of media violence on attitudes, emotions, and cognitions. *Journal of Social Issues, 42*(3), 29–50.

Rushton, J. P. (1988). Television as a socializer. In M. Courage (Ed.), *Readings in developmental psychology* (pp. 437–456). Peterborough, Ontario, Canada: Broadview.

Rutherford, P. (1988). The culture of advertising. *Canadian Journal of Communication, 13*(3 & 4), 102–113.

Rutherford, P. (1994). *The new icons? The art of television advertising.* Toronto, Ontario, Canada: University of Toronto Press.

Salomon, G. (1981a). *Communication and education: Social and psychological interactions.* Beverly Hills, CA: Sage.

Salomon, G. (1981b). Introducing AIME: The assessment of children's mental involvement with television. In H. Kelly & H. Gardner (Eds.), *Viewing children through television* (pp. 89–102). San Francisco: Jossey-Bass.

Salomon, G. (1983). Television watching and mental effort: A social psychological view. In J. Bryant & D. R. Anderson (Eds.), *Children's understanding of television* (pp. 181–198). New York: Academic.

Salomon, G. (1984). Investing effort in television viewing. In J. P. Murray & G. Salomon (Eds.), *The future of children's television* (pp. 59–64). Boys Town, NE: Father Flanagan's Boys' Home.

Salomon, G. (1990). Cognitive effects with and of computer technology. *Communication Research, 17,* 26–44.

Salomon, G., & Leigh, T. (1984). Predispositions about learning from print and television. *Journal of Communication, 34,* 119–135.

Salutin, R. (2003, March 7). Bye, Mr. Rogers: It wasn't just his niceness to kids. *The Globe and Mail,* p. A15.

Santrock, J. W., & Yussen, S. R. (1992). *Child development* (5th ed.). Dubuque, IA: Brown.

Sarcasm doesn't click with young minds. (2003, January 13). *The Record,* p. D1.

Saunders, D. (1996, December 7). Babes in TVland. *The Globe and Mail,* pp. C1, C7.

Sawin, D. B. (1990). Aggressive behavior among children in small playgroup settings with violent television. In K. D. Gadow (Ed.), *Advances in learning and behavioral disabilities* (Vol. 6, pp. 157–177). Greenwich, CT: JAI.

Scheer, R. (1995). Media violence should not be censored. In C. Wekesser (Ed.), *Violence in the media* (pp. 62–66). San Diego, CA: Greenhaven.

School board considers deal to swap ads for computers. (2000, April 7). *New York Times,* p. A1.

Schooler, C., Feighery, E., & Flora, J. A. (1996). Seventh graders' self-reported exposure to cigarette marketing and its relationship to their smoking behavior. *American Journal of Public Health, 86,* 1216–1221.

Selnow, G. W. (1986). Television viewing and the learning of expectations for problem resolutions. *Educational Studies, 12*(2), 137–145.

Selnow, G. W., & Bettinghaus, E. P. (1982). Television exposure and language level. *Journal of Broadcasting, 26,* 469–479.

Shapiro, M. A., & McDonald, D. G. (1992). I'm not a real doctor, but I play one in virtual reality: Implications of virtual reality for judgments about reality. *Journal of Communication, 42*(4), 94–114.

Sherry, J. (2001). The effects of violent video games on aggression: A meta-analysis. *Human Communication Research, 27,* 409–431.

Sherry, J., de Souza, R., Greenberg, B. S., & Lachlan, K. (2003). *Why do adolescents play video games? Developmental stages predicts video game uses and gratifications, game preference, and amount of time spent playing.* Retrieved July 4, 2003, from http://web.ics.purdue.edu/~sherryj/videogames/VG&age.pdf

Sherry, J., Holmstrom, A., Binns, R., Greenberg, B. S., & Lachlan, K. (2003). *Gender and electronic game play.* Retrieved July 4, 2003, from http://web.ics.purdue.edu/~sherryj/videogames/VG&Gender.pdf

Sherry, J., Lucas, K., Rechsteiner, S., Brooks, C., & Wilson, B. (2001). *Video game uses and gratifications as predictors of use and game preference.* Paper presented at the International Communication Association, Video Game Research Agenda Theme Session Panel. Retrieved July 4, 2003, from http://web.ics.purdue.edu/~sherryj/videogames/VGUG.pdf

Shrum, L. J. (1995). Assessing the social influence of television: A social cognition perspective on cultivation effects. *Communication Research, 22,* 402–429.

Shrum, L. J. (1996). Psychological processes underlying cultivation effects. Further tests of construct accessibility. *Human Communication Research, 22*(4), 482–509.

Signorielli, N. (1987). Children and adolescents on television: A consistent pattern of devaluation. *Journal of Early Adolescence, 7*(3), 255–268.

Signorielli, N. (2001). Television's gender role images and contribution to stereotyping: Past, present, future. In D. G. Singer & J. L. Singer (Eds.), *Handbook of children and the media* (pp. 341–358). Thousand Oaks, CA: Sage.

Signorielli, N., & Bacue, A. (1999). Recognition and respect: A content analysis of prime-time characters across three decades. *Sex Roles, 40,* 527–544.

Silvern, S. B., & Williamson, P. A. (1987). The effects of video game play on young children's aggression, fantasy, and prosocial behavior. *Journal of Applied Developmental Psychology, 8,* 453–462.

Singer, J. L., & Singer, D. G. (1983). Implications of childhood television viewing for cognition, imagination, and emotion. In J. Bryant & D. R. Anderson (Eds.), *Children's understanding of television* (pp. 265–295). New York: Academic.

Singer, J. L., & Singer, D. G. (1986). Family experiences and television viewing as predictors of children's imagination, restlessness, and aggression. *Journal of Social Issues, 42*(3), 107–124.

Singer, J. L., & Singer, D. G. (1998). Barney & Friends as entertainment and education: Evaluating the quality and effectiveness of a television series for preschool children. In J. K. Asamen & G. L. Berry (Eds.), *Research paradigms, television, and social behavior* (pp. 305–367). Thousand Oaks, CA: Sage.

Singer, J. L., Singer, D. G., & Rapacynski, W. S. (1984). Family patterns and television viewing as predictors of children's beliefs and aggression. *Journal of Communication, 34*(2), 73–89.

Singer, M. I., Miller, D. B., Guo, S., Flannery, D. J., Frierson, T., & Slovak, K. (1999). Contributors to violent behavior among elementary and middle school children. *Pediatrics, 104*(4), 878–884.

Singer, M. I., Slovak, K., Frierson, T., & York, P. (1998). Viewing preferences, symptoms of psychological trauma, and violent behaviors among children who watch television. *Journal of the American Academy of Child and Adolescent Psychiatry, 37,* 1041–1048.

Slaby, R. G., Barham, J. E., Eron, L. D., & Wilcox, B. L. (1994). In L. D. Eron, J. H. Gentry, & P. Schlegel (Eds.), *Reason to hope: A psychosocial perspective on violence and youth* (pp. 447–461). Washington, DC: American Psychological Association.

Slater, M. D., Rouner, D., Domenech-Rodriguez, M., Beauvais, F., Murphy, K., & Van Leuven, J. K. (1997). Adolescent responses to TV beer ads and sports content/context: Gender and ethnic differences. *Journalism and Mass Communication Quarterly, 74,* 108–122.

Smith, J. D., & Kemler-Nelson, D. G. (1988). Is the more impulsive child a more holistic processor? A reconsideration. *Child Development, 59*(3), 719–727.

Smith, S. L., & Boyson, A. R. (2002). Violence in music videos: Examining the prevalence and context of physical aggression. *Journal of Communication, 52*(1), 61–83.

Smith, S. L., & Donnerstein, E. (1998). Harmful effects of exposure to media violence: Learning of aggression, emotional desensitization, and fear. In R. G. Geen & E. Donners (Eds.), *Human aggression: Theories, research, and implications for social policy* (pp. 167–202). New York: Academic.

Smith, S. L., Nathanson, A. I., & Wilson, B. J. (2002). Prime-time television: Assessing violence during the most popular viewing hours. *Journal of Communication, 52*(1), 84–111.

Smith, S. L., & Wilson, B. J. (2000). Children's reactions to a television news story: The impact of video footage and proximity of the crime. *Communication Research, 27,* 641–673 [Abstract]. Retrieved December 20, 2002, from http://giorgio.ingentaselect.com/v1=18800786/c1=17/nw=1/rpsv/wwwtemp/c117+mp90.ht

Sobieraj, S. (1996). Beauty and the beast: Toy commercials and the social construction of gender. *Sociological Abstracts,* 044.

Sohn, D. (1982). David Sohn interviews Jerzy Kosinski: A nation of videots. In H. Newcomb (Ed.), *Television: The critical view* (3rd ed., pp. 351–366). New York: Oxford University Press.

Some video games boost perception. (2003, May 28). Retrieved May 28, 2003, from http://abcnews.go.com/wire/US/ap20030528_1055 .html

Spicer, K. (1995, October 3). TV can have a positive influence on children. *Kitchener-Waterloo Record,* p. A9.

Sprafkin, J., & Gadow, K. D. (1986). Television viewing habits of emotionally-disturbed, learning disabled, and mentally retarded children. *Journal of Applied Developmental Psychology, 7*(1), 45–59.

Sprafkin, J., Gadow, K. D., & Abelman, R. (1992). *Television and the exceptional child: A forgotten audience.* Hillsdale, NJ: Lawrence Erlbaum Associates, Inc.

Sprafkin, J., Gadow, K. D., & Dussault, M. (1986). Reality perceptions of television: A preliminary comparison of emotionally disturbed and nonhandicapped children. *American Journal of Orthopsychiatry, 56*(1), 147–152.

Sprafkin, J., Watkins, L. T., & Gadow, K. D. (1986). *Curriculum for Enhancing Social Skills through Media Awareness.* Unpublished curriculum, State University of New York at Stony Brook.

Sprafkin, J., Watkins, L. T., & Gadow, K. D. (1990). Efficacy of a television literacy curriculum for emotionally disturbed and learning disabled children. *Journal of Applied Developmental Psychology, 11,* 225–244.

Stanger, J. D. (1998). *Television in the home 1998: The third annual national survey of parents and children.* Philadelphia: University of Pennsylvania, Annenberg Public Policy Center.

Stead, D. (1997, January 5). Corporations, classrooms and commercialism. *The New York Times,* p. 31.

Steele, J. R. (2002). Teens and movies: Something to do, plenty to learn. In J. D. Brown, J. R. Steele, & K. Walsh-Childers (Eds.), *Sexual teens, sexual media: Investigating media's influence on adolescent sexuality* (pp. 227–252). Mahwah, NJ: Lawrence Erlbaum Associates, Inc.

Stern, S. (2002). Sexual selves on the World Wide Web: Adolescent girls' home pages as sites for sexual self-expression. In J. D. Brown, J. R. Steele, & K. Walsh-Childers (Eds.), *Sexual teens, sexual media: Investigating media's influence on adolescent sexuality* (pp. 265–285). Mahwah, NJ: Lawrence Erlbaum Associates, Inc.

Steuer, J. (1992). Defining virtual reality: Dimensions determining telepresence. *Journal of Communication, 42*(4), 73–93.

St. Peters, M., Fitch, M., Huston, A. C., Wright, J. C., & Eakins, D. J. (1991). Television and families: What do young children watch with their parents? *Child Development, 62,* 1409–1423.

Strasburger, V. C. (1993). Children, adolescents, and the media: Five crucial issues. In V. C. Strasburger & G. A. Comstock (Eds.), *Adolescent Medicine: State of the Art Reviews, 4*(3), 479–493. American Academy of Pediatrics. Philadelphia: Hanley and Belfus.

Strasburger, V. C. & Donnerstein, E. (1999, January). Children, adolescents, and the media: Issues and solutions. *Pediatrics, 103,* 129–139.

Strasburger, V. C. & Wilson, B. J. (2002). *Children, adolescents and the media.* Thousand Oaks, CA: Sage

Straus, M. (1991). Discipline and deviance: Physical punishment of children and violence and other crime in adulthood. *Social Problems, 38,* 133–154.

Subrahmanyam, K., & Greenfield, P. M. (1994). Effect of video game practice on spatial skills in girls and boys. *Journal of Applied Developmental Psychology, 15,* 13–32.

Subrahmanyam, K., Greenfield, P., Kraut, R., & Gross, E. (2001). The impact of computer use on children's and adolescents' development. *Applied Developmental Psychology, 22,* 7–30.

Subrahmanyam, K., Kraut, R., Greenfield, P., & Gross, E. (2000). The impact of home computer use on children's activities and development. *The Future of Children: Children and Computer Technology, 10*(2), 123–144.

Subrahmanyam, K., Kraut, R., Greenfield, P., & Gross, E. (2001). New forms of electronic media: The impact of interactive games and the Internet on cognition, socialization, and behavior. In D. Singer & J. Singer (Eds.), *Handbook of children and the family* (pp. 73–99). Thousand Oaks, CA: Sage.

Sutton, M. J., Brown, J. D., Wilson, K. M., & Klein, J. D. (2002). Shaking the tree of knowledge for forbidden fruit: Where adolescents learn about sexuality and contraception. In J. D. Brown, J. R. Steele, & K. Walsh-Childers (Eds.), *Sexual teens, sexual media: Investigating media's influence on adolescent sexuality* (pp. 25–55). Mahwah, NJ: Lawrence Erlbaum Associates.

Talbot, M. (2003, February 16). Turned on, tuned out. *The New York Times Magazine,* pp. 9–10.

Tamborini, R., Eastin, M., Lachlan, K., Fediuk, T., Brady, R., & Skalski, P. (2000, November). *The effects of violent virtual video games on aggressive thoughts and behaviors.* Paper presented at the 86th annual convention of the National Communication Association, Seattle, WA. Retrieved July 4, 2003, from http://web.ics.purdue.edu/~sherryj/videogames/papers.htm

Tamborini, R., Eastin, M., Lachlan, K., Skalski, P., Fediuk, T., & Brady, R. (2001, May). *Hostile thoughts, presence and violent virtual video games.* Paper presented at the 51st annual convention of the International Communication Association, Washington, DC. Retrieved July 4, 2003, from http://web.ics.purdue.edu/~sherryj/videogames/papers.htm

Tamborini, R., Mastro, D. E., Chory-Assad, R. M., & Huang, R. H. (2000). The color of crime and the court: A content analysis of minority representation on television. *Journalism and Mass Communication Quarterly, 77,* 639–653.

Tarpley, T. (2001). Children, the Internet, and other new technologies. In D. G. Singer & J. L. Singer (Eds.), *Handbook of children and the media* (pp. 547–556). Thousand Oaks, CA: Sage.

Thompson, T., & Zerbinos, E. (1997). Television cartoons: Do children notice it's a boy's world? *Sex Roles: A Journal of Research, 37,* 415–433.

Tiggemann, M., Gardiner, M., & Slater, A. (2000). "I would rather be a size 10 than have straight A's": A focus group study of adolescent girls' wish to be thinner. *Journal of Adolescence, 23,* 645–659.

Troseth, G. L., & DeLoache, J. S. (1998). The medium can obscure the message: Young children's understanding of video. *Child Development, 69,* 950–965.

Trotta, L. (2001). Children's advocacy groups: A history and analysis. In D. G. Singer & J. L. Singer (Eds.), *Handbook of children and the media* (pp. 699–719). Thousand Oaks, CA: Sage.

Tuggle, C. A., Huffman, S., & Rosengard, D. S. (2002). A descriptive analysis of NBC's coverage of the 2000 Summer Olympics. *Mass Communication and Society, 5,* 361–375.

Unequal access to computers a "concern," StatsCan says. (2003, June 11). *The Record,* p. A8.

Valkenburg, P. M., Cantor, J. & Peeters, A. L. (2000). Fright reactions to television: A child survey. *Communication Research, 27,* 82–99.

Valkenburg, P. M., & Soeters, K. E. (2001). Children's positive and negative experiences with the Internet: An exploratory survey. *Communication Research, 28,* 652–675.

Valkenburg, P. M., & Van der Voort, T. H. A. (1994). Influence of TV on daydreaming and creative imagination: A review of the research. *Psychological Bulletin, 116,* 316–339.

Valkenburg, P. M., & Van der Voort, T. H. A. (1995). The influence of television on children's daydreaming styles: A 1-year panel study. *Communication Research, 22,* 267–287.

Van der Voort, T. H. A. (1986). *Television violence: a child's eye view.* Amsterdam: North-Holland.

Van Evra, J. (1984). *Developmental trends in the perception of sex-role stereotypy in real life and on television.* Unpublished manuscript.

Van Evra, J. (1995). Advertising's impact on children as a function of viewing purpose. *Psychology and Marketing, 12,* 423–432.

van Schie, E. G. M., & Wiegman, O. (1997). Children and video games: Leisure activities, aggression, social integration, and school performance. *Journal of Applied Social Psychology, 27,* 1175–1194.

Varsity TV created for teens. (2003, July 29). *The Record,* p. B4.

"Videogames." (2003, June 9). *The Globe and Mail,* p. A14.

Violent music boosts aggressive thoughts. (2003). Retrieved May 4, 2003, from http://abcnews.go.com/wire/US/reuters20030504_240.html

Vivian, J. (1997). *The media of mass communication* (4th ed.). Boston: Allyn & Bacon.

Waisglas, E. (1992, February). Listen to the children. *Canadian Living,* p. 59.

Walma van der Molen, J. H., & Van der Voort, T. H. A. (2000). The impact of television, print, and audio on children's recall of the news: A study of three alternative explanations for the dual-coding hypothesis. *Human Communication Research, 26,* 3–26 [Abstract]. Retrieved February 9, 2003, from http://hcr.oupjournals.org/cgi/gca?gca=26%2F1%2F3 &gca26%2 F1%F75&sendit=Get+A

Walsh-Childers, K., Gotthoffer, A., & Lepre, C. R. (2002). From "just the facts" to "downright salacious": Teens' and women's magazine coverage of sex and sexual health. In J. D. Brown, J.

R. Steele, & K. Walsh-Childers (Eds.), *Sexual teens, sexual media: Investigating media's influence on adolescent sexuality* (pp. 153–171). Mahwah, NJ: Lawrence Erlbaum Associates, Inc.

Ward, L. M. (1995). Talking about sex: Common themes about sexuality in the prime-time television programs children and adolescents view most. *Journal of Youth and Adolescence, 24,* 595–615.

Ward, L. M., & Greenfield, P. M. (1998). Designing experiments on television and social behavior: Developmental perspectives. In J. K. Asamen & G. L. Berry (Eds.), *Research paradigms, television, and social behavior* (pp. 67–108). Thousand Oaks, CA: Sage.

Warren, R., & Bluma, A. (2002). Parental mediation of children's internet use: The influence of established media. *Communication Research Reports, 19,* 8–17.

Wartella, E. (1986). Getting to know you: How children make sense of television. In G. Gumpert & R. Cathcart (Eds.), *Inter/media: Interpersonal communication in a media world* (3rd ed., pp. 537–549). New York: Oxford University Press.

Webster, J. G. (1989). Television audience behavior: Patterns of exposure in the new media environment. In J. L. Salvaggio & J. Bryant (Eds.), *Media use in the information age: Emerging patterns of adoption and consumer use* (pp. 197–216). Hillsdale, NJ: Lawrence Erlbaum Associates, Inc.

Weidner, J. (2003, July 10). UW program entices girls to computers. *The Record,* p. B1.

Wiegman, O., Kuttschreuter, M., & Baarda, B. (1992). A longitudinal study of the effects of television viewing on aggressive and prosocial behaviors. *British Journal of Social Psychology, 31,* 147–164.

Wiegman, O., & van Schie, E. G. M. (1998). Video game playing and its relations with aggressive and prosocial behavior. *British Journal of Social Psychology, 37,* 367–378.

Williams, F., Phillips, A. F., & Lum, P. (1985). Gratifications associated with new consumer technologies. In K. E. Rosengren, L. A. Wenner, & P. Palmgreen (Eds.), *Media gratifications research: Current perspectives* (pp. 241–252). Beverly Hills, CA: Sage.

Williams, T. M. (1986). Summary, conclusions, and implications. In T. M. Williams (Ed.), *The impact of television: A natural experiment in three communities* (pp. 395–430). Orlando, FL: Academic.

Willis, E., & Strasburger, V. C. (1998). Media violence. *Pediatric Clinics of North America,45,* 319–331.

Wilson, B. J., Colvin, C. M., & Smith, S. L. (2002). Engaging in violence on American television: A comparison of child, teen, and adult perpetrators. *Journal of Communication, 52*(1), 36–60.

Wilson, B. J., Hoffner, C., & Cantor, J. (1987). Children's perception of the effectiveness of techniques to reduce fear from mass media. *Journal of Applied Developmental Psychology, 8,* 39–52.

Wilson, B. J., Smith, S. L., Potter, W. J., Kunkel, D., Linz, D., Colvin, C. M., & Donnerstein, E. (2002). Violence in children's television programming: Assessing the risks. *Journal of Communication, 52*(1), 5–35.

Wilson, B. J., & Weiss, A. J. (1993). The effects of sibling coviewing on preschoolers' reactions to a suspenseful movie scene. *Communication Research, 20,* 214–248.

Winn, M. (1985). *The plug-in drug.* New York: Penguin.

Wood, W., Wong, F. Y., & Chacere, J. G. (1991). Effects of media violence on viewers' aggression in unconstrained social interaction. *Psychology Bulletin, 109,* 371–383.

Wright, C. R. (1986). *Mass communication: A sociological perspective* (3rd ed.). New York: Random House.

Wright, J. C., Huston, A. C., Murphy, K. C., St. Peters, M., Pinon, M., Scantlin, R., & Kotler, J. (2001). The relations of early television viewing to school readiness and vocabulary of children from low-income families: The early window project. *Child Development, 72,* 1347–1366.

Wright, J. C., Huston, A. C., Ross, R. P., Calvert, S. L., Rolandelli, D., Weeks, L. A., Raeissi, P., & Potts, R. (1984). Pace and continuity of television programs: Effects on children's attention and comprehension. *Developmental Psychology, 20,* 653–666.

Wright, J. C., St. Peters, M., & Huston, A. C. (1990). Family television use and its relation to children's cognitive skills and social behavior. In J. Bryant (Ed.), *Television and the American family* (pp. 227–251). Hillsdale, NJ: Lawrence Erlbaum Associates, Inc.

Wroblewski, R., & Huston, A. C. (1987). Televised occupational stereotypes and their effects on early adolescents: Are they changing? *Journal of Early Adolescence, 7,* 283–297.

Young, B. M. (1990). *Television advertising and children.* Oxford, England: Clarendon.

Zillmann, D. (1985). The experimental exploration of gratifications from media entertainment. In K. E. Rosengren, L. A. Wenner, & P. Palmgreen (Eds.), *Media gratifications research. Current perspectives* (pp. 225–239). Beverly Hills, CA: Sage.

Zillmann, D., aust, C. F., Hoffman, K. D., Love, C. C., Ordman, V. L., Pope, J. T., & Seigler, P. D. (1995). Radical rap: Does it further ethnic division? *Basic and Applied Social Psychology, 16,* 1–25.

Zillmann, D., & Bryant, J. (1985a). Affect, mood, and emotion as determinants of selective exposure. In D. Zillmann & J. Bryant (Eds.), *Selective exposure to communication* (157–190). Hillsdale, NJ: Lawrence Erlbaum Associates, Inc.

Zillmann, D., & Bryant, J. (1985b). Selective-exposure phenomena. In D. Zillmann & J. Bryant (Eds.), *Selective exposure to communication* (pp. 1–10). Hillsdale, NJ: Lawrence Erlbaum Associates, Inc.

Zillmann, D., & Bryant, J. (1986). Exploring the entertainment experience. In J. Bryant & D. Zillmann (Eds.), *Perspectives on media effects* (pp. 303–324). Hillsdale, NJ: Lawrence Erlbaum Associates, Inc.

Zillmann, D., & Bryant, J. (1994). Entertainment as media effect. In J. Bryant & D. Zillmann (Eds.), *Media effects: Advances in theory and research* (pp. 437–461). Hillsdale, NJ: Lawrence Erlbaum Associates, Inc.

Author Index

Subject Index

A

Academic achievement, 67–74 *See also* Reading
  amount of viewing and, 67, 69–70, 73
  California Assessment Program, 67–68, 70
  computers and, 177–178, 185–186
  media use and, xxiii, 235
  positive effects of TV viewing on, 70, 163–164
  school versus television, 70, 72–73
  socioeconomic level and, 68, 70, 95
Access to information, 7, 176, 235–236
Advertising, 116–128
  alcohol use and, 119, 234
  behavior changes and, 120, 127–128
  celebrity endorsement, 121
  comprehension of, 118, 122
  critical viewing skills and, 127
  developmental level and, 122, 124, 234
  disclaimers in, 118, 124
  emotional appeals in, 119, 120, 123
  exposure to, 117–119
  formal features in, 123, 125
  gender differences and, 125
  information in, 123
  Internet, 183, 233
  premiums, 124
  program-length commercials, 121
  prosocial behavior and, 161, 162
  retention of, 120, 126
  sterotypes in, 107–108, 126–127
  tobacco use and, 119, 234
  viewer needs and, 125

Aggressive behavior, *See also* Violence
  amount of viewing and, 91, 94
  arousal and, 84, 85, 204
  exceptional children and, 165–166
  family background and, 94
  initial levels of, 91–92, 205
  intelligence and, 90
  perceived realism and, 166–167
  relational aggression, 87, 88, 91, 231
  types of aggression, 90–91, 237
AIME *see* Mental effort
Alcohol use. *See* Health issues
Amount of viewing, 18
  achievement and, 67–69, 73
  aggressive behavior and, 91, 94
  body image and, 152
  cultivation and, 6, 11, 17, 101
  developmental level and, 7, 17, 89
  gender differences in, 105
  and obesity, 153
  racial factors and, 105
  social interaction and, 159–160
  socioeconomic level and, 95
Anorexia. *See* Health issues
Anxiety. *See* Fear and anxiety
Arousal effect, 84–85, 99, 204, 237
Attention, 35–38 *See also* Information processing
  arousal level and, 37
  auditory and visual attention, 36–37
  comprehension and, 35–36
  developmental level and, 36–37, 122
  formal features and, 39
  gender differences in, 37–38
  stimulus characteristics and, 37, 43, 44
attributional biases, 87–88